SEEING THROUGH EVERYTHING

Seeing Through Everything

ENGLISH WRITERS 1918-1940

William H. Pritchard

FABER AND FABER

3 Queen Square

London

First published in 1977
by Faber and Faber Limited
3 Queen Square London WC1
Printed in Great Britain by
Butler & Tanner Ltd
Frome and London

British Library Cataloguing in Publication Data

Pritchard, William Harrison
  Seeing through everything.
  1. English literature—20th century—History
  and criticism
  I. Title
  820'.9'00912   PR471

ISBN 0-571-10167-4

To Marietta, who discriminates

Contents

Author's Note and Acknowledgements

In this book I largely refrain from recounting the plots of novels or naming the themes and images of a poem, as if English literature between the two world wars is at the tip of everybody's recollection. This does not mean that my only fit audience is made up of professional students and readers of that literature; I should hope someone who, at some point in life, read a novel by Huxley or an Auden poem, could read with interest and profit my account of the writer in question. Although in most cases this account can be designated as Introductory, I have tried to introduce in the literal senses of the word: to bring into play reader and text; to lead the reader into relationships with distinctive styles and voices. This kind of activity seems to me usefully practised only in the presence of the novel or poem; so there is liberal quotation, followed by commentary, all of which takes space but is done in the belief that the part, carefully considered, can serve for the whole.

There is also liberal quotation from and reference to other critics, and here an eyebrow might be raised at any pretence to be writing for the intelligent general reader. Particularly in the Lawrence and Eliot chapters, hosts of secondary names crop up, or perhaps get in the way. My excuse is that they—these critics, that 'secondary' material— are in *my* way; but they enter this book I hope only to enable me to make a further, more refined point about the artist's procedures. I have been careful to supply page references and editions only when it seemed important for the general reader to know about them, or when the review or article had special claims to be looked up or was obscurely placed.

STE—A*

    The suggestion that this book be written was made to me by Charles
Monteith for whose subsequent kindnesses and encouragement I owe
much thanks. In 1973–4 I was recipient of a John Simon Guggenheim
Fellowship, and record my gratitude here, Frank Kermode generously
provided me with an Honorary Research Fellowship which allowed me
to use the welcome facilities of University College, London. I should
also like to thank Warner Berthoff, C. J. Fox, Christopher Ricks and
Julian Symons for their solicitude and their critical responses to the idea
of this book. Mr. Symons deserves particular acknowledgement for his
insistence that having started the book I should finish it. Mrs. James
Crosson typed the manuscript; Francis Murphy and Marietta Pritchard each read it through and made useful, in an instance or two
usefully deflationary, comments. No doubt more of that is in order.
Finally I should like to express my immense debt to Reuben A.
Brower whose lifetime defense of reading and whose imaginative
questionings of what a reader does, have I hope made their mark on
this book. My sadness is that he could not live to read it.

Speaking as an American whose experience of modern English writers
did not begin until the 1950s, I recognize my distance from the
literary heroes of this book. A stanza from Donald Davie's 'Remembering the Thirties' comes to mind:

> It dawns upon the veterans after all
> That what for them were agonies, for us
> Are highbrow thrillers, though historical;
> And all their feats quite strictly fabulous.

It has also dawned upon me, and so apologies to the veterans. But in
writing about them I have tried at least to disdain the 'neutral tone'
Davie goes on to speak of, in favor of subjectivity, preference, the
belief that some writers and works of literature are better than others.

Introduction

1

This is a book without a thesis or overarching idea which holds together and makes comprehensible the fact of English literature between the two world wars. Without such a unifier, why then write another book about some literary figures—poets, novelists, critics—whose productions have already been extensively and sometimes intelligently discussed? For it is not merely the major figures, such as Eliot or D. H. Lawrence, about whom hundreds of books and articles have been written; even writers of less than major rank—Huxley Forster, Auden—have received at least their due, have had their books recalled, their plots and themes traced, images noted, symbolic continuities delineated. And if there is no dearth of books on individual talents, the period's writing as a whole has been surveyed a number of times: in Walter Allen's *Tradition and Dream*, in W. W. Robson's *Modern English Literature* and in Martin Seymour-Smith's *Guide to World Literature*. The conspicuous lack is of a book, neither survey, history, nor intensive treatment of two or three writers, which attempts to move more or less chronologically through the period and come to terms with its most significant and enduring literary monuments. Such a book—which the present one tries to be —would presume to deal with the fifteen or so most important English writers over the years 1918–40. Unlike surveys pressed for space, its commentary would not be hurried, would not mention the names of all Huxley's novels nor furnish one or two lines in capsule summary of their themes and content. Rather, it would direct itself towards the problematic element in the individual writer and attempt to raise fundamental questions about what it is like to read Huxley or

Ford or Orwell, both as individual talents with distinctive styles and as writers who take their places beside one another in a literary and social climate.

That it is these and not some other writers who take their places beside each other here is due in part to the critic's exercise of judgement. Lawrence or Eliot could scarcely be excluded from any such treatment; but what about Dylan Thomas, and why Anthony Powell at some length rather than Graham Greene or Henry Green? Various moments of nervously defensive explanation within this book will suggest that I found the problem of exclusion a troubling one and that particular solutions bring less than full satisfaction. But some general lines for exclusion can be laid down at the outset: first the omission, except through glancing reference, of three major 'modernist' writers—Yeats, Joyce and Pound. They are not English born, but neither was T. S. Eliot who figures prominently in these pages; their work has elicited much commentary but not more than some others discussed here. At a later point I address myself to why this is a book about writers other than in Wyndham Lewis's phrase, 'The Men of 1914' and why, since there is no comparable presiding genius, these years between the wars can't be called—as Hugh Kenner called the years just before 1920—The Pound Era or anybody else's era. Practically I could find no way to include Pound, Yeats and Joyce without committing myself to the grossest simplification of their work— compressed treatment to the point of useless or oblique gesture. Moreover, and unlike the two other Men of 1914, these three writers were simply not *in* England during these years; the realm of myth and heroic literature was their true place of residence. Whether in Sligo or Paris or Rapallo, they climbed to the top of their respective towers and, in the Yeatsian phrase, preoccupied themselves with 'mere images'—even though Pound and Yeats also considered themselves to be profound analysts of the modern world.

Eliot and Wyndham Lewis, on the other hand, did not go so far upstairs, or at least came down to answer the doorbell when some rash intruder rang. These two writers, the central pillars of strength as well as—to confess it now—my own favorite modern literary men, are preeminently on the scene, in journalistic and critical as well as 'creative' ways. They saw themselves as guardians and sceptical critics of literary and cultural, of 'liberal' values; each took himself to be Matthew Arnold's successor in that line. And unlike Yeats or Pound or Joyce, their thought and their argument are not fiercely transformative—even with Eliot's religion and Lewis's god-appointed sense of personal mission—of ordinary, common-sense controversy. They argued, that is, with Lawrence or Virginia Woolf or Forster in ways that didn't take the debate into another realm. And though cosmopolitan and unprovincial enough in their attitudes, they never made, in Pound's ironic phrase about *Hugh Selwyn Mauberley*, 'so distinct a farewell to London' that we have to remind ourselves they are English writers. In this sense Eliot and Lewis are the main supports and instructors of my own criticism; they help me to believe that English literature between the wars is something more than an academic convenience.

Other omissions have simpler or cruder reasons behind them: a disinclination to break out of or say farewell to London in order to consider the work of David Jones or Hugh MacDiarmid or even Dylan Thomas; a lack of conviction that still unacknowledged 'genius' writers like T. F. or John Cowper Powys, like Dorothy Richardson or Edith Sitwell, are geniuses indeed, or that they provide imaginative satisfactions of an order provided by my chosen writers; a simple regret that interesting novelists who emerged in the 1930s—like Elizabeth Bowen or Henry Green—are allowed no room here. What began with a resolve not to confine the notion of imaginative writing merely to novels and poems, turned out to be more bound by those genres, and by literary criticism, than is no doubt healthy: thus the absence of T. E. Lawrence or R. G. Collingwood, or any of the lively autobiographies and memoirs from the late 1920s and '30s by Graves, Lewis and Ford, or a book of literary-social criticism such as Woolf's *A Room of One's Own*. Except for Shaw, no dramatists are considered.

The survivors are roughly seventeen in number and come in for varying amounts of attention, with Lawrence, Eliot and Lewis receiving most of it. An attempt is sometimes made here to characterize or speculate about literary climate—as with English poetry and criticism in the 1920s, or satirical fiction in the next decade—but never to explain the books by generalizations about The Age. I am myself surprised how little good it does, when trying to pay attention

to a poem by Auden or a novel by Waugh, to fortify oneself with
truths about the condition of England at that time, the 'social back
ground' we sometimes pretend lies behind works of art. Wherever
such background does or doesn't lie, useful commentary about literature has all it can do to cope with the pleasures and difficulties of the
text itself; with, certainly in the case of these writers, what lies on the
surface of the prose or poetry. Eliot should be thanked for saving the
word 'superficial' from simple connotations of unworthy and shallow
triviality, by reminding us instead that a solid superficies can be a
thing of beauty. From Shaw to Graves to Orwell, English literature
between the wars shows at least that virtue, whatever the resonances
or adequacies of its deeper tones.

A word about method should introduce an unmethodological book.
Although F. R. Leavis comes in for some animadversions in these
pages, I have no desire to gainsay what seem to me the inescapable
formulations about the function of criticism he made in his chapter
'Literary Studies' from *Education and the University*:

> Literary history, as a matter of 'facts about' and accepted
> critical (or quasi-critical) description and commentary, is a
> worthless acquisition; worthless for the student who cannot
> as a critic—that is, as an intelligent and discerning reader—
> make a personal approach to the essential data of the literary
> historian, the works of literature (an approach is personal or
> it is nothing: you cannot take over the appreciation of a poem,
> and unappreciated, the poem isn't 'there').

It is good to have the student in this paragraph because so much of my
own argument about and discussion of books takes place in a classroom
'where I am saying, 'This is so, isn't it?' waiting for somebody to reply
Yes, but', or 'No, not exactly'. Leavis of course opens the gates to the,
'student'—or to whatever we call ourselves—by holding up the 'personal approach' as a *sine qua non* of literary response. And though
there is always the danger of elevating the personal approach into a
substitute for accurate remarks about texts, that danger will be risked.
I read Leavis's final sentence here—'you cannot take over the appreciation of a poem, and unappreciated, the poem isn't "there" '—as
an interesting reminder that one builds on the appreciations of
earlier readers but can't use them as established truth about the text,

and has instead to perform the work of 'appreciation' over again, or as if for the first time. So I plan to engage in such appreciation here, exercised quite selectively on single books or passages from books whose authors wrote more than I begin to take account of.

One further principle, expressed in R. P. Blackmur's statement about the 'relativism' of the critic:

> He knows that the institution of literature, so far as it is alive, is made again at every instant. It is made afresh as part of the process of being known afresh; what is permanent is what is always fresh, and it can be fresh only in performance—that is, in reading and seeing and hearing what is actually in it at this place and this time . . . the critic brings to consciousness the means of performance.
>
> ('A Burden for Critics')

Whether or not Blackmur meant it, the ideal place for such performance—'reading and seeing and hearing what is actually in it at this place and this time'—is in a classroom with students; lacking them, one's critical performance tries to bring literature to consciousness without vocal and gestural aids. But like Leavis, Blackmur insists that we behave as if the book were not a settled thing with meanings to be pronounced upon or a literary structure noted and outlined; we must speak back to the book, try, in Emerson's phrase, to draw a 'circle' around it and thus, though only for the moment, hold it in a new relation.

It is perhaps vain to believe that the institution of literature, as it reveals itself to us during the years 1918–40, can be made afresh by an individual act of juxtaposing what one sees as the best writers and best books of that age; but, with such admirable and available writers and books who would want to attempt less? Empson tells us that all good poetry is ambiguous; the best poetry, novels and criticism written during these years is ambiguous in a way that resists any brisk, surveying commentary which would pin down their art in a page or two. They need rather to be seen, however briefly, in their vulnerabilities and weaknesses, the better to arrive at a sense of their strengths. And of their strangenesses: raised as they are beyond the ordinary by their exemplary displays of wit, of sanity, of hopeless yearning, of high contempt.

2

Pronouncements by one writer on another, or on the character of a literary period, make special claims on our interest—especially if we respect the writers in question. I want to begin consideration of some English writers whose work falls between the two world wars by consulting what three of them—George Orwell, Virginia Woolf, Wyndham Lewis—said about the change which came over English literature some time between 1910 and the end of World War I. And although there is no reason to believe that later scholars or critics have explained what happened any better than those who were on the scene, I shall consider one recent attempt to compare postwar English writers with their modernist contemporaries.

Orwell's fine essay 'Inside the Whale', written in 1940, is itself a work of art, an endlessly rereadable three-part sequence that begins with an appreciation of Henry Miller, moves on to define some differences between pre- and post-World War I literature, then between 1930s writers and those of the previous decade, finally coming back to Miller and out to general statements about the writer and politics. Orwell dwells rather exclusively on Housman as a powerful writer on the imagination of those who were adolescents in 1910–25, then identifies a postwar group of writers of 'completely different tendency' from Housman and the Georgian nature poets. This postwar group is seen as comprising Joyce, Eliot, Pound, Lawrence, Wyndham Lewis, Huxley and Lytton Strachey. They form 'the movement', and if (Orwell argues) Yeats is outside it and Forster really predates it and Somerset Maugham should be added even though literarily he doesn't 'belong', those exceptions substantiate its identity as *the* significant group of men of letters after 1918— Virginia Woolf going unmentioned by Orwell. He admits that this group doesn't look like a group since many of the writers would have resented being coupled with each other, indeed were actively antipathetic to each other; yet what holds them together is, in Orwell's phrase, *pessimism of outlook*.

Orwell tries out other terms to characterize the thread holding this group together: 'tragic sense of life', but that seems too stiff and portentous; hostility to the idea of progress—the belief that it ought *not* to happen; most valuably, the sense that these writers 'see through' all systems and ideals under which their predecessors had enlisted themselves. This last term provides a useful, if dangerously abstract, way of holding Orwell's 'modern' writers together. For example, take the following list of works published 1918–21 (some had been written earlier)—'Gerontion', *Hugh Selwyn Mauberley*, *Women in Love*, *Tarr*, *Crome Yellow*, *Eminent Victorians*—and consider how much of their imaginative energy is generated out of seeing through, as Stephen Dedalus put it, those big words which make us so unhappy. Orwell doesn't exploit the possibilities of the phrase 'seeing through' as much as he with justice might have; for if its main thrust is towards a piercing exposure of pretense, an unmasking of what passes for high and commendable motive, it offers also the possibility of a further step towards the visionary: you may see through a flimsy structure of lies in order to glimpse, behind the façade, more compelling motives and truer objects of allegiance. Surely the figures of Gerontion, Hugh Selwyn Mauberley, Rupert Birkin, Frederick Tarr, Stephen Dedalus himself, have yearnings to establish life-giving contact with something beyond the merely social, mundane and therefore, in their absolutist vision of things, inevitably corrupted world. So there is at least the possibility, and one which their creators are active in exploring, that seeing through something results in seeing something more worth seeing.

The clever turn in Orwell's discussion of what he terms the postwar era of 'cosmic despair', 'the skulls and cactuses, the yearning after lost faith and impossible civilisations', comes when he asks rhetorically whether this phenomenon might not have occurred precisely *because* it was an exceedingly comfortable time, those postwar years: 'Everyone with a safe £500 a year turned highbrow and began training himself in *taedium vitae*. It was an age of eagles and of crumpets, facile despairs, backyard Hamlets, cheap return tickets to the end of the night.' This is lively and engaging polemic, yet beyond mentioning one novel Orwell doesn't specify the sorts of merely fashionable works he has in mind, and presumably his major moderns didn't write them, since their despair was authentic. In any case the sweeping analysis leaves out or explains too much to be fully acceptable. Of the major writers in the period 1918–30, Orwell insists that their 'purpose' is very much up in the air; they don't attend to urgent problems, don't have any politics to speak of, avert their eyes from 'the places where things are actually happening'. He goes on to argue that 'thirties writers as typified by Auden and Spender will reverse this cultivation of detached unconcern.

It depends on how you define purpose. For Virginia Woolf, in her famous essay 'Mr. Bennett and Mrs. Brown' (1924), it was that the purpose of literature had changed, or rather had recovered itself about 1910 when the new novelists (she lists Joyce, Eliot, Forster, Strachey, Lawrence and herself) began to reestablish contact with the novel's true concerns which had been obscured for a generation by the Edwardians: Wells, Bennett and Galsworthy. This trio had concentrated on external matters such as how the fictional Mrs. Brown was dressed or what the carriage in which she rode looked like, or they had used her as a human instance from which to generalize or on which to impose their utopian or humanitarian concerns. But none of them was able to capture her spirit; they could not penetrate the soul-dimension. This penetration is what the new novelists, along with Strachey and T. S. Eliot, are engaged in, and for that purpose their art must be complex, difficult, no doubt often inchoate: 'We must reconcile ourselves to a season of failure and fragments', runs the oft-quoted sentence. Though Wyndham Lewis jumped on this argument (in *Men Without Art*) as self-servingly apologetic and mocked Virginia Woolf's attempt to sensitize robust writers like Lawrence and Joyce, her essay has nevertheless become a heavily anthologized classic, perhaps because it provides such a neat way for the lecturer to make his transition from prewar to postwar English writing, Edwardianism to Modernism, materialism to spiritualism. As a statement about Virginia Woolf's own developing art it does very well; much less so when one considers, as Margaret Drabble has done most fully in her recent biography of Arnold Bennett, the justice and point of Mrs Woolf's claims in relation to that particular Edwardian. One could compile an anthology of moments in which postwar modernists put down their elders, including Eliot's derogatory re-marks about the Georgians, his frequent jabs at Shaw, Bertrand Russell and Wells, or Pound's ignorant dismissal of Bennett (later partially apologized for), or Lawrence's passionate dissection of

Galsworthy. It is necessary for revolutionaries to characterize then cast out their immediate predecessors as forces of inertia and un-enlightenment. But it is more interesting to see how both Orwell and Virginia Woolf built up the myth that prewar English writing was innocent: innocent of the perspicuity Orwell attributes to the newer writers; innocent of the demands of self and soul for expression within the novel that Virginia Woolf and the other moderns were attempting in her view to satisfy.

Finally there is Wyndham Lewis's claim, in his 1937 memoir *Blasting and Bombardiering*, that the significant modern writers were the Men of 1914, consisting of Joyce, Pound, Eliot and himself. In contrast to prewar writers like Shaw and Wells, for whom being an artist was subordinate to some further, public purpose, the Men of 1914 cared only to produce Art and cultivated a detachment Lewis is eager to term classical. For Lewis, whose *Men Without Art* had already explored the general discrediting of serious work he felt was occurring in the 'proletarizing' of literature, Modernism and the Men of 1914 had failed, not through any fault in the men but rather because of the world which with its wars, revolutions and economic depressions had sold out art. We were 'the first men of a Future that has not materialized', so his nostalgic account runs. Actually Lewis's position is not all that different from Virginia Woolf's. Substitute Pound and himself for Lawrence, Strachey and Forster, and you get essentially the same argument for the sufficiency unto itself of great art, its remoteness from public or political purpose—although Virginia Woolf would stress the soul in contrast to Lewis's emphasis on the external. But Mrs. Woolf's list (with herself included) is much more hospitable towards English writers, while Lewis pretends not to speak from his position as an English writer and is the reverse of embarrassed at the relatively international flavor of his group.

Recently one has encountered the argument that most of the literature written by Englishmen between the wars is an embarrass-ment and second-rate, that the truly vital work was done by non-Englishmen. So George Steiner proclaims that at present the real creative achievement is taking place in American rather than English writers; he would doubtless be willing to assign a minor status to most native English writers since 1918, though not to John Cowper Powys.

And in a recent book by Terry Eagleton, significantly titled *Exiles and Emigrés*, the single Englishman allowed major status is D. H. Lawrence, who joins the Men of 1914 group of Pound, Joyce and Eliot, but with Yeats included and Lewis omitted. Eagleton poses the question of why the great works of modern English literature, many of them falling between the deaths of James in 1916 and of Conrad in 1924, 'should have been the work of foreigners and emigrés'. Why is it that these foreigners best convey the 'sense of impending or actual collapse', the 'felt disintegration' of civilization? He attempts to give substantiation to the claim by individual treatments of some of these writers, but of more interest here is his analysis of why the natives failed to be good enough. They illustrate

> the inability of indigenous English writing, caught within its partial and one-sided attachments to 'totalise' the significant movements of its own culture. That literature responded to the crises of its society either with an external cynicism, or with a sense of disgusted futility which was itself a symptom, rather than a creative interpretation of disturbance.

Evelyn Waugh and Aldous Huxley are adduced as examples of this cynical disgust, while for the creative interpretation of disturbance we are to go to members of the above group—to works like *Mauberley*, *The Tower*, *Ulysses*, *The Waste Land*.

This group at present commands mainly unqualified reference from university courses, teachers and students. Yet surely things could be seen in another way and Eagleton's language in the above quotation scrutinized in a way he doesn't himself provide. English writing between the wars, so the argument runs, was unable to 'totalise' the 'significant movement' of its own culture; it gave us, except for the example of Lawrence, disgust and futility rather than a 'creative interpretation' of our modern disturbance. Leaving aside the complaint that counters like 'cynicism' and 'disgust' are quite inadequate to characterize the fictional operations of such 'indigenous, partial and one-sided' English writers as Graves or MacNeice or Waugh or Huxley or Henry Green (to name some poets and novelists of the period who failed, we may agree, to 'totalise'), why should we identify the ambitious, often pretentious and sometimes hysterical, sometimes achieved, efforts of Pound or Yeats or Lawrence, or the

dislocated brilliance of Eliot's 'The Hollow Men', as the only legiti-
mately creative interpretations of disturbance? Remember that three
of Eagleton's group are poets, and that at least Joyce's later work can't
be adequately understood as that of a novelist's; isn't it possible that
such 'totalising' comes off better when the artist is removed from the
social, novelistic necessity of somehow dealing with the world out
there? And what is wrong with very human attitudes like cynicism
and futility, especially when they are refined and expressed with the
sharpness of a writer who turns them into something more?

The collective achievement of the Men of 1914 is immense, and
we are still learning how to take it in. But one can't consort with the
party of genius all the time; there are simply far more readerly needs
and curiosities than can be satisfied by repeated and extended study
of the *Cantos* or *The Tower* or *Finnegans Wake*. English writers
between the wars succeeded brilliantly in speaking to some of these
needs. It is a literature of marvelous satiric and comic vitality, certainly in its prose, but to some extent in its poetry and most surely in
its criticism also. As for lamenting the spectacle of a literature somehow hiding its head in the sand and callously ignoring the crisis of its
society, when, in retrospect, is any society not headed for some crisis?
We love the things we love for what they are; the best English novels
and poetry in the period 1918–40 insisted on being splendidly themselves and not another thing.

I
England Seen Through

Of the older writers who lived on and published work in the postwar decade and beyond, Bennett, Shaw and Forster stand out, indeed may be the only ones whose later productions we still return to with admiration. Conrad's last readable novel is *Victory* (1915), and it creaks more than a bit; James is dead; Kipling and Chesterton have already given us the fiction for which they will be remembered; Galsworthy and Maugham are in my judgement, and in Nabokov's phrase about the former, 'stone-dead' writers—at any rate not demanding of much criticism. H. G. Wells continues to be a fascinating and prolific author, but a reader of his postwar books would probably be mainly concerned with documenting and tracing the journey of his mind to the end of its tether. Certainly the best novels —*Tono-Bungay*, *Kipps*, *Mr. Polly*—are well behind him; there are entertaining moments in *Mr. Britling Sees It Through* (1916) and some affectingly pathetic ones (the death of Britling's son in the war) but it is mainly, as Wells described his own *Boon* to Henry James, a 'wastebasket'—though, as always, with items made lively by the writer's energy and intelligence. But the postwar book for which Wells should be most remembered is his *Experiment in Autobiography* 1934).

1. Bennett and Shaw

Bennett and Shaw present different challenges to the critic. About postwar Shaw—the Shaw of *Heartbreak House* and *Saint Joan*— there is no critical accord. Is *Saint Joan* his best play or a slick and

rather soft piece of whimsical charm? Does *Heartbreak House* ask to
be considered along with modernist visions of chaos and treated with
high seriousness as a prophetic work, or is it one last fling of irresponsible, sporadically amusing chatter? Depending on how one
asks and answers these questions, Shaw is either crowned by the two
plays or remembered rather as the author of *Pygmalion*, *Man and
Superman* and *Major Barbara*. By contrast Bennett's best postwar
books, *Riceyman Steps* (1923) and *Lord Raingo* (1926), are not going
to dethrone *The Old Wives' Tale* or *Clayhanger* from the heights of
Bennett's excellence as a realist. But neither are they unmistakable
fallings-away from early excellence, and the critical challenge they
present is not to explication or interpretation, but to the matter of
whether any criticism of such highly readable books is at all to the
point. With a book like Maugham's *The Moon and Sixpence* criticism
has little to do; it has its solid virtues if you can bear the ingratiating
(so he hopes) narrator and his unflustered attitudes toward experience.
Adultery, the lonely struggle to paint, and eventually death are
exciting events to gaze at from afar; but little exercise of intelligence
and complication is called for on the reader's part since everything is
limited and contained within the suave narrator's tone of worldly
wisdom.

Bennett's Later Novels

Bennett's novels are a different story, as entertaining in their ways as
Huxley's written during the same period. It is also likely that anyone
who admired *The Good Soldier* or *Nostromo* or Henry James, and
who in 1926 was reading Joyce and Virginia Woolf, might well have
groaned and thrown Bennett's *Lord Raingo* out of the window. A
cruder, more energetically vulgar book than *Riceyman Steps*, it
tailors its narrative to the hero's unvarnished warts-and-all character.
But the crudity is not just Sam Raingo's; Bennett hacks the book into
eighty-seven chapters, all of them short and snappy to ensure read-
ability and titled with pointers like 'Sam's Fright', 'The Situation
Made Clear' or 'The Clue'. Nothing could be clearer than that the
author thoroughly enjoys and vigorously participates in his hero's
successes and failures as a member of the war cabinet, his toils with

wife and mistress and son, the hearty pleasure of his meal-taking at the Savoy or cigar at the club. The scenes of wartime London, life in the Strand, Pall Mall, Berkeley Square, are easily accepted and strongly placed for our inspection. And even if Sam's deathbed rattle goes on a bit beyond our capacities for sympathetic response, it is exhilarating to hear him cough his last while we live on to read another novel.

Lord Raingo asks to be talked about in irreverent ways because it is decidedly unreverent about itself. What Bennett did was to think up a plausible story, drawing upon his own experience in the public and private sectors—from war cabinet to wife to mistress—and let Raingo air to others and himself the restless perplexities, the daily enthusiasms and depressions, of an imperfect human being to whom we're invited to bring our own imperfections. When the book was published Virginia Woolf had already made her pronouncement that Bennett couldn't portray anybody's soul, could only do the material outsides of things. Yet this novel gives us quite a full picture of Sam Raingo's 'soul', not the Woolfian luminous halo or still centre, but the groans and satisfactions of an organism dealing with the world daily on its usual complicated and unsatisfactory terms. Nobody I think would accuse the book of lacking its full quotient of human nature. That it is generally unknown and likely to remain so may suggest Bennett couldn't muster enough art to make human nature live; it may also suggest that there is pleasure to be taken in fiction alien to the modernist books Mrs. Woolf plugged for and others have subsequently deified.

Riceyman Steps, on the other hand, can be defended as an 'art' novel in its concentrated treatment of the life, late marriage and death of a miser, Henry Earlforward, Clerkenwell bookseller. In his excellent little book on Bennett, Walter Allen speaks of *Riceyman Steps* as outside the tradition of English fiction in that its 'distillation of all the possibilities of a single theme' (though not, Allen adds, its technique) is like the Conrad–Ford insistence on rendering the 'affair', the *progression d'effet*. The book was extremely successful, perhaps due overmuch to the enthusiasm with which Bennett's portrait of the servant-girl Elsie was received—her anguished thieving of bits of steak or an egg at midnight in the Earlforward residence was evidently much appreciated as a glimpse of warmhearted human foible. But, as Allen rightly points out, the heart of the book is Earlforward, in his miserliness, his fascination with the physical appearance of books, his middle-age romance with a woman who does not quite bend to his will and mysteriously suffers illness and death just before the miser himself.

Readers of *Riceyman Steps* surely find unforgettable its vivid placing of Clerkenwell as, at the outset, Earlforward looks down the road to King's Cross:

> —a hell of noise and dust and dirt, with the County of London tramcars, and motor-lorries and heavy horse-drawn vans sweeping north and south in a vast clangour of iron thudding and grating on iron and granite beneath the bedroom windows of a defenceless populace.

As with that word 'defenceless', Bennett's writing in the book is the reverse of toneless or blandly objective; his fine ability to penetrate the spirits of places like 'the huge red Nell Gwynn Tavern, set on the site of Nell's still huger palace, and displaying printed exhortations to buy fruity Portuguese wines and to attend meetings of workers' with ironic intelligence and a sense for disproportion, is equally in play when human character rather than Clerkenwell is the subject. Walter Allen speaks of the 'subtle distortion' by which Bennett acts as an ironic intermediary between the reader and the awfulness of events, and Allen invokes as literary antecedents the humorous– grotesque contributions of Jonson, Smollett and Dickens. But there is nothing reassuringly 'odd' or quaint about Earlforward, nothing in Bennett's presentation of him that signals or winks at us as if to say we needn't confuse this fiction with life. As the doctor confides to the already fatally ill Mrs. Earlforward his suspicion that her husband has cancer at the cardiac end of the stomach (Earlforward's miserly starving of himself expressing itself physically), our attention is directed to the invalid:

> The doctor would undoubtedly charge double for a night visit. And the fire, choking and roasting him! He saw himself in the middle of a vast general lunacy and conspiracy, and he alone maintaining ordinary common-sense and honesty. He felt the

whole world against him; but he could fight the whole world. He had perfect confidence in the fundamental hard strength of his nature.

There is nothing here which invites the reader to detach himself from the man in trouble—no literary and verbal diversions to substitute for the pains of righteous suffering.

Rather, the distortion Allen speaks of is a larger matter that does not appear noticeably in individual sentences. And there is cause for wondering about some of this distortion; for example, does Bennett mean to put forth some 'real', Norman Mailerish connection between miserliness and cancer? More troublingly, is it possible within the compass of a short (very short for Bennett) novel with its marvelously realistic furniture—the London borough, the bookstore, the bedroom —to take two recently married people swiftly into death without our questioning the whole thing as too much of a put-up job? Bennett never lacked wilfulness as a novelist, but the great leisured spaces of *The Old Wives' Tale* and the *Clayhanger* sequence made operations of his will seem but the natural unfolding of events in time. Here in *Riceyman Steps*, 'distortion' is evident to the extent that we may feet the arbitrariness of it all, hence be less than naturally moved by Earlforward's sickness unto death.

If this is a felt difficulty it doesn't make the book less interesting, indeed accounts in part for its specialness as something more than good entertainment. Speaking adversely again, it is true also that when Bennett comes to write about the obsessed Earlforward's inner life (as in the passage quoted above) he relies on the straightforward strength of his narrative punch; one sentence after another begins with 'He' and tells us in no uncertain terms what 'He' felt and what he thought. When Walter Allen says that Bennett's flat technique is unlike the Ford–Conrad way of rendering impressions, he doesn't go on to consider whether such flatness is a limitation, a virtue, or somehow both. If the fact of an unshakeable narrative voice constitutes part of what is admirable about *Riceyman Steps* and to a lesser degree *Lord Raingo*, it also makes the act of appreciating Bennett as a surviving, realist voice in the midst of postwar modernism, a somewhat delicate one. We may pull back from making too high claims for *Riceyman Steps* by recalling that *Ulysses* appeared in the previous year, a book which did away forever, it would seem, with the un-shakeable narrator in whose trustworthy hands we place ourselves and wait to find out what happens next. *Riceyman Steps* and *Lord Raingo* mean to brim with life; but we never lose sight of the professional operator behind them, coolly getting on with the story that will end only in the toils of death. For a moment we side with Virginia Woolf and say, yes, these novels are solid products, but 'life' has stolen away in the making of them.

Yet only for a moment. It might at first thought seem odd to compare Bennett's work in the 1920s with the fast-rising Aldous Huxley's, apostle of the new cynicism and anatomist of the new value-lessness. Surely next to Huxley, Bennett seems old-fashioned; yet they liked each other and admired each other's work.[1] Behind *Those Barren Leaves* or *Antic Hay*, as much as the two Bennett novels discussed, stands a secure narrative intelligence. That intelligence is not sceptical about its own creations, does not (like Joyce) subordinate character and story to literary superstructures or verbal brilliance, does not (like Ford) attempt an exploration into the mysteries of story-telling itself. Bennett, like Huxley, knew what he was up to. Although this security now strikes us, as it did many back then, as the reverse of experimental, not risking as much as was to be risked by greater books in the 1920s, it also guided and informed the honourable, fully-told books he wrote.

Shaw and *Heartbreak House*

If Shaw exists at all as a postwar writer he does it through *Heartbreak House* (1919) and *Saint Joan* (1924), although the former, written during the war, was withheld from publication until afterwards either because—as Shaw variously accounts for it—of economic circumstances or because the war effort couldn't abide the satiric exposure of English shams while young men were dying for their country. His lively preface, dated June 1919, includes a comparison of the play with Chekhov and Tolstoy, an insistence that *Heartbreak House* is 'cultured, leisured Europe before the war', plus an analysis of how this culture was separated from 'power' (the barbarians of Horseback Hall) and a description of the 'four terrible years' just concluded in which life became as 'crude theatrical farce' as was to be found in the theater. Perhaps in part because of the preface's large claims, there has grown up a tradition of taking *Heartbreak House* to be something more than just another Shavian wit-combat; as if here finally he touched on deeper, more serious matters about which his vision might be understood as tragically disillusioned. Yet Shaw is also a master at seeing through everything. Even more than Bennett or Huxley, he is adept at exposing eccentricities of character while imaginatively delighting in them; and like the novelists he is not out to annihilate them.

In *Heartbreak House* Shaw, if we are to take his preface seriously, sees through 'cultured, leisured Europe' before the war and the literary triviality of lives whose currents have lost the name of action and express themselves solely through a stock of words, courtesy of the dramatist, which can be turned this way and that. The play teases us but also itself, mainly through the character of Captain Shotover, with the notion that there is a deep wisdom to be glimpsed beyond appearances. 'What am I to do?' asks Hector Hushabye, and the Captain tells him to learn his business as an Englishman: 'Navigation. Learn it and live; or leave it and be damned.' But already the Captain's seventh degree of concentration has turned out to be indistinguishable from 'Rum', while various other illusions have been disrobed, seen through particularly by the once-innocent Ellie Dunn as she progresses toward experience, undergoes education. Ellie decides eventually that she wants 'Life with a blessing'; and in response to Boss Mangan's confessing he doesn't understand a word of what she's saying, she replies with 'Neither do I. But I know it means something.'

The reader is really no better nor worse off than Ellie. As the play draws to its operatic close, with Beethoven, the German planes and all the stagecraft summoned to bear on death in the dynamite pits— while life at the house consists only in hoping that the planes will come again—Shaw makes no bones about pretending he has anything to hand on in the way of wise guidance. He gives Shotover a splendid speech to Ellie:

> A man's interest in the world is only the overflow from his interest in himself. . . . In old age the vessel dries up; there

is no overflow: you are a child again. I can give you the memories of my ancient wisdom: mere scraps and leavings; but I
no longer really care for anything but my own little wants and
hobbies. I sit here working out my old ideas as a means of
destroying my fellow-creatures. I see my daughters and their
men living foolish lives of romance and sentiment and snobbery. I see you, the younger generation, turning from their
romance and sentiment and snobbery to money and comfort
and hard common sense. I was ten times happier on the
bridge in the typhoon, or frozen into Arctic ice for months in
darkness, than you or they have ever been. . . .

No doubt, but 'rum' as well: the speech is attractive and stirring
wholly because of its rhetorical panache—it wants to be said out
boldly, accompanied by gestures and appropriate music. When Ellie
replies, sensibly, with the feminist perception that 'They won't let
women be captains', the whole business trails off, the subject gets
changed. And really that is what the whole play amounts to—one
change of subject after another, made with enough cleverness and
grace to distract us from pausing too long and asking difficult questions.

   Heartbreak House flirts with apocalypse and with the notion of life
as tragedy, but never succumbs to such notions because finally there
is still the charming (intolerable for some) presence of Bernard Shaw
at the play's helm. If this account is accepted it makes somewhat
empty the preface's boast about how the play *is* cultured Europe before
the war, or *is* England—is anything except the virtuoso bag of tricks
and pleasure which the resourceful master trots out for our delecta-
tion. It is all atmosphere and pointed speech and disillusioned,
'understanding' wit; but such wit is a good deal harder to come by
than the quick dismisser of Shaw realizes. It seems silly to make up a
story about how the play anticipates *The Waste Land*, if that means
taking Shaw seriously as an apocalyptic or tragic seer. On the other
hand, if one were willing to revise the nature of claims made for
Eliot's poem as a solemn judgement on modern civilization, then
(though Eliot would doubtless be displeased) there may be room for
him and Shaw as comparable creators of grotesques whose creations
live through the rhetorical brilliance of their language.

   It should be emphasized that Shaw's great gift for putting together
human voices in argument, in teasing, in momentary harmony, is as

evident in *Arms and the Man* as in the later plays. Surely *Saint Joan* is wonderfully distinguished for its ability to set forth characters with different purposes and weave those purposes into the fabric of speech by which they make them known or try to conceal them. W. W. Robson says the play restored Shaw to critical favor, perhaps because he seemed to have given up teasing and was sympathizing with the simple and good; Robson also terms it Shaw's greatest play and praises him for, for once, not avoiding strong drama:

> The forces opposed to Joan are impressive, and taken seriously. The play is Shaw's version of Dostoyevsky's 'Grand Inquisitor'. Can we afford a saint? Do we want one? Shaw asks real questions.[2]

Perhaps, yet I wonder whether the strong drama Robson praises, and which is undeniably there right down to the crackling of flames, does not make of less account the teasing, irresponsible, but invigorating flirtation with ideas that my favorite Shaw—*Man and Superman*, *John Bull's Other Island*, *Pygmalion* and *Heartbreak House*—show in abundance. *Saint Joan* is so beautifully engineered, so masterfully led down all avenues to its end, then so winningly turned about in the Epilogue, that the reader is left speechless, admiring the perpetrator of all this wondrous construction but not in the least concerned to consider seriously the 'real questions' Shaw supposedly asks about sainthood. It is a play filled with questions and counter-questions, ideas and purposes in conflict; yet its well-made nature leaves us quite outside any encounter with the doubts and uncertainties greater works engage with. Wyndham Lewis evidently saw the play in its early days of production, and he provides a hint to its limitations:

> The strangely unreal geniality and playfulness of *St. Joan*, again (that seems written to be played by a cast of elderly anglican curates), is a deadly atmosphere for such a heroic subject, of course, and produces a most painful effect. Indeed, as it was presented first in London, it was difficult to escape from the feeling that most of the actors—with all their very 'kindly' but, of course, mischievously twinkling eyes, and breezy, capable manners—were not in reality of a more elevated calling than that of an actor; and that for some reason they had decided—attracted perhaps by the 'religious' nature of the subject—to take part in that performance.[3]

Still, and unlike its predecessor *Back to Methuselah*, it remains a piece of work able to charm and delight. We should stop patronizing Shaw and stop speaking as if the writers whose work became prominent after the war possessed some new apprehensions of reality that, unlike his, have not dated. It may well turn out that *Heartbreak House* and (to a lesser degree) *Saint Joan* have not dated at all, show very little subservience to any spirit of the age or literary tendency. Which is to say that Shaw was a rare sort of writer whose like we shall not come upon again.

2. Huxley, Strachey, Lewis

Huxley's Early Novels

With the possible exception of D. H. Lawrence, no English novelist during the ten years which followed the war's end was treated with as much respect and admiration as Aldous Huxley: 'No other writer of our time has built up a serious reputation so rapidly and so surely,' Edwin Muir said about him in his 1926 collection of essays, *Transition*. Huxley was widely read by intelligent people and he if anyone addressed himself in fiction to many issues, in private life and in public, which the thoughtful 'modern' man or woman was thinking about. His novels and stories from the 1920s, most particularly and extendedly *Those Barren Leaves* and *Point Counter Point*, discuss and inspect attitudes toward love, sex, ennui, poetry, death, that anyone living in Oxford or Chelsea found perfectly familiar and very much to the point; thus the books are first-rate material for cultural historians interested in how the English intelligentsia talked. We are to understand them, most writers on Huxley have agreed, as embodying the 'deflationary, mocking spirit of the post-war generation' (W. W. Robson), and Huxley is also seen as symptomatic of and a prey to the malaise and disgust he could not master. It is not surprising that a writer who can be summed up this easily should be now pretty much unread. In America, at least, it is *Brave New World* by which Huxley is known, along with some later traffickings with mysticism and the drug-and-mushroom trade; while *Crome Yellow* and *Those Barren Leaves* are noticed only by graduate students of postwar English satire.

Huxley's works do not, fifty years later, stand high as imaginative creations; yet he is an obvious place from which to begin considering some 'new' English writers. And his early books in particular should be read and appreciated more than they perhaps are. In *Enemies of Promise*, that brilliant and extremely useful attempt to arrange and comment upon the books of this period, Cyril Connolly found Huxley typical of a generation, 'typical in his promise, his erudition, his cynicism and in his peculiar brand of prolific sterility', and claimed further that his nature was 'a very English one, that of the divided man, the lover of beauty and pleasure dominated by the puritan conscience'. Connolly is happiest with the earliest Huxley stories and *Crome Yellow*, where the spirit of the dandy prevails. After these books, and culminating in the long, ambitious *Point Counter Point* (1928), the novelist like his heroes suffers increasingly the agonies of the 'split-man' (Wyndham Lewis's phrase) to the detriment of the novels and especially to their prose style. But Connolly, though admiring of Huxley's gifts in the early fiction, doesn't go far enough in examining that fiction or in describing why readers did and still should take pleasure in it.

One of Huxley's earliest published stories (collected in *Limbo*, 1920) is titled 'Happily Ever After' and is directly concerned with World War I as a human fact. It is the stuff of which television dramas are made; the mutilation of one man and the death of another in the war, the grief of the bereaved heroine, the detached disillusionment or crudely patriotic fervour of others in response to such horrors. The story is written in an extremely direct, telegraphic manner—not at all the elaborated 'Mandarin' (Connolly's term) which was increasingly to be Huxley's vehicle. Originally designed as a play, it ends with a punch-line feeling as the one-legged survivor, George, finds himself kissing Marjorie who has just received news of her betrothed's death. They claim they will remember only the marvelous things about him:

> 'Perhaps our darling Guy is with us here even now,' said Marjorie, with a look of ecstasy on her face.
> 'Perhaps he is,' George echoed.
> It was at this point that a heavy footstep was heard and a hand rattled at the door. Marjorie and George moved a little

further apart. The intruder was Roger, who bustled in, rubbing his hands with an air of conscious heartiness, studiously pretending that nothing untoward had occurred. It is our English tradition that we should conceal our emotions. 'Well, well,' he said, 'I think we had better be going in to luncheon. The bell has gone.'

This 'strong curtain', as the objectionable phrase has it, can only make a reader feel complacent (if he is with Huxley) or embarrassed (if he is not). Perhaps the 'It is our English tradition' remark by the narrator should be seen as merely an early infelicity on the part of a young writer; but behind the words lies a firm narrative will which Huxley never lost. Although we have been earlier invited to hold Roger, the patriotic curate, in contempt, we can now smile a bit too at Marjorie and George telling each other stories about how they will remember poor Guy. We know better; in fact we, like Huxley, know all about the vanities and foibles of human wishes and promises. Except for such a knowing intrusion, Huxley in this early story is a self-effacing and omniscient narrator who provides no stylistic energies that might impede telling of 'the story' or transform it into something more than a carefully engineered television drama. It hardly feels like reading at all. Using hindsight, we can say that he must have found this narration simply not imaginative enough, if the making of art rather than acceptable slick-fiction was desired. There is nothing in 'Happily Ever After' beyond the talents of tale-tellers like Galsworthy or Maugham.

Crome Yellow is a different and more interesting matter. Huxley's first novel is still admired, when it is read, but perhaps not enough for its wholly individual charm. Cyril Connolly sees it as one novel in a postwar genre he titles 'The Clever Young Man and the Dirty Deal', in which genre the young man suffers from being unable to seduce a woman, competes with and loses to rivals, is advised by a father figure (or a father) whose advice he can't quite understand. As other examples of the genre Connolly cleverly, if rather abstractly, names Norman Douglas's *South Wind* along with 'Prufrock', Joyce's *A Portrait of the Artist as a Young Man*, Hemingway's *The Sun Also Rises* and Huxley's other 'twenties novels. Actually Douglas's book is the only one which really should be compared to *Crome Yellow*, and only then if they are distinguished rather soon. For Douglas's book, despite its amusing scenes and sprightly invectives on the part of the Douglas-spokesman, Keith, is overlong, badly paced, and too quickly falls into separable styles—travel or nature writing, anecdote, doctrinal persuasion. *Crome Yellow* also has different styles or genres but keeps under two hundred pages and consistently carries itself with high-spirited grace.

To link the book with ones by Eliot, Joyce and Hemingway is justified if one takes seriously the notion that 'Prufrock', like the three novels, has a Hero who suffers from a Problem. But as with the poem, that notion quickly evaporates when you locate the most interesting parts of *Crome Yellow*. Insofar as Huxley exhibits his sensitive Oxford poet, Denis, trying to make it among the human types at Crome, we are provided only with the mildly amusing pleasures of seeing the timid soul discomfited by his female love-object, or outdone by his rival, or seen-through by the deaf Jenny Mullion, or pestered by the would-be intellectual Mary Bracegirdle (to whom Huxley allows Denis an unexpected riposte when, on being questioned as to his three favorite modern poets, he confides that they are Blight, Mildew and Smut). The really memorable things in *Crome Yellow* occur when Huxley gives his inventive powers freedom from getting on with the story and allows them to develop a fantasy. These creative fantasies live intensely within their language and are unrelated to the novelese which would eventually take over Huxley's style. For example, early in the book the assembled guests contemplate a newly-delivered sow with her litter of fourteen, grunting and squelching about in the mire. 'Old Rowley', described as the most venerable of farm-labourers and resembling a great English nineteenth-century statesman, joins them. After regarding the pigs for a bit:

> 'Look at them, sir,' he said, with a motion of his hand towards the wallowing swine. 'Rightly is they called pigs.'
> 'Rightly indeed,' Mr. Wimbush agreed.
> 'I am abashed by that man,' said Mr. Scogan, as old Rowley plodded off slowly and with dignity. 'What wisdom, what judgement, what a sense of values! "Rightly are they called swine." Yes. And I wish I could, with as much justice, say, "Rightly are we called men." '

If this were Peacock somebody would then answer Mr. Scogan and there would follow an exchange of speeches in which the limitations of each eccentric viewpoint were unveiled. Instead Scogan misquotes Old Rowley—or improves his diction—but we don't need to be busy seeing through Scogan's pretension and abstractness since our ears are still delighted by Rowley's magnificent salute: 'Rightly is they called pigs.' This is a joke about language and life, if you will, but it is not made at Old Rowley's expense, nor at his master's (Mr. Wimbush) who adds a 'Rightly indeed'. Huxley's comedy here is extraordinarily unembittered, does not seek to expose human beings as knaves or fools. And in fact everybody in *Crome Yellow* is given good lines at one time or another, the sense being that there are enough of them to go around, their author generously equipped by nature. It is the spark of language—'Rightly is they called pigs'—that makes the atmosphere exhilarating.

Continuous with a moment like this one about the pigs are the splendid set-pieces built around the genealogical researches done by Crome's present owner, Sir Henry Wimbush. These involve most memorably an account of how the builder of the house, an Elizabethan gentleman named Sir Ferdinando Lapith, was preoccupied by one thought—sanitation—and how his little, now rare book called 'Certaine Privy Counsels . . .' treated 'with great learning and elegance' the matter of how privies should be placed as far away from the sewage arrangements as possible, namely at the top of the house. The tale is unfolded in much lovely detail by Sir Henry who suddenly ceases and the narrator comments:

> The contemplation of the glories of the past always evoked in Henry Wimbush a certain enthusiasm. Under the grey bowler his face worked and glowed as he spoke. The thought of these vanished privies moved him profoundly. He ceased to speak; the light gradually died out of his face, and it became once more the replica of the grave, polite hat which shaded it. There was a long silence; the same gentle melancholy thoughts seemed to possess the mind of each of them. Permanence, transience—Sir Ferdinando and his privies were gone, Crome still stood.

The charm of such a moment can't be usefully accounted for by invoking terms like satire; instead it lies in the creative fantasy Huxley has woven, and participated in himself through expressive pacings and rhythms of language which move us. And Sir Ferdinando's privies are only a prelude to the book's *tour de force*—the story of the three-foot four-inch dwarf, Sir Hercules Lapith, the furnishing of Crome for him and his tiny wife in the image of dwarfness, a dream all to be shattered by the birth of a son who grows up normal-sized (' "Ferdinando goes *crescendo*," ' wrote Filomena in her diary, ' "It seems not natural" ') and eventually, with his loutish and similarly large friends, makes life no longer worth living for the tiny pair. The tale is exquisitely told, both absurd and oddly sad in its effect. Huxley's genius, insofar as these and other bits from *Crome Yellow* reveal it, is closely associated with a species of pathos and silliness (of a sort recently seen in Nabokov) that is unafraid to exploit itself, to see where it will lead. Such 'digressions' to my mind constitute the heart of the book.

Crome Yellow was written, Huxley tells us, in a creative flurry of two months. But clearly a novelist as concerned with ideas, the state of society, and the progress of man's soul as Huxley was, could not feel comfortable indulging himself for long with the likes of Sir Ferdinando and his privies or Sir Hercules and his tiny horses. Already in a letter of 24 August 1921 he has 'plans to do a gigantic Peacock in an Italian scene'. *Those Barren Leaves* would be the title, in which the 'ideas'—mainly confined in *Crome Yellow* to Mr. Scogan's scientific fantasies—are allowed much fuller play and divided up among three characters with the same first letter to their names: Cardan, Chelifer, Calamy. The book which eventually resulted is now one of Huxley's lesser-read ones: lengthy and leisurely compared to *Crome's* brisk pace, it is really a series of juxtaposed operations in now professionally competent Huxleyan modes: some fine travelogue of Italy, a portentous ending in which the possibilities of mystical contemplation are put forward through Calamy's retreat to the mountains, a rewriting of 'Swann in Love' called 'The Autobiography of Francis Chelifer', some good discussions of matters like parasitism or the baroque in which ideas are played with and interestingly developed as they might be in good conversation. But what it all adds up to one wouldn't try to say. Huxley himself in a letter to Naomi Mitchison (25th February 1925) after the book was published spoke of it as 'tremendously accomplished, but in a queer way, I now feel, jejune and shallow and off the point'. This was an incisive comment made with what seems his typical ability at self-scrutiny which neither brags nor lacerates. Tremendously accomplished *Those Barren Leaves* most certainly is, perhaps beyond the reach of any novelist in England at that time. The attempt to think seriously about life, to set oneself historically in a period after the great warcrisis, to imagine (within the admittedly narrow confines of leisured, upper-class characters) different ways of experience, above all to entertain—this is a considerable achievement. But yes, like *Crome Yellow*, in a 'queer way off the point'—if that point was to be located as one at which profound vision of the modern world were to be found.

Huxley's attempt to get *on* the point resulted eventually in *Point Counter Point*, where novelese triumphs over style; but already in his second novel, *Antic Hay* (1923), he felt he had done something different, perhaps more serious, than the delicate fantasies which make up the best parts of *Crome* and *Those Barren Leaves*. A letter to his father shows him wounded by Leonard Huxley's distaste for *Antic Hay*, defends it as a book 'written by a member of what I may call the war-generation for others of his kind . . .', and says it was intended to reflect the 'violent disruptions of almost all the standards, conventions and values current in the previous epoch'. The interesting thing about Huxley's language here is that it differs not a bit from the way he is talked about in guidebooks; in drawing himself up to confront his father he reached out for 'official' language to characterize and supposedly dignify what he had created in a novel. Since in one sense I agree with Leonard Huxley and find *Antic Hay* a good deal less attractive than the novels which precede and follow it, I am inclined to look sceptically on Aldous Huxley's defense. Or rather, to suggest that it is a long step from imagining Henry Wimbush's contemplation of the glories of vanished privies, or the sad story of Sir Hercules, to imagining something like *The Waste Land*, another work which is talked about officially in the terms Huxley uses. It is true that *Antic Hay* breaks new ground—in Rosie's seduction by Gumbril and her subsequently displayed psychology—for the exploration of sexual fantasies, ennui and disgust which *Point Counter*

Point quite ambitiously cultivates. But too much of the earlier book is summed up in the aimless peregrination about London performed at its end by Gumbril and Mrs. Viveash: 'Tomorrow will be as awful as today' says that lady, too invitingly turning herself and the book into a cultural symbol supposedly having deep point about the modern world.

In fact, *Antic Hay* is as brittle as *Crome Yellow* but largely without the sanely witty charm of the earlier novel. No one would want to take issue with what Evelyn Waugh (in a 1955 *London Magazine* symposium on Huxley) said about *Antic Hay*, that it was 'Henry James's London possessed by carnival', though one might demur at accepting all three of Waugh's adjectives for the book—'frivolous and sentimental and perennially delightful'. Angus Wilson, also a contributor to the symposium, was given the book at the age of fifteen and testifies to the excitingly liberating effect it had on him. I should guess that was so partly because the 'satire' in the book is more easily taken in, more obviously a matter of the creator indifferently paring his fingernails somewhere out there behind his creations. In a word, *Antic Hay* is the sort of book which might, in Eliot's response to I. A. Richards's phrase about *The Waste Land*, provide a generation with the *illusion* that they were disillusioned. At any rate it is interesting that, on Angus Wilson's own testimony, he moved on from his early fascination with *Antic Hay* to a later preference for *Crome Yellow* and *Those Barren Leaves*, books in which Wilson acutely detects and appreciates an 'exultation', since as he puts it, 'despite himself and his rejection of the world, Mr. Huxley communicates a satisfying acceptant quality which enchants'. That 'acceptant' quality which is also enchanting makes Huxley's way of seeing through the world much more than complacent and brittle, or cynical and disgusted. We put him down sorry that the book is ended, not that the world is so bad.

Strachey and *Eminent Victorians*

> It is perfectly possible that the presentation of such spectacles as Comedy presents may prove, in certain circumstances, undermining to the virtue of the spectators.
>
> (Lytton Strachey, *Portraits in Miniature*)

Strachey is of course the arch underminer, and *Eminent Victorians* his best book. *Queen Victoria*, and much less so *Elizabeth and Essex*, are graceful and vigorous performances; indeed one may admire the moralist who frequently appears in *Queen Victoria* more than the comic writer who saw through certain Victorian eminences. But the earlier book, with its brilliant surface, has a way of provoking interesting literary questions, since we are sometimes as virtuous readers cleverly undermined—to the disgust of some, the delight of others. F. R. Leavis has probably been Strachey's main disparager, linking him (as if it were bad company) with Gibbon (the 'Strachey–Gibbonian manner') as dealers in destructive irony. Leavis casts contempt on Strachey's Leslie Stephen lecture on Pope, though he does have a small word of praise for his remarks about Shakespeare's final plays; in fact both essays reveal Strachey's acuity and his willingness to direct attention to formal effects in Pope and Shakespeare's verse. But it is mainly the 'Bloomsbury' cleverness which Leavis detests, and he does not accord Strachey the dignity of real criticism.[4]

I avoid the arguments, fully and sensibly dealt with by Michael Holroyd's biography, about the degree to which Strachey was fair to his Victorian subjects. All satire is unfair, and if we do not propose to read Purcell's *Life of Cardinal Manning* in order to check out what Strachey added or suppressed or intimated, we are left with only the ring of his sentences themselves and the question of whether or not they force belief. Just what sort of 'belief' do we give to Strachey anyhow? The question raises itself immediately and most vividly with regard to the first eminent Victorian, Cardinal Manning, whose life as a young archdeacon is described in these often-quoted and sometimes mistrusted sentences:

> In his archdeaconry, Manning lived to the full the active life of a country clergyman. His slim, athletic figure was seen everywhere—in the streets of Chichester, or on the lawns of the neighbouring rectories, or galloping over the downs in breeches and gaiters, or cutting brilliant figures on the ice. He was an excellent judge of horseflesh, and the pair of greys which drew his hooded phaeton so swiftly through the lanes were the admiration of the county. His features were already beginning to assume their ascetic cast, but the spirit of youth had not yet fled from them, so that he seemed to combine the

attractions of dignity and grace. He was a good talker, a sympathetic listener, a man who understood the difficult art of
preserving all the vigour of a manly character and yet never
giving offence.

Thus it is no surprise that his sermons are crowded and a bishopric
predicted for him. No one would deny these to be finely cut and paced
sentences; yet the feeling may be that they somehow undermine
Manning's purity by so exaggerating his social and worldly attributes.
A troubled reader could focus on the 'seemed', in 'seemed to combine
the attractions of dignity and grace', to suggest that the qualities may
have gone no deeper than what met the eyes of the country folk as
Manning skated about the ice, cutting his brilliant figures. This
seeming–being contrast could also be worked up around the other
Victorian figures; thus Strachey's technique would be that of the
debunker, the penetrator of glittering appearance to reveal the soul,
or lack of it, within.

It can't be denied that at times Strachey does so penetrate and mock
his subject, as when he says of Florence Nightingale that her con-
ception of God was not orthodox, that she felt 'towards Him as she
might have felt towards a glorified sanitary engineer', and (falling
further into alliterative fun) that she seemed hardly 'to distinguish
between the Deity and the Drains' and that if 'He is not careful she
will kill Him with overwork'. But something more interesting than
deflation is taking place in the paragraph about Manning and in the
best parts of Strachey's essays. To amend a phrase, his prose sets out
to convince us that seeming is believing; that if Manning *seems* to
combine dignity and grace, then he *does* combine them, if the sentences putting forth these qualities are memorable enough stylistically. Here it is the 'slim, athletic figure' in the streets of Chichester,
or in breeches and gaiters, or driving the fine pair of greys, which
catches our imagination. In competition with these appearances,
notably incised by Strachey's language, who would care to moralize
dully about how Manning was too worldly in that men of God are
supposed to be something more?

To invoke a distinction made at about this time by T. S. Eliot in
his essay on Dryden: Strachey's 'satire' is creative rather than critical. It doesn't issue in a precise, analytical treatment by which its

subject's vices are unmasked, his inner self laid bare for our condemnation; rather the words are seen to 'create the object which they
contemplate'. As Dryden memorably created Achitophel—'A fiery
soul, which working out its way,/Fretted the pigmy body to decay/
And o'er informed the tenement of clay'—so analogues might be
drawn with Strachey on Manning, on 'Chinese' Gordon or Florence
Nightingale—the shorter, relatively hostile treatment of Thomas
Arnold reveals Strachey's critical animus more simply. Michael
Holroyd's reservations about the portrait of Manning, and about the
whole of *Eminent Victorians*—that its treatment of the figures is
cold, made strictly in rational terms, too intellectual—doesn't at all
account for the vigorous warmth of, say, the wonderful ecclesiastical
portraits in 'Cardinal Manning'. A memorable one of Cardinal
Wiseman, whom Manning was to replace as Archbishop of West-
minster, is introduced as follows:

> Cardinal Wiseman was now obviously declining towards
> the grave. A man of vast physique—'Your Immense,' an
> Irish servant used respectfully to call him—a sanguine
> temperament, of genial disposition, of versatile capacity,
> he seemed to have grafted upon the robustness of his English
> nature the facile, child-like and expansive qualities of the
> South.

In rejecting the analogy between Wiseman and Browning's Bishop
Blougram, Strachey admits that he resembles Browning's character
in one way—'his love of a good table'. 'Some of Newman's disciples
were astonished and grieved to find that he sat down to four courses
of fish during Lent. "I am sorry to say," remarked one of them
afterwards, "that there is a lobster salad side to the Cardinal." '
Strachey needs to be quoted at length in order to recall how much
'unnecessary' bits like 'Your Immense' and the 'lobster salad side'
humanize the portrait of Wiseman. As for Newman, Strachey can
admire in more complex ways, but no less warmly, *Apologia Pro Vita
Sua* for 'its transparent candour, its controversial brilliance, the
sweep and passion of its rhetoric, the depth of its personal feeling . . .
recognised at once as a classic, not only by Catholics, but by the whole
English world'. No snickers here, nor are there any in the brilliant and
chilling three-page description of the hospital conditions at Scutari,

near Constantinople, when in 1854 Florence Nightingale arrived to begin her great work.

This is not to attempt a whitewash or to say that Strachey always resists the cheap or too-easy jab—such as his emphasis on Clough's weak ankles, Thomas Arnold's 'slightly puzzled expression', or the silly bathos about Newman with tears streaming down his face repeatedly muttering 'Oh no, no!' to the Curate of Littlemore.[5] As with other writers his books show signs of human imperfections. Gerald Brenan, in a letter written to Strachey on the publication of *Queen Victoria*, claimed the books did not show such signs, and mock-chastised him for never 'sinking' as did all other artists, even Shakespeare occasionally. Brenan added that 'I prefer Joyce to you: he does not taunt me, but leads me on, points to very far horizons and shows me a way that leads there. He promises new discoveries, new methods, new beauties—you don't promise anything. You just are.'[6] Precisely, and this just-is-ness, the sense of a Strachey object as completely made, rounded off, knowing just what it's about and attempting no more, makes him rather resistant or impervious to the sort of literary analysis which rehashes the organization of an essay or classifies its various characters. That organization and those characters are most clearly revealed to us by the lucid biographer himself.

Gerald Brenan also predicted a new age in English literature, with *Eminent Victorians* standing on the border-line between new and old. It is difficult to make much of this prediction; insofar as Strachey's style is 'perfect', his vision complete, then he cannot be placed in the company of major novelists of the 1920s who were none of them stylistically secure or intellectually complete, but were on the contrary in quest of new discoveries, new values, new beauties. Still, Strachey can be seen as an innovator, as 'experimental' as any other artist of his generation, if we look behind the style and try to imagine the kind of labor which went into its creation. Virginia Woolf did this in an excellent perception from the 'Mr. Bennett and Mrs. Brown' essay, when she compared Strachey with Macaulay, saying that the latter wrote with the strength of his age behind him, which strength went straight into his work, whereas Strachey had to open our eyes, 'to search out and sew together a very artful manner of speech'. Mrs. Woolf finds the effort makes his work therefore less forceful and his scope more limited; but, we might ask, who would not seem limited in comparison with Macaulay? As for Strachey's influence on later writers, some have surely felt it as liberating; although imitation of the knowing manner without Strachey's lovely command of anecdote and detail or his extraordinary sense of fun and mischief, is bound to make the imitator sound just complacent or perhaps sour. Cyril Connolly predicted, in *Enemies of Promise*, that Strachey's gifts would one day be rescued from 'the neglect into which, by his spectacular success, they were too soon precipitated'. Thirty-five years after Connolly, one wants to promote this operation, suggesting fancifully that the best way to rescue Strachey from neglect would be to re-institute the practice of reading aloud.

Lewis's *Tarr*

Lewis makes the first of his personal appearances here solely on the basis of his first novel. *Tarr*, published in 1918 but written earlier, then rewritten in its present form (the one referred to here) in 1928, is unique among Lewis's novels. It is, as V. S. Pritchett remarked, a 'considerable comic creation'; but rather than dealing with it as the first step in Lewis's career as a novelist, I have chosen it as the last in this group of postwar 'seeing-through' books. By all measurements *Tarr* is the strangest and most difficult of them, and Lewis the oddest writer. Although his *Childermass* and *The Apes of God*, published in the late 1920s, show an even more harshly elaborate style, *Tarr* remains a formidable book to read. Evidence that readers have felt this way can be gathered from the fact that while most students of modern literature have heard of *Tarr*, few would swear to having read it through. And it is not, as *Eminent Victorians* might well be, likely to be 'rediscovered' as a modern classic. The reasons for this are worth exploring and take precedence here over analysis of its design or interpretation of its significance.

The book was written at the time when Lewis was busy producing *Blast* and inaugurating Vorticism, an art movement which committed itself above all to Energy, to a dynamic union of stillness and movement, and to vigorous use of the artist's material. If the material was words then words must be made to reveal new potentials through their brilliant juxtaposition in sentences, and through the surprises and electric shocks communicated by one sentence to its neighbour. On the second page of *Tarr* the hero meets a fellow-artist named Hobson:

> They met in a gingerly, shuffling fashion: they had so many good reasons for not slowing down when they met, numbers of antecedent meetings when it would have been better if they had kept on, all pointing to *why* they *should* crush their hats over their eyes and hurry forward, so that it was a defeat and insanitary to have their bodies shuffling and gesticulating there.

This meeting is no more than a gingerly shuffling, insanitary defeat, conveyed by a prose only less filled with gesticulations than other examples could show. In this respect the 1918 version of *Tarr* is more abrupt and uningratiating towards the reader than the smoothly engineered revised version; Lewis originally went so far as to provide marks between sentences (—) to make sure the reader wouldn't pass too easily from one to the next.

When from the perspective of forty years he looked back (in his memoir, *Rude Assignment*) on this first novel, Lewis said it was the occasion at which 'Writing—literature—dragged me out of the abstractist cul-de-sac'; in other words, that it was impossible and undesirable to attempt non-human, non-representational creation in a medium and genre traditionally devoted to telling a story about man in society. The interesting thing is that the novel Lewis wrote turns out to be about the lesson learned; in the alternating careers of two very different artists, Tarr and Kreisler, we see Lewis making comedy—sometimes on the edge of tragi-comedy—out of the attempt to effect balances and truces, or to engage in all-out struggle with the 'life' that art attempts to master and shape. But Lewis's retrospective sentence, as well as my continuation of it, is something quite different from the modernist mythology foisted upon the work, partly by Lewis himself but more prominently by his allies, Pound and Eliot. Pound linked *Tarr* with Joyce's *Portrait of the Artist* as the decade's two significant novels which had arisen as it were to banish Wells-Shaw-Bennett from the scene.

Of course to compare *Tarr* with Joyce's novel, even without considering the immense boost of interest added to it by Joyce's later work, instructs one in why *Portrait* is read by everyone, *Tarr* by a good many less than that. For all the ironic placing of its hero and the stylistic imitativeness of many passages (where again Joyce could be said to be 'framing' his hero) Joyce's book is told very much from the inside of Stephen's head, heart, and sensitive soul. Childhood memories, pains of adolescence, guilt, sin, illicit sex, romance, religious conversion, lapse into sin again, rejection of church–state–fatherland, commitment to Art—these are matters the young reader wants to hear about, and no book ever made a stronger impact on youth aged sixteen to twenty than Joyce's *Portrait*. To invoke the famous phrase, one can *identify* with Stephen Dedalus. But one would have to be of a rather special fibre to succeed in identifying either with Tarr or with Kreisler—in that sense Lewis, unlike Joyce, keeps us outside the book. Even more important than the refusal to provide a hero to identify with is *Tarr*'s style of address—or lack of it—to the reader; and here Lewis's whole mode of narrative behavior differs strikingly from his contemporaries. Without minimizing their many differences from each other, Huxley, Strachey, Shaw, and Bennett are all painstakingly aware of their reader to the extent of entertaining, flattering and stirring him to indignation or approval. Their operations are never carried on in private; they mean to be read.

While it's absurd to say that Lewis's novel is not meant to be read, it goes about its business in a strangely independent way. There are no winks, elbows in the reader's ribs, nor subtler forms of ingratiation; when jokes get made, appearances painted in, rhetorical high moments achieved, they seem always to occur without reference to anybody who might look to the novel for amusement or edification. Nor is *Tarr* a very good story; even its revised version sometimes feels lumpish in construction, while its sentences can't always be read aloud with a clear sense of emphasis and speech rhythm. Pound's way of distinguishing Lewis from Joyce, twenty years after their novels appeared, was to argue that 'Lewis's renovation of the word was a vigorous renovation and not a diarrhoetic imitation of Mr. Joyce's leisurely flow and murmurous permuting. Lewis's renovation was conceptual. Joyce's merely, in the main sonorous, an attraction of the half-awake consciousness to and by similar sounds.'[7] And if one thinks of Stephen Dedalus's paradigm for the ideal artist, retired behind his creation, sitting there indifferent and paring his fingernails, one would not identify him with the creator of *Portrait*, but—if Stephen's definition were not so weary-ninetyish—with the author of *Tarr*.

We are familiar enough with Pound's iterated emphasis, at least as far back as 'A Few Dont's by an Imagiste' (1913) on how art should be hard and clear, should present, rather than explain or preach. Eliot picked this up to the extent that, writing in the *Athenaeum* in April 1919, he praised Hawthorne for what other American writers didn't have—'the hard coldness of the genuine artist'; and in one of his most striking formulations a month later said in the same magazine in a review of Kipling that

> It is wrong, of course, of Mr Kipling to address a large audience; but it is a better thing than to address a small one. The only better thing is to address the one hypothetical Intelligent Man who does not exist and who is the audience of the Artist.

This is a clever hit against 'communication' whether to the mass or the happy few; you don't speak directly to the 'one hypothetical Intelligent Man', for how would you speak, what would you say to him? An address to Him is different in kind from more easy, because tonally classifiable ones; so it makes sense to claim that Lewis's highbrow effort in *Tarr* was partly designed to avoid vulgar speakings to a known audience. He didn't have an audience, didn't know to whom he was speaking, and wrote a novel which tried to make those circumstances into virtues.

Whenever physical movement is involved, or a person's appearance, or the look of a restaurant, or the Luxembourg Gardens, Lewis's style discovers much that is new in the objects and refreshes our perception of them. Even a less than crucial moment like the following in which Kreisler, out of control himself, creates a scene at a genteel English club in Paris where Germans go to dance, is rendered memorable by the energies of style that wheel the widow Bevelage about

> . . . with ever-increasing velocity, round the large hall, and at the third round, at breakneck speed, spun with her in the direction of the front door. The impetus was so great that she,

although seeing her peril, could not act sufficiently as a brake on her impetuous companion to avoid the disaster. Another moment and they would have been in the street, amongst the traffic, a disturbing meteor, whizzing out of sight, had not they met the alarmed resistance of a considerable british family entering the front door as Kreisler bore down upon it. It was one of those large featureless human groups built up by a frigid and melancholy pair, uncannily fecund, during an interminable intercourse. They received this violent couple in their midst. The rush took Kreisler and his partner half-way through, and there they stood embedded and unconscious for many seconds. The british family then, with great dignity, disgorged them, and moved on.

This will have to serve as representative of Lewis's 'metaphysical' satire which cares only about the outsides and interactions of things behaving as if they were people. A poem of Pound's like 'Les Millwin' operates on the same principle, but Pound's juxtapositions seldom seem as deadpan and disengaged as Lewis's—to the latter's advantage I should say. As a comedy of wild bodies colliding, *Tarr* is superb and different from other English novels to the extent that, as suggested earlier, readers still don't know quite what to make of it.

We might guess that Lewis himself did not know, when he began to write the book or even later on, quite what to make of it. Clearly, and in the broadest sense, it is about the artist Tarr's attempting and eventually failing to hold life at bay, 'life' meaning especially the lures of sex, the body, action rather than contemplation, the pitfalls of time-bound man headed for death. Against these forces stands the artist as lonely hero, as detached maker of timeless, 'cold', intellectual forms. Kreisler is the artist as failure, become the wild body that yearns to be swallowed up into the chaos and dissolution he finally achieves in hanging himself. Tarr's fascination with Kreisler takes up much of the latter part of the novel and is inexplicable even to Tarr himself; unable to forego him, as he is unable also to forego his fiancée Bertha Lunken, Tarr in a characteristically energetic passage puts together the two affairs:

> His sardonic dream of life got him, as a sort of quixotic dreamer of inverse illusions, blows from the swift arms of windmills and attacks from indignant and perplexed mankind. But he—

unlike Quixote—instead of having conceived the world as more chivalrous and marvellous than it was, had conceived it as emptied of all dignity, sense and generosity. *The drovers and publicans were angry at not being mistaken for a legendary chivalry, for knights and ladies!*

He is a sufferer, he decides, from 'the curse of humour'—'anchoring him at one end of the see-saw whose movement and contradiction was life.'

One can see from this paragraph alone, in its eager analysis of Tarr's case, how the novel in which he's set is more than simply hard and cold in its demeanour towards life. Insofar as the book is *about* trying to be hard and cold, Lewis warms to the subject. If Tarr (and Lewis) suffers from the curse of humor, perhaps all true artists—at least novelists—must so suffer. In his review of the book (*Egoist*, September 1918) Eliot made the interesting claim that 'humour' was in fact a distinctly English trait, that 'The intelligent Englishman is more aware of loneliness, has more reserves, than the man of intelligence of any other nation.' This may be true—at least Eliot has a way of making it sound true—and at any rate provides an excellent gloss on the combination of arrogance, wit, loneliness, verbal bluster and idealistic fervour which makes up the character of Tarr. It is true also, as Eliot pointed out, that things are wound up too smartly and neatly in the novel; Lewis shows a streak of smart-aleckism in comparison to which the efforts of Shaw or Huxley or Strachey are mild. But *Tarr* deserves at least the attention given it here, not simply as the first step in an interesting career, but as an original book of great resourcefulness which continues to reveal itself after repeated readings. Not always successful or even attractive, it nonetheless seems to me a work of genius, just as much so as *Portrait of the Artist*, and in a quite distinctive way. And our attempts to become the 'hypothetical Intelligent Man' whom Eliot evokes as the only audience for the true artist, make for the reader a varied and surprising experience.

Crome Yellow, Eminent Victorians and, most complicatedly, *Tarr* are in their distinguishable ways exhilarating books which are not filled with postwar despair, do not put forth for our weary approval attitudes of disgust and rejection, find by implication at least that the modern world of England in 1920 is at least no worse than England in 1870 or Paris in 1900 or life as lived back in the days of Sir Hercules Lapith and his ungrateful son. To group the books under some deadly category like 'postwar satire' is a mistake insofar as it immediately sets up stock responses that can only get in the way of hearing and delighting in their truly individual styles and voices. If we are to read them, in Leavis's phrase about the Donne poem, as we read the living, then best to try and see each for what it is and not another thing. And since the last phrase is stolen from Eliot, we may end by suggesting that the great 'totalising' poem about to be published—*The Waste Land*—can be better understood in terms similar to the ones used for Huxley, Strachey and Lewis, than as a complexly human expression of despair or a lament over past richness compared to present sterility. For demonstrations of which we move on to Eliot.

II

T. S. Eliot: 1918-1922

One of the 'London Letters' Eliot wrote for the *Dial* in 1921–2, briefly addressed the phenomenon of Lytton Strachey's extraordinary popular success with *Queen Victoria*. Eliot does not attempt to debunk that success, indeed is generous to Strachey to the point of invoking his illustrious forbears: his style is a compound of 'Gibbon in the irony, Macaulay in the romance'. But Eliot is at pains to undermine what was already the growing legend in 1921: that Strachey was the prototypical 'icy' analyst, not in the least taken in by the people he selected to write about. On the contrary, Eliot insisted: 'Strachey has a romantic mind . . . he deals with his personages not in the spirit of "detachment" but by attaching himself to them.' Admittedly the statement is made about *Queen Victoria*, which is in fact a book more genial and sentimental towards its key figure than *Eminent Victorians*; still, as can be seen from inspecting key passages in the earlier essays on Manning, Florence Nightingale and the others, Strachey is anything but detached from his heroes. After reading about one of the eminent Victorians a reader is able neither to approve nor deplore the figure, not because of balanced argumentative fairness on the part of an impartial 'detached' historian, but because the figure has been turned into a 'character', animated into what Wyndham Lewis called—speaking of his own satirical creations—an 'exuberant, hysterical truth'. Eliot does not take Strachey to task for so attaching himself to his heroes; yet one knows, fortified by similar remarks made by Eliot in the immediate postwar years, that he did not conceive of his own creative work in these terms; nor is he in principle friendly to the romantic, personalizing attachments favoured by some writers. He talks as if Strachey has been rather lucky to bring it off as well as he did.

The trouble with *Queen Victoria*, in the terms Eliot had set down in the Kipling review quoted earlier, was that Strachey had succeeded in addressing too large an audience; there were too many readers out there with a hunger for romance, eager to identify with the feelings of Melbourne or Disraeli or the queen herself, as Strachey so artfully displayed and orchestrated them. The 'hypothetical Intelligent Man' who didn't exist but was the audience of the Artist, hardly reared his non-existent head. In other words Strachey had too much of a winning tone, too charmingly ingratiated himself with a good many more readers than was salutary; whereas Lewis's *Tarr* resolutely went its own way, cultivating what Pound called an 'active unpleasantness' of style in regard to its audience. Eliot too, in the five years beginning in 1918 capped by publication of *The Waste Land*, went his own way with a vengeance: proposing, dispensing, relegating others to limbo or worse, making it seem as if to be a true Artist were a vocation fit— in these modern times—for almost no one but Eliot himself. 'Stendhal's scenes, some of them and some of his phrases, read like cutting one's own throat', he confided in an *Athenaeum* review of 30 May 1919; by comparison even work as accomplished as *Queen Victoria* or *Saint Joan* or *Crome Yellow* would feel demonstrably more cozy, and lacking what Hawthorne displayed—'the hard coldness of the genuine artist'.

'Crabbe, Blake, Landor and Jane Austen are precisely the spirits who should have guided and informed the period of transition from the 18th century'; thus Eliot saluted four of the 'greatest minds' who remained apart from the general ideas of, as his review titled it, 'The Romantic Generation'. If another period of transition was in progress in July 1919 when Eliot wrote the sentence, he set out, if not to guide and inform it, at least to attempt in his essays and reviews some sceptical criticism of the new time's general ideas, or lack of them. In the essays collected to make *The Sacred Wood* (1920) and in the dozens more uncollected and little-known ones scattered over the years in the *New Statesman, Egoist*, Middleton Murry's *Athenaeum*; in his 'London Letters' written home to America for the *Dial*; in his anonymous, enormously influential revaluations of Ben Jonson, Marvell, the Metaphysical Poets, and Dryden written for the *TLS*, Eliot put together an achievement of literary journalism unmatched or at least unexceeded in its brilliance and point by any other critic. When it is recalled that these were the years of the publication of 'Gerontion' (in *Poems, 1920*) and of *The Waste Land* two years later, this half-decade asks to be seen as the most interesting and crucial one of Eliot's career. Earlier there had been the bold performances of 'Prufrock' and 'Portrait of a Lady'; afterwards the extension of concern into social and religious philosophy, into the poetic drama and finally the writing of *Four Quartets*. But in the five years *aetat* thirty to thirty-five, his literary opinions were expressed with a daring flair, with harshness or suaveness depending on the occasion, which he seldom attempted later on. And the two longer poems, plus the series of quatrain ones, represent his most difficult and intransigent creative work.

Undoubtedly he said things that, from his later, seasoned retrospection he must have regretted slightly, like the following dismissal tossed off in a *Dial* 'London Letter' of April 1922 about certain contemporary American poets, among them Robert Frost: 'Mr. Frost seems the nearest equivalent to an English poet, specializing in New England torpor; his verse, it is regretfully said, is uninteresting, and what is uninteresting is unreadable, and what is unreadable is not read. There, that is done.' Had he really read, as he could have done by this time, 'An Old Man's Winter Night', 'Home Burial', 'Mowing', or 'Putting in the Seed'? Or was he just following Pound in crossing Frost off the list of poets worth taking seriously? (Pound was no longer interested in Frost.) What is significant about Eliot's remark—aside from the deplorable note struck by 'his verse, it is regretfully said, is uninteresting' (as if Eliot couldn't help speaking the sad truth)—is that Frost, like Lytton Strachey, was having and would continue to have an immense popular success, indeed would address perhaps the largest audience commanded by any poet of this century. Frost had already said, scornfully, a few years before that he had no interest, like Pound, in being 'caviare to the crowd'. As with the thoughts of Queen Victoria, so New England torpor, leisurely dispensed in unpretentious blank verse, seemed to attract readers not to be confused with the hypothetical Intelligent Man. These readers would not, on the other hand, find much to interest them in the 'art-emotion' of 'Burbank with a Baedeker; Bleistein with a Cigar' or of 'A Cooking

Egg', to name perhaps the two least approachable specimens of the quatrain poems Eliot had recently been publishing. Putting it one further and extreme way: Strachey and Frost, plus a good many others named and unnamed, were all-too-readable; the true Artist had to guard, above all, against this quality. He had on the contrary to find his niche next to Pound's early *Cantos*, *Tarr* and the strange short stories Lewis was publishing—above all, next to the chapters from *Ulysses* which were appearing in the *Little Review*.

'Gerontion'

Thus it is not surprising but fitting rather that a recent essay on 'Gerontion' should describe the poem as 'literally unreadable'.[1] What the critic, Gabriel Pearson, means by his claim is that Eliot's poem, unlike a dramatic monologue by Browning, forces us to concentrate on 'words, syntax, grammar associations' to the extent that we cannot follow sentences and understand them as piecing together a psychological state; there is no 'human being' with a problem we are enabled to intuit, comprehend and sympathize with through the power of poetry. My own experience shows it a mistake to think of 'Gerontion' as a 'difficult' poem which has to be carefully studied and worked out, perhaps in a classroom, in order for its meaning to reveal itself. What, for example, do the opening lines, pondered long, eventually yield in the way of perceived truth?

> Here I am, an old man in a dry month,
> Being read to by a boy, waiting for rain.
> I was neither at the hot gates
> Nor fought in the warm rain
> Nor knee deep in the salt marsh, heaving a cutlass,
> Bitten by flies, fought.
> My house is a decayed house,
> And the Jew squats on the window-sill, the owner,
> Spawned in some estaminet of Antwerp,
> Blistered in Brussels, patched and peeled in London.
> The goat coughs at night in the field overhead;
> Rocks, moss, stonecrop, iron, merds.

These lines tell us what the old man didn't do and where he wasn't, in a verse which has no affinities with ordinary speech or syntax ('Bitten by flies, fought') and is curiously alliterative to the extent where 'the Jew'—for many years in lower case type—is much odder than any mere anti-semite could make him: 'Blistered in Brussels, patched and peeled in London.' A reader cannot take seriously, think seriously about 'the Jew' any more than, a bit later on, he can consider for long what 'Hakagawa, bowing among the Titians' was really up to, or whether Fräulein von Kulp 'Who turned in the hall, one hand on the door', was making an invitation or just saying good-night. And if the purely verbal associations of 'patched and peeled' aren't enough, we go on from the Jew to the goat, also residing in the vicinity, but coughing 'at night in the field overhead' rather than squatting on the windowsill. It is not clear whether the goat has a touch of flu; but after the semi-colon he coughs up 'Rocks, moss, stonecrop, iron, merds', a resilient quintet, but to be found particularly at night when the field is 'overhead' one's house?

If the poem is unreadable, if instead we read words, let us be clear about what a readable poem looks like; here are the opening lines from one about an old man written only a few years before 'Gerontion' by the poet of New England torpor:

> All out-of-doors looked darkly in at him
> Through the thin frost, almost in separate stars
> That gathers on the pane in empty rooms.
> What kept his eyes from giving back the gaze
> Was the lamp tilted near them in his hands.
> What kept him from remembering what it was
> That brought him to that creaking room was age.
>   ('An Old Man's Winter Night')

If into his own bin of 'interesting' poetry Eliot would admit poems like 'Gerontion' or the quatrain ones (different from one another as they are) then the soberly humorous directness of Frost's narrative would surely be uninteresting—though not in fact unread. Frost's poem is readable because of its controlled unfolding through measured cadences of an intelligible and intelligent narrator, presenting a character; by contrast the 'I' of 'Gerontion' is brilliant, throws off many exciting rhetorical sparks, but is hardly intelligent, nor is he intelligible, nor is he a 'he'.

Yet as Eliot's best critic Hugh Kenner reminds us, Gerontion, though he has no particular voice, is all Voice:

> The old man with neither past nor present, reduced to a Voice, employs that Voice, fills up the time of the poem with the echoes and intermodulations of that Voice, draws sustenance from the Voice and existence itself from the Voice for as long as he can animate the silence. . . . For the protagonist has no voice but a collective past which he has never made his own by great labor, which consequently uses him, blows him with restless violence through phrase after phrase without substance or satisfaction. It is a great grotesque conception, greatly achieved. . . .[2]

Swept up by this Voice, we cannot assume that any specifically human character lies behind it, even though we may refer to 'the old man'. A passage such as the one beginning 'After such knowledge, what forgiveness?' is unforgettable, asks to be admired for the powerful rhetorical marvel it is; yet we note the urgent buttonholing, the 'think now' and 'think' repeatedly hanging there at line-end without a true syntactical connection with what follows: 'Think/Neither fear nor courage saves us.' Are we being told any more than that history is a snare and a delusion, is a cheating whore (Kenner cleverly unravels the skein of sexual imagery) and that we had better 'Think at last', even if it's not clear exactly what we are to think about? Kenner would have Eliot the master craftsman as detached from his speaker as is Joyce from Stephen Dedalus in *Ulysses* who says, Gerontion-like, 'Weave, weaver of the winds' and hears 'the ruin of shattering glass and toppling masonry'. And Gerontion, like Stephen, is victim and prey to all the literary echoes from the past which Eliot, in 'Tradition and the Individual Talent' (1919) wants the poet to be aware of.

But Gerontion employs, or is employed by those echoes like a Shakespearian or Jacobean tragic hero, intent on cheering himself up:

> I would meet you upon this honestly
> I that was near your heart was removed therefrom
> To lose beauty in terror, terror in inquisition.

These lines stand at the centre of feeling in the poem. They could be read as indicating Gerontion's self-delusion, his penchant for making large, vague and impressive gestures towards sincere communication of something, then his withdrawal into self-pity and self-laceration. But does Eliot understand all this and is he detachedly, 'coldly' rendering it with the true artist's impersonal vision? I doubt such an account will do at all to explain the way the poem tugs at one. For it does so tug because we cannot sit back and entrust ourselves to the capable hands of a detached poet setting forth the agonies of somebody whose problem he understands. There is no 'character' named Gerontion anywhere; the voice which speaks could belong to no human being existing on land or sea. How then should we expect to intuit an 'Eliot' who is clearly distinct from his poetic stooge? The one thing this poem does not do is meet anybody upon anything 'honestly', surely because the 'I' and 'you' who would supposedly do this are not only fictions but transparent ones. It is not clear what they would talk about if they did meet.

Certain scenes in Stendhal, Eliot said, read like cutting one's own throat: they are 'a terrible humiliation to read, in the understanding of human feelings and human illusions of feeling that they force upon the reader'. I think it wrong to speak of 'Gerontion' in comparable terms, though it is surely a disturbing and dislocating poem to read. But if Stendhal's detachment or coldness as an artist is not in question, Eliot's most assuredly is. The Voice which swells to command the passage from the poem's middle about the deceptions of History, seems to come from the center of Eliot's being; there is here no cool appraisal or witty setting-forth of an obsessed mind. Admittedly, later on, Eliot-Gerontion seems to know what he's up to and how he's entertaining or titillating himself:

> These with a thousand small deliberations
> Protract the profit of their chilled delirium
> Excite the membrane, when the sense has cooled,
> With pungent sauces, multiply variety
> In a wilderness of mirrors.

The lines read as an accurate gloss on the whole poem; and since the reader has been similarly excited, similarly dazzled by seeing variety multiplied in a wilderness of verbal mirrors, he can only assent— exhausted, but with no complex understanding of human feeling or human illusions of feeling gained. Eliot's art in 'Gerontion' seems less overtly moral—in its worried playing-off of the claims of human feeling against the claims of art—than it was in 'Portrait of a Lady' or 'La Figlia che Piange' or in the 'Do I dare' hesitancies of 'Prufrock'. Gabriel Pearson maintains in his essay that Eliot 'took the logic of Symbolism to an extreme and then attempted to return it to experience by connecting the word with the Word'. Certainly 'Gerontion' represents an extreme which even the term 'Symbolism' may be inadequate to encompass; and it would be wrong also to lump the poem together with *The Waste Land* as twin examples of imprisonment within the word, with the possibilities of release shining ahead in the post-conversion poetry. 'Symbolism' cannot explain the distinct strangenesses of these two most difficult poems; but a look at the great criticism Eliot was writing during the years 1918–22 may help to.

Eliot's Criticism

Discussion of Eliot's criticism has traditionally focused on 'Tradition and the Individual Talent', the 'Hamlet' essay, and his appreciations of the Metaphysical poets and Marvell. These essays contain striking formulations which have proved too overwhelming to resist: 'The continual extinction of personality' which the artist was supposed to perform; the 'objective correlative' needed—and missing in *Hamlet*— to express feelings precisely in words; the dissociated sensibility and the corrective wit (tough seriousness allied with slight lyric grace)— these influential notions have provoked counter-attacks and sceptical analysis of them (by Winters and Leavis and Kermode), or they have simply fallen into disrepair. It is too bad that many readers never extend their sense of Eliot's critical writing beyond these particular anthologized essays, marvelous as they are. For after reading them one needs to sit down with *The Sacred Wood*; while the uncollected journalism from these years shows Eliot in an even more flamboyant and informally daring mode than the anthologized pieces.

Kenner's chapter on the criticism is particularly valuable because it tries to imagine the circumstances under which it was written: almost entirely as reviews of individual books, severely limited as to available space, subtly shaped to the expectations (often subverting them) of a particular audience—whether the avant-garde *Egoist*, the more respectable *Athenaeum*, or the anonymous *TLS*. Eliot's ironic and parodic style is delineated, his Flaubertian imitation of idiocies, as in the faked *Athenaeum* correspondence supposedly written by various pious, well-intentioned citizens with an interest in keeping up literary standards. But it is with regard to 'Gerontion' that Kenner makes the most essential point about *The Sacred Wood* and the mass of uncollected reviews from those years, remarking with reference to the 'After such knowledge' passage that 'No other Eliot poem exploits an ambiguity of dissolving key-words to this degree. There is no up nor down, no ground on which declaration may stand.'

This remark points to how Eliot's criticism during these years is mainly a dissolvent, sometimes of key words but more generally of any attempt at literary writing that has emanated from less knowing and less disillusioned minds than his own. For example, in an *Athenaeum* review called 'The Education of Taste' (27 June 1919) we are informed that

> To communicate impressions is difficult; to communicate a co-ordinated system of impressions is more difficult; to theorize demands vast ingenuity, and to avoid theorizing requires vast honesty. Also, there is the generality, which is usually a substitute for both impression and theory.

Here the hopeful critic is faced with a severe round of choices. Whatever he choose to engage in it will be difficult or will demand vast ingenuity (unless he refrains from doing it, in which case vast honesty is required). He can always fall in with generality-mongering, a substitute for the demanding activities which proved too defeating for him to perform them. To readers surrounded by a wash of comfortable, genial or disgruntled reviewing, by reviewers who knew what they liked, weren't bothered by fine points of critical argumentation and were never at a loss for words, this sort of warning or advice might have seemed heady stuff indeed. Here was a critic who let one know what really to respond to Stendhal's sentences might be like; or to whom the appearance of the *Georgian Anthology* demanded superlative terms of appreciation—its 'dullness' was 'original, unique'; who let it be known that the most interesting artistic work, *circa* 1920, was being done not by English poets and novelists but by Picasso, by Stravinsky (in *The Rite of Spring*), by a cave man like Wyndham Lewis or a wild man like Pound. Or by Marie Lloyd and other representatives of the music-hall tradition Eliot so much admired and aggressively flaunted, as if to say *this* is what the Artist admires, not the poetry of John Drinkwater. As for English literary men, when Walter Raleigh was to be replaced as Professor of Poetry at Oxford in June 1922, Eliot ran through a list of possible English candidates, summed up their limitations, then brought forth the name of an ornery American professor, Irving Babbit; a more intelligent man, says Eliot, and with a more coherent and serious set of principles than any of the Englishmen he has named.

Sceptical dissolving of terms is most ingeniously practised in *The Sacred Wood*, a revolutionary book which deserves to be read as a whole though it is in fact an artfully stitched-together series of items. Yet even after Eliot published his *Selected Essays*, incorporating much material from it, the earlier book has continued to be reprinted. I remember the awed excitement with which in my early university days I borrowed it from the library and when other work was done sat down to try and read it. Exactly to what purpose it was hard to say, since I knew scarcely any of the texts or writers Eliot referred to. But the message came through even then: criticism was a very serious business, was usually slovenly performed or not at all, and we had better get down to 'comparison and analysis' while attempting to *ériger en lois*. The book is now framed by the preface to its 1928 edition in which poetry is defined as 'a superior amusement'. A true definition? No, says Eliot, not true, but 'if you call it anything else you are likely to call it something still more false'—like 'emotion recollected in tranquility' or 'criticism of life', say. Or you may be tempted to think that it inculcates morals or directs politics or acts as a surrogate for religion. But if poetry is what it is and not another thing, then the attempt to say what it is in other terms will issue only in a 'generality', a substitute for impression or for theory. In his introduction, Eliot permits himself to wish that Matthew Arnold had resisted the temptation to 'put literature into the corner, until he cleaned up the whole country first' and had given us more criticism, comparison and analysis of individual writers. What sort of thing does Eliot wish Arnold had done? He might have 'shown his contemporaries exactly why the author of *Amos Barton* is a more *serious* writer than Dickens, and why the author of *La Chartreuse de Parme* is more serious than either'. From our knowledge of Eliot's own criticism we remind ourselves that he never took the time to show us why Dickens was less serious than 'the author of *Amos Barton*' (and why not, by the way, the author of *Middlemarch*?) nor did he ever demonstrate Stendhal's greater seriousness. Nor, I think, did he show his own contemporaries 'exactly' why Joyce or Lewis was more 'serious' than Huxley or D. H. Lawrence.

The point is made not to confute Eliot, rather to suggest that 'serious' criticism, like 'poetry', is not to be defined, except insofar as the critic's practice gives us a sense of what it can mean. The casual-seeming remark about grades of seriousness in George Eliot, Dickens and Stendhal does not demonstrate anything, but may well nudge the reader into trying to see for himself just what 'seriousness' in *The Charterhouse of Parma* could amount to. By contrast one might say of F. R. Leavis that he attempted in *The Great Tradition* to show 'exactly' how George Eliot was more 'serious' than Dickens; but after having assimilated Leavis's criteria for seriousness one is tempted either to swallow them whole, as does the disciple, or reject them as personal and idiosyncratic, perhaps Puritan. Eliot's hints and paren-thetical jabs, his 'I could, if I had the time, a tale unfold' air, has a healthy way of leaving things open and up for argument.

There is, further, the even more complicated matter of finding a proper language in which to criticize poems: where in fact does one begin? One begins, Eliot says, 'with poetry as excellent words in excellent arrangement and excellent metre':

> That is what is called the technique of verse. But we observe that we cannot define even the technique of verse; we cannot say at what point 'technique' begins or where it ends; and if we add to it a 'technique of feeling,' that glib phrase will carry us but a little farther. We can only say that a poem, in some sense, has its own life . . .

These fascinatingly put-together sentences reveal the typically Eliotic critical operation. First the impeccably useless definition of 'technique of verse' as 'excellent' this and that, which definition seems to dissolve and exhaust the word. 'That is what is called [no doubt by certain glib writers] the technique of verse', as if you marshalled some good ideas together, then worked up your technique so as to come out with a good poem. By this time Eliot is himself using the word 'technique' in quotation marks, introducing a 'glib phrase' only to reject it. Since 'we cannot say' at what point 'it' begins or ends, then we had best not trust to 'generality'—as with 'poetry' or 'serious' the word 'generality' might turn out to be less useful or true than the confusion and uncertainty in which we were groping. 'So we cannot stop at any point' he goes on to say in concluding the 1928 preface. This motto represents for me, Eliot at his most typical and very best: the stubbornly playful and self-critical refusal to hand out definitions and wisdom about matters he could be trusted to know a lot about. Instead of depressing and discouraging a reader it has, or should have, the opposite effect, should make one eagerly alive to the mystery of poetic creation and curious about testing oneself against the next poem to be read.

The dissolving of key terms, the listings of definitional pitfalls or simplifications to avoid, the scrutinizing of an idea until it is seen to be only itself, not another thing like the Truth—it is a profoundly witty procedure. Like Huxley and Strachey, Eliot had put in his time at Ottoline Morrell's Garsington. And wit, we remember from the essay on Marvell, finally emerges after a short seminar on what it is not (not erudition, not cynicism) as 'a recognition, implicit in the expression of every experience, of other kinds of experiences which are possible'. This 'definition' was taken up by some New Critics and wielded like a triumphant sword. But as Eliot formulates it, it can be of no use to anybody trying to get the goods on some poem; indeed it is vague and veiled, all implicit recognition. Yet to formulate it any more precisely might well result in something less true; we might contrast Cleanth Brooks's rigid use of the word 'paradox' with Eliot's supple fluidity. The latter's criticism seldom gives its readers a place to stop and rest secure, even when he may think he has found one.

The Waste Land

The Sacred Wood threw new light on Marlowe, Ben Jonson, Swinburne; Eliot was shortly to follow with even more influential essays on the Metaphysicals, Marvell, and Dryden which have persuaded countless readers to look at these poets in Eliot's way. Yet there is another end to the scale, at which we can read the essays as works of art 'in themselves', becoming less interested in whether the statement about Dryden is true than in the artfulness with which Eliot's critical operation is carried on: the jokes, the sly comparisons, the booby traps—all the strategical rhetoric that is also a source of complex pleasure. Somewhere between our interest in what the essays tell us about writers, literature and criticism, and in what they show of Eliotic guile and showmanship, comes their importance and usefulness in understanding the poems he was himself writing. Particularly with regard to 'Gerontion', the interests and impulses of Eliot's criticism were deeply intertwined with his poetic concerns—'Tradition and the Individual Talent' helps us read 'Gerontion' and vice versa.

More recently, Kenner has argued convincingly that Eliot's essay on Dryden, published when *The Waste Land* was about to issue forth, is of prime importance in understanding that poem's origin as a satiric, 'social' poem about London which then turned into something else—an apocalyptic and mythological one. But an even more useful approach to the poem can be made instead through the Ben Jonson essay, by stressing the theatrical and caricatural aspects of Eliot's art, while guessing that the virtues he admired so much in Jonson's plays were precisely the ones he himself was attempting to get into the new long poem which was occupying him in 1921.[3] In these terms one looks at *The Waste Land* as, in Eliot's phrase about Jonson's work, a 'titanic show' and emphasizes the literally 'superficial' aspects of the poetry, the presentation of 'characters' (really more like Jonsonian humours) who possess no 'third dimension'—as, for Eliot, Jonson's characters also did not, though Shakespeare's did:

> The simplification consists largely in reduction of detail, in the seizing of aspects relevant to the relief of an emotional impulse which remains the same for that character, in making the character conform to a particular setting. The stripping is essential to the art, to which is also essential a flat distortion in the drawing; it is an art of caricature, of great caricature, like Marlowe's.

There are a number of passages in which this 'stripping' and dis-tortion can be observed. but the most brilliant one and the one which

has drawn most adverse criticism is the encounter between typist and
young man carbuncular in 'The Fire Sermon':

> A small house agent's clerk, with one bold stare,
> One of the low on whom assurance sits
> As a silk hat on a Bradford millionaire.
> The time is now propitious, as he guesses,
> The meal is ended, she is bored and tired,
> Endeavours to engage her in caresses
> Which still are unreproved, if undesired.
> Flushed and decided, he assaults at once;
> Exploring hands encounter no defence;
> His vanity requires no response,
> And makes a welcome of indifference.

It is sometimes said that this is a sordid passage, conveying nothing
so much as Eliot's personal shudder at loveless sex, actively snobbish
about clerks and typists, and lacking the true poise of complex art.
Yet the verse does not shudder but rather elevates the mundane,
'sordid', decidedly unheroic material into an object of admiration—
and remember that Eliot is composing here in the 'heroic stanza'
(though the quatrains aren't separated) of Dryden's 'Annus Mirabilis'
or Gray's 'Elegy'. We experience a flawless, stunning simplification
of behavior that gives no complex insights into real people, nor offers
praise or blame for their behavior. This absence of insightful sympathy
is the condition of Eliot's art in the poem, to be appreciated for its
bold strokes, rhythmic felicity and splendidly chosen diction which,
like Eliot's own description of Jonson's creations, make 'a great caricature which is beautiful'.

Eliot consistently pushed for 'simplification' in the art he hoped to
see more of around him. There is an interesting though not always
lucid essay called 'The Possibility of a Poetic Drama' which appears
in *The Sacred Wood* but not in *Selected Essays*, where the presen-
tational aspect of art (rather than its reflective possibilities) is insisted
upon as necessary for any permanent literature. Flaubert, unlike
Thackeray in *Vanity Fair*, is praised for putting his art into statement,
for refraining from reflection and moralization, for 'keeping out a
great deal that Thackeray allowed to remain in' (Hemingway looms
on the horizon), for making a book that, like Henry James's mind, no
idea could violate. In comparing present possibilities with the achieve-

ment of Elizabethan poetic drama, Eliot concluded by saying that 'our problem should be to take a form of entertainment, and subject it to the process which would leave it a form of art. Perhaps the music-hall comedian is the best material.' Immediately he draws back a little, confessing that he's made a 'dangerous' suggestion. But it was that suggestion on which he acted in composing *The Waste Land*. Evident too, particularly in the essays on Ben Jonson and Dryden, is the implied fact that Eliot's medium was verse rather than the novel. However much *L'Education Sentimentale* was admired, however much Flaubert left out, a poem written in 1921 would incline towards what Eliot called 'creative' rather than the 'critical' fiction of which Flaubert's book is the distinguished example.[4] After all, the poet does not have hundreds of pages in which to build up, through statement and image, the society Flaubert anatomized. His relation to the actual world will be, in Eliot's term from the Jonson essay, more 'tenuous', his satire will originate from no precise intellectual attitude held towards the actual world. Like Dryden and Jonson's poetry it will be 'creative', enhancing rather than diminishing the characters—more precisely the caricatures—it sets down in broad and simple strokes.

If this much at least is granted, that Eliot attempted in *The Waste Land* to realize some of the virtues he found in poets and music-hall entertainers he admired (or even if it was in fact the other way around —if his admirations were symptomatic of deeper poetic impulses), then an approach to it quite other than one conducted through scrutiny of the 'Notes', analysis of the Fisher King-Grail motif, or paraphrase and translation of its caricatures into some assumed 'meaning' with reference to the modern world *circa* 1922, is demanded. Yet many readers did and still do take it as a profound poem about the death of civilization, are moved, even terrified by its vision of life; and perhaps it is itself an unsalutary critical simplification to say, fifty years later, look, *this* is the kind of poem it really is and something other than you took it for. The French proletariat who rioted at the *Comédie Française* production of Eliot's favorite Shakespearian play, *Coriolanus*, may have been simpleminded and misguided in their response, yet they so responded and the cultural meaning of the play was added to. Two questions about *The Waste Land* need now to be investigated further: first, whether there are in fact demonstrable elements in the poem which do not fit the notion of it as simplified caricature, a titanic entertainment displayed by a clever showman; second, whether it is reasonable, even morally necessary, to complain that the poem is inadequate because it so severely limits its sympathies, acting as if poetry were a superior amusement (and let them eat cake) in the face of which 'the actual world' must fend for itself as best it can.

I think the answer to the first question is yes, the answer to the second one no, provided one accepts that there are ways of being 'human' in poetry other than through expressing complex sympathies with one's fellow human beings. At any rate there are moments in the poem which can't be accounted for by using terms like 'poetry of the surface' or 'caricature' or 'simplification', and by speaking of Eliot's poetry as an employment of the methods of Ben Jonson or Dryden. Those two poets seldom if ever touch the deepest terrors and desires, as Shakespeare did and as Eliot had already attempted to do in 'Prufrock' and 'Gerontion'. That part of *The Waste Land* where the poetry is most painfully evocative, most stirring and disturbing of the feelings, is Part V, 'What the Thunder Said', with its vision of falling towers and its unreal cities which crack and reform and burst in the violet air. But, to take one example from earlier in the poem, what is to be made of the moment in the public bar in Lower Thames Street, after the young man and typist have gone their ways and the narrator hears

> The pleasant whining of a mandoline
> And a clatter and a chatter from within
> Where fishmen lounge at noon: where the walls
> Of Magnus Martyr hold
> Inexplicable splendour of Ionian white and gold.

These lines and the words which compose them are so familiar we can hardly see them to read; yet the 'statement' those words make is quite impossible to articulate. What, for example, is the precise weight of that colon which separates the fishmen from the splendours of Magnus Martyr? Are church and pub ironically juxtaposed, and if so to what purpose? At any rate the lines invite a surge of feelings, and not negative feelings either; there is something strongly attractive about the pub and strongly stirring, inexplicably so, about what the walls of Magnus Martyr hold. It has nothing to do with Grail legends and precious little, except in the crudest sense, with Fisher Kings. The poetry is what it is, and not another thing; memorable and affecting, but hardly translatable into meaningful, rational statement.

A passage like this, admittedly one of the few which displays 'positive' feelings, should not be adduced as an indication that Eliot's attitude towards human life really wasn't so gloomy after all; especially since if the poetry does matter, then depressing life-situations like that of the typist returning home to entertain her clerk are transformed into something beyond depression. But there are also, particularly in the final section, equally strong passages of 'negative' feeling (these adjectives reveal their inadequacies) about the 'dry sterile thunder', the 'hooded hordes swarming', the 'bats with baby faces in the violet light'; or passages filled with a mixture of yearningly romantic accessions of hopeless sadness:

> In this decayed hole among the mountains
> In the faint moonlight, the grass is singing
> Over the tumbled graves, about the chapel
> There is the empty chapel, only the wind's home.

Here the surface exists only to be dreamed through towards something we know not what that lies deeper. So we are invited, after the thunder speaks, to think of the key and confirm our prison, or we are promised a what-might-have-been in which

> . . . your heart would have responded
> Gaily, when invited, beating obedient
> To controlling hands

and are finally asked to contemplate the narrator shoring fragments against his ruins. With earlier figures like Mr. Eugenides, or the portraits of different ladies, we could admire the bold authority with which presences are struck off, and be more interested in what they *were* than in anything they might mean when plugged into a scheme of explanation. But 'What the Thunder Said' is a different story that bids for grander, more chilling revelations.

This final section moves away from the tight control of earlier portraits into more plangent complaint and regret. It might be deplored as a falling-off from Augustan brilliance, but I should rather see it as a finding of direction into a less critically detached, more vulnerably human lamentation. At least the great and culminating passage on the towers upside down in air, the bats crawling head downward, the voices singing out of empty cisterns and exhausted wells is that: the most profound moment of lonely, visionary desperation in the poem. Hell is here not for other people only; and it is from this point in the poem (and from its subsequent elaboration in 'The Hollow Men') that one goes on to read 'Ash-Wednesday' and *Four Quartets*. For this reason we must reject a recent unfavorable version of *The Waste Land* given by Ian Hamilton (*A Poetry Chronicle*, 1973) in which he argues that 'Eliot's technique . . . is to proffer personal disabilities as impersonal talents, to allow emotional weaknesses to masquerade as moral strengths.' This criticism would have point if only the first three books (and particularly books II and III) were considered; although even there I think the 'impersonal talents' Hamilton refers to are much more strange and impressive than he finds them. But it's significant that he studiously avoids any mention of the final section, in which impersonal talent is not at all the phrase which springs to mind as we read this patently personal distension of the nerve-ends. 'It is impossible to say just what I mean!/But as if a magic lantern threw the nerves in patterns on a screen': so Prufrock explained himself. In 'What the Thunder Said' the nerves thrown on screen are placed at no comfortable distance outside the man who is suffering from them.

Eliot, like Lewis, kept protesting the virtues of impersonality, coldness, harshness, bold simplifications and broad strokes. But as early as *Tarr* Lewis displayed mixed feelings about his curse of humor and about the 'life' over against which it stood. Neither should it be forgotten that Eliot's 'Tradition' essay, after the famous lines about how poetry is an escape from emotion and personality, turns around to confide that 'Of course only those who have personality and emotions know what it means to want to escape from these things.' The escape is not as perfectly successful in *The Waste Land* as Eliot the critic might have liked; it may for that very reason be a poem human beyond anything imagined by those who chastise him for inadequately responding to life. The poems he wrote later on have their own logic and virtues; but there is no way to get around *The Waste Land* by setting it aside as a cultural document or a quaint poem which once was 'difficult' and is now destined merely to be studied in classrooms. Frank Kermode put the matter best when he once said about the poem that it was there for Eliot the dreams crossed, the dreams in which began responsibilities.

III

D. H. Lawrence: 1920-1930

Lawrence doesn't fit in anywhere, refuses to be bracketed with post-war 'satirists', would make an unhappy consort with the Men of 1914 (he disliked *Ulysses*, thought Lewis a purely negative writer, seems not even to have bothered forming an opinion of Eliot's or Pound's work), and is neither sympathetic towards Bloomsbury nor nostalgic for the solid entertainments of Wells or Bennett. I speak here of the Lawrence who pronounced on these matters in essays, letters and the fiction written in that period from war's end and the publication of *Women in Love* (1920) to his death in 1930. This leaves out of account the great Lawrence; even if one can't decide finally whether *Women in Love* is more a work of inspiriting genius or a shrill and grotesque piece of murderous disintegration, *The Rainbow* and *Sons and Lovers* will remain and Lawrence be remembered as a great realistic novelist of the family and the sexual struggle. I feel less guilty than otherwise I might about confining my own commentary—much of it adverse— to the postwar, progressively embittered Lawrence, for two reasons: first that there is much fascination in sorting out conflicting responses to the stories, novels, poems, invectives and essays written from *Women in Love* until his death; second, that there has recently appeared an excellent discussion by Roger Sale of Lawrence's three major works—*Sons and Lovers*, *The Rainbow*, *Women in Love*— which makes the fullest, most convincingly imaginative defense and explanation of his career, as revealed in those books.[1]

On the other hand, Mr. Sale gives short shrift to Lawrence's work after *Women in Love*, indeed treats it as no more than a brief and largely unsatisfactory postscript to a completed story. A few tales and the book on American literature are all he cares to salvage from the general stridency and wreckage of those years. Such an accounting of a great artist's production, when it spans the years from age thirty-five to his death is not easy to understand and accept. Lawrence was dying, at least was seriously ill from 1925 on, was not acclaimed as a great writer by everyone, was harassed by censors and other culture-morons; still, others have been as ill, have suffered as many slings and arrows without causing us to invoke outrageous fortune as an answer to what went wrong in a writer during the years which should have been the most creatively distinguished ones of his life. Or perhaps nothing *did* go wrong, at least in the books which came from Lawrence's pen during this last decade. It is common to wish that he were less doggedly insistent in his saying of valuable things. It is also common to argue as John Carey has in the conclusion to his acute essay on Lawrence's 'doctrine', where after extracting and ridiculing that doctrine Carey pulls himself up a step short of total condemnation; even though abstractly conceived it may well be 'disgusting, dangerous or satanic', it becomes something else in the books themselves, namely 'alive':

> Extracted, schematized, it loses its shifting, paradoxical quality: the luminous visual and verbal power marshalled to attack the visual and verbal; the intellect deriding the intellect; the sensitivity and callousness fused together. It loses, too, its personality, its human smell—and that is a vital consideration, for it is the final paradox of Lawrence's thought that, separated from his warm, intense, wonderfully articulate being, it becomes the philosophy of any thug or moron.[2]

These two positions are not as far apart as at first they sound: one admires the good things Lawrence says but is put off by the messianic style; the other insists that the things he had to say are only good when they smell human and occur as the expression, in a book, of a 'warm, intense, wonderfully articulate being'. It is surely right to look for what is live and shifting and undeniably expressive of Lawrence's personality; such looking for and pointing out is to be preferred to further 'objective' analysis or readings of individual books. But when Lawrence of 1920–30 is inspected for moments when, in Carey's terms, the human smell is most evident, these moments very often turn out to be ones of rejection, disgust at others and at self expressed through the passionate but chilling cry of *noli me tangere*: moments in which the reek of the human reeks of the grave, where in the words of his fine poem 'Hymn to Priapus' Lawrence cannot 'And will not forget./ The stream of my life in the darkness/Deathward set!'

In a review of Edward Dahlberg's *Bottom Dogs* written toward the end of Lawrence's life he made this judgement on a contemporary: 'Wyndham Lewis gives a display of the utterly repulsive effect people have on him, but he retreats into the intellect to make his display. It is a question of manners and manners. The effect is the same. It is the same exclamation: They stink! My God, they stink!' No one would deny that Lewis created some unlovely specimens of things behaving like persons in his satiric fiction; but it is primarily in Lawrence's own writings from the 1920s that the really violent and reproachfully negative emotions are directed, in scorn and profound depression, at the way other people behave. A letter written on 22 December 1913, filled with acute comments about Walt Whitman, ended with Lawrence criticizing Whitman's generalizing rhetoric by saying that 'One *doesn't* feel like that—except in the moments of wide, gnawing desire when everything has gone wrong' and going on to speak of Whitman's poetry as 'Just a self revelation of a man who could not live, and so had to write himself.' At the risk of being unfeelingly glib it is hard to avoid turning these remarks back on post-*Women in Love* Lawrence, as when things went wrong—censorship, bodily decay, the deterioration of things with Frieda—his desire to set other people straight, to chastise the world for being out of step, reached its widest and most gnawing proportions. As the life became ever more dissatisfied, transient and tortured, so the books poured out faster, the 'self revelation' increased to epic scale. And the 'clear-sighted and mocking vivacity . . . quite without animus', which F. R. Leavis found in Lawrence's criticism and letters, more and more seems a figment of Leavis's imagination rather than anything encountered in the pages of Lawrence's books.

Of course if Leavis had found more 'animus' in Lawrence, less clear-sighted vision and more obsessive rage projected on his human surroundings, he could not have admired him as the apostle of health and sanity presented to us in the pages of *D. H. Lawrence: Novelist*.

Yet whether or not we esteem Lawrence's work in the 1920s it is inescapably there, disturbing us by its refusal, its inability to be, among other things, great literature. For rather than appearing as Dr. Leavis's supreme novelist, the Lawrence of this decade often is scarcely a novelist at all, impatient with everything that makes the novel what it is and not another thing. This does not make his work less interesting. Twenty years after Leavis's book, we no longer have to answer, as he did, Eliot's charge that Lawrence was a corruptor, 'rotten and rotting others', by insisting that on the contrary he was the sanest and healthiest English writer of this century. Nor are his views now felt by the young to carry with them the possibilities for profound changes of conviction in regard to sexual and social behavior, although *Lady Chatterley's Lover* and *Women in Love* are read interestedly and argued about disinterestedly in university classrooms, without recriminations. This disinterestedness could be interpreted as a sign that Lawrence's power to convert is diminished; as one who twenty years ago thought he was converted, I do not lament this possibility, and think that present-day cooler heads may well be better readers of his books than I was.

Women in Love

One of the truths about *Women in Love* is true also of Lawrence's other prophetic fictions: that rereading the novel over a period of years, one more and more treasures incidental things, while passing over the big moments with a sense that one has been there before. There is a chapter called 'Continental' which is not strictly necessary to develop the tale or characters but simply tells how Ursula and Birkin leave England and travel across Belgium. In the darkness they see the lights of Ghent station and Ursula is reminded of her childhood at the Marsh and her servant Tilly 'who used to give her bread and butter sprinkled with brown sugar in the old living-room where the grandfather clock had two pink roses in a basket painted above the figures on the face'. Now she is 'travelling into the unknown with Birkin, an utter stranger', and the distance between now and childhood 'was so great, that it seemed she had no identity, that the child she had been, playing in Cossethay churchyard, was a little creature of history, not really herself'. In this lovely passage, and in much of the chapter, Lawrence reverts to a narrative not strikingly different from the one employed in *Sons and Lovers* and at times in *The Rainbow*, so it may be retrograde to admire it. Yet often-made claims that the central narrative technique of *Women in Love* is something we must appreciate in its own, new terms should not be too quickly accepted.

Lawrence tells us in the preface to *Women in Love* that we should approach our soul with a 'deep respect', that nothing in the passional self can be bad, and that 'This struggle for verbal consciousness should not be left out in art' since it is a great part of life. The last, strange sentence has its own art, reads as if 'art' is exactly the kind of finished thing liable to leave out the 'struggle for verbal consciousness'. By opting for a style that would express the 'pulsing, frictional to-and-fro which works up to culmination', the crucial struggle will be presented as it deserves to be. But Lawrence also adds, as if in nervous self-justification, that in portraying this struggle he is not out to superimpose a theory, rather to give us life as it is most deeply felt. This is exactly the way he talks in his preface to the American edition of *New Poems* (1918) which sets up the fluid pulse of his own Free verse in rather crude opposition to the fixities and rigidities of 'the old poetry', and puts life against death, the organic against the mechanical.

One sees why Lawrence insisted that he wasn't superimposing a theory, since he most surely had a theory about the nature and destiny of Gudrun and Gerald. Towards the end of *Women in Love*, in the 'Snowed Up' chapter where crucial steps in Gudrun's progression towards mechanical corruption and Gerald's towards polar annihilation have to be made, the narrator says with regard to Gudrun:

> Cross the threshold, and you found her completely, completely cynical about the social world and its advantages. Once inside the house of her soul, and there was a pungent atmosphere of corrosion, an inflamed darkness of sensation, and a vivid, subtle, critical consciousness, that saw the world distorted, horrific.
>
> What then, what next? Was it sheer blind force of passion that would satisfy her now? Not this, but the subtle thrills of extreme sensation in reduction. It was an unbroken will reacting against her unbroken will in a myriad subtle thrills

of reduction, the last subtle activities of analysis and breaking
down . . .

Aside from the crudity of its style—why should one *not* find fault with
the unimaginative repetition of 'subtle', or the attempt to pass off
'pungent atmosphere of corrosion' as convincingly about anything?—
the trouble with the passage is that only a few chapters before we have
seen Ursula and Gudrun taking a last look at their parents' house
and agreeing that they are not eager for another 'home':

> 'But a home, an establishment! Ursula, what would it mean?
> —think!'
> 'I know,' said Ursula, 'We've had one home—that's enough
> for me.'
> 'Quite enough,' said Gudrun.
> 'The little grey home in the west,' quoted Ursula ironically.
> 'Doesn't it sound grey, too,' said Gudrun grimly.

In 'Why the Novel Matters' Lawrence says that only in the Novel
are '*all* things given full play', that 'out of the full play of all things
emerges the only thing that is anything, the wholeness of a man,
the wholeness of a woman, man alive and live woman'. One must
consult his own sense of what is or isn't full play, but I submit that
something like it is heard in this exchange between the sisters and in
Gudrun's final 'Doesn't it sound grey, too,' said 'grimly' but with a
saving wit and sanity such as is found in Lawrence's best letters. By
contrast, the other passage's insistence on how only the 'subtle thrills of
extreme sensation in reduction' will satisfy her (and which the sculptor,
Loerke, supposedly represents) sounds like a put-up job. Isn't it
possible that a girl who was capable of making the remark about the
greyness of a grey home in the west might possess the saving touch of
complication which would allow her to be seen as more than illustrative of the 'vivid, subtle critical consciousness' that is wholly dis-
integrative and reductive?

Lawrence abuses Tolstoy (in 'Morality and the Novel') with respect
to *Anna Karenina* and to the creation of Pierre, for putting his 'thumb
on the scale' and interfering with life—the full play of all things; yet
he could not heed his own warning in the books beginning with
Women in Love. Gerald and Gudrun are hunted down and done in
by an author who has imposed a scheme upon the novel that these

characters are not permitted to disrupt. The freedom of disruption is reserved instead for Birkin and Ursula, and it is remarkable in the case of these successful lovers how their conversational and social individuation is so strong, their 'full play' so evident after prolonged struggle with each other. It even survives the embarrassing language Lawrence reaches for in the famous 'Excurse' chapter. The struggle for verbal consciousness with respect to Ursula and Birkin is present in carefully worked-out scenes where different ways of expression are tried out, rejected, come back to: in their struggle the novel succeeds in putting us in touch with the 'wholeness' of man alive and live woman. It is a tribute to Lawrence's full sense of life then that even though he writes about Birkin (in 'Excurse') that 'a lambent intelligence played secondarily about his pure Egyptian concentration in darkness' the book shucks off such cant; we *know* there is a truer reality of character here than any talk about 'suave loins of darkness' or 'pure mystic nodality of physical being' or 'star-equilibrium' can suggest. And there are poignant post-'Excurse' moments in the book, where it becomes clear that Lawrence can't bring Birkin and Ursula any closer together, where we know that even what they shared in 'Excurse' is only momentary and not enough—especially when something more, like Birkin's failed man-to-man relation with Gerald Crich, is contemplated.

With respect to Birkin and Ursula the book survives its doctrinal superimpositions; with respect to Gudrun and Gerald it does not, though there is much interesting analysis of Gerald in relation to industrial society, to family, and to the condition of England. What it's most difficult to excuse Lawrence for—particularly in the light of the books to come—is his badgering of characters, most blatantly evident in the case of Hermione Roddice. Although Lawrence is usually praised for his creation of this supposedly liberated woman who is but a mouthpiece for Birkin's doctrines, in fact the exposure of her is crude. As revealed most fully in the 'Classroom' chapter, Lawrence's method is to have Hermione go on at great length about how knowledge and the mind are killing us:

... Then, pulling herself together with a convulsed
movement, Hermione resumed, in a sing-song, casual voice:

> 'But leaving me apart, Rupert; do you think the
> children are better, richer, happier, for all this
> knowledge; do you really think they are? Or is it
> better to leave them untouched, spontaneous? Hadn't
> they better be animals, simple animals, crude, violent
> *anything*, rather than this self-consciousness, this
> incapacity to be spontaneous?'

As she goes on and on, repeating the same catch-phrases, we are asked
to notice 'a queer rumbling in her throat', a 'clenched' fist 'like one in
a trance', another 'convulsed movement of her body' all of which go
to make up her 'queer rhapsody' which she 'drawls' to Ursula in a
'queer resonant voice'. Eventually, taking a deep breath, Birkin
assumes command and destroys her, exposing the arguments as
shibboleths only. Or so we are supposed to feel. In fact one finds oneself embarrassed and eventually annoyed at the slovenly butchering
of Hermione. No worry about revealing 'the full play of all things'
here—supposedly this woman is *only* a mouthpiece, wholly entranced
by her own 'queer' rhapsody, incapable of a word of truth or honest
response to anything. To take sides with Birkin and exult in his
triumph is a debasement of intelligence; the triumph is hollow because
the fight has been staged, allowed to be conducted only within certain
rigidly circumscribed limits. Admittedly Lawrence does permit Hermione to bash Birkin with the piece of lapis lazuli not too long afterwards; and as long as we direct the blow towards Lawrence, as well
as his hero, perhaps the writer is vindicated. But the book's 'satire',
if meant to be a lively and engaging battle of wills and ideas, sadly
fails to be such. The word for it instead is one Lawrence uses frequently and in this book—'jeering'.

Women in Love is largely free of such jeering because Lawrence
has not yet totally despaired of regenerative possibilities, perhaps
even the creation between men and women of a new world—'the joint
work of men and women' of which he spoke to Garnett in 1914 and
which the novel set out to express. Seven years later, in another letter
to Garnett (19 October 1921) the following postscript occurs: 'I hear
I am in worse odour than ever, for *Women in Love*. But, pah! what
do I care for all the *canaille*.' It was a refrain to be heard often over the
remainder of his life. And the 'joint work of men and women' of which

he spoke so hopefully in 1914, while struggling to realize it in his
marriage to Frieda, might be recalled in juxtaposition with the following extract from a letter to Koteliansky in March 1919:

> I am not going to be left to Frieda's tender mercies
> until I am well again. She really is a devil—and I
> feel as if I would part from her for ever—let her go
> alone to Germany, while I take another road. For it is
> true, I have been bullied by her long enough. I really
> could leave her now, without a pang I believe. The time
> comes, to make an end, one way or another. . . .

Look, we have come through, and I can't stand it. But somehow he
kept going and in the grip of a 'wide, gnawing desire when everything
has gone wrong' undertook a savage pilgrimage or, if one prefers, a
journey with genius, while attempting (in his early phrase about *Sons
and Lovers*) to shed his sickness in the books which he poured out.

1920–25

Lawrence's major fictional expression of these years I take to be *St.
Mawr* (1925) which Leavis first proclaimed a masterpiece comparable
with *The Waste Land* and is now included in the *Oxford Anthology
of English Literature*. But before considering *St. Mawr* let us examine
the tone and direction of certain essays and short novels which
appeared during these post-*Women in Love* years. As the quotation
from 'Why the Novel Matters' suggested, Lawrence as critic-
philosopher of the form is in favour of Life, against rules and 'Thou
Shalt Nots', against schemes of morality and superimposed systems of
explanation; he is against the intellect of the novelist insofar as it
tries to dictate to the passional self, tries to force the blood to obey its
prescriptions. So Tolstoy cheated in *Anna Karenina* by making Anna
pay, and created the 'dull' Pierre in *War and Peace* who has too many
ideas and is not 'quick' enough. He is also against too much 'purpose'
in modern novelists: 'They've all got it: the same snivelling purpose.
They're all little Jesuses in their own eyes, and their "purpose" is to
prove it. Oh Lord!—*Lord Jim*! *Sylvestre Bonnard*! *If Winter Comes*!
Main Street! *Ulysses*! *Pan*!' No attempt is made to elucidate the
'purpose' that somehow links Conrad to Sinclair Lewis, Joyce, and

some others, but the jeering tone ('Oh Lord—*Lord Jim*!) is heard at length in the same essay ('The Novel', 1924) in Lawrence's baiting of 'Leo' (Tolstoy) and Leo's insufficiently alive creations—Pierre, and the Prince in *Resurrection*. This habit of jeering, of baiting and teasing authors had been fully developed in the just-published *Studies in Classic American Literature*, and there it often works brilliantly: destructively and amusingly in the Franklin essay; more complicatedly critical in the essays on two writers towards whom Lawrence had the deepest feelings—Melville and Whitman. Along with their harsh wit these essays reveal a critical disinterestedness and impersonality which, if it were general in Lawrence's work, would make him the great critic Leavis salutes.

But perhaps the American writers were sufficiently distant in time and space for Lawrence not to feel threatened by them or in competition with them. Not so with *Ulysses*, nor with Proust, who is jeered at along with other too 'personal' novelists because they keep writing about whether they feel twinges in their little toe. Even the Russians who admittedly meant so much to him come in for their licks: as early as 1916 he charged Tolstoy, Dostoyevsky, Turgenev, Chekhov (a 'Willy Wet-Leg') with showing 'a certain crudity and thick, uncivilised, insensitive stupidity about them', and he realizes 'how much finer and purer and more ultimate our own stuff is'. By the 1920s 'our own stuff' had pretty much boiled down to the works of D. H. Lawrence; even *A Passage to India*, just about the only novel by a contemporary Englishman Lawrence is caught admiring, makes him 'wish a bomb would fall and end everything. Life is more interesting in its undercurrents than in its obvious; and E. M. does see people, people and nothing but people: *ad nauseam*' (23 July 1924). Novels should be about something more than people, should be 'finer and purer and more ultimate' than those Russian novels with their 'certain crudity' perhaps smelling too much of people. Novelists should not, on the other hand, do dirt on life like Flaubert or Thomas Mann did, nor be deliberately dirty-minded like Joyce, nor be resigned like Arnold Bennett (who is referred to as 'a pig in clover') nor be clever and negative like Lewis or Huxley. At the same time Lawrence seems to have been impressed with his own work, particularly with *Women in Love* which he liked best, but also with *Lady Chatterley*,

The Man Who Died and no doubt others. We can presume that he was attempting to transcend the limitations of other novelists and to create in his own works what he found lacking in theirs.

It would be easy but unprofitable to treat Lawrence's fiction during these years as failing to live up to his principles: no artist should be expected to practise what he preaches. Still it is instructive—perhaps only as illustrating the gap between promise and performance—to hear him loudly declaring (in 'Morality and the Novel', 1925) that if you try to 'nail anything down' in the novel it 'gets up and walks away with the nail', and that it is a sin for the novelist to put his 'thumb in the pan'. His own most recent novels, *Aaron's Rod* and *Kangaroo*, had shown a very heavy thumb in the pan indeed; nor was anyone likely to be unaware of doctrinal designs in his just-completed *The Plumed Serpent*. While essential reading for the student of Lawrence, these novels all seem to me disastrous ventures that no one would recommend to an ideal common reader. *Aaron's Rod* is shapeless and wandering, filled with invitations to connect a name with some real-life friend or enemy of Lawrence's, and of course providing (in the Aaron-Lilly relationship) the leader-follower business which interested Lawrence so much in those years and which now seems only dreary and embarrassing. *Aaron's Rod* begins wonderfully with the hero's walkout on his family, shocking yet natural in its execution. Later on there are some good moments in London and later still some interesting travelogue. But the whole doesn't add up to a novel; nor does *Kangaroo* which is part leader-follower dialectic, part good writing about Australia, plus the famous and detachable insert of Lawrence's nightmare physical examination for the army. And while *The Plumed Serpent* might appeal to some readers with anthropological interests or a soft spot in the heart for mornings in Mexico, it seems to me at the very bottom of all Lawrence's work—an often hateful and more often boring tract. It must have been this book, or work related to it, which moved Wyndham Lewis to refer on a later occasion to the tiresomeness of Lawrence's 'arty voodooism'.

More attractive to our hypothetical common reader are the longer stories (or shorter novels) from these years, notably 'The Fox', 'The Captain's Doll', 'The Princess', and 'The Woman Who Rode Away'. The first two have been praised as masterpieces by Leavis, while

Graham Hough puts 'The Woman Who Rode Away' at the very summit of Lawrence's art. All of them contain flashes of vivid creation, but they do not get up and walk away with the nail Lawrence has hammered through them. More troublingly, they set forth with evident sympathy, even with some relish on their author's part, certain aggressively cruel actions we are asked to assent to, or at least to believe have more 'life' in them than the deadness they sweep out of the way. It is not surprising that Kate Millett, preoccupied with hunting down Lawrence in *Sexual Politics*, should gleefully pounce on 'The Princess' with its dark-blooded rapist, Romero, who serves the prim Princess with what Lawrence evidently thinks she deserves. Nor that Millett should read 'The Woman Who Rode Away' as reminiscent of hard-core pornography in its carefully-graduated stripping-down of the woman in preparation for the final to-be-welcomed-as-her-destiny thrust of the dark-blooded Indian's knife. What price landscape, symbolic journeys, mythical translation beyond the social world, if to get them you have to endure a happening simply beyond sympathetic comprehension? One doesn't have to be a feminist to find it absurd, or to deplore our assumed situation as a watchful reader of all those Indians watching the white lady. No struggle towards verbal consciousness, no full play of all things: only a toneless narration, rhapsodic and drugged in its assent to the 'inevitable'.

The earlier short novels written in the backwash of *Women in Love* are much more humanly interesting; the possibility of love and marriage between man and woman was then still a real one in Lawrence's mind, and so he did not have to search out a character's fulfilment in the most remote, unhuman circumstances. Yet even here, in the social comedy of 'The Captain's Doll' which Leavis admires so much, or in the fine renderings of March, Banford and Henry in 'The Fox', a new relationship between man and woman is possible only after great violence has been done to the world, or to its representatives—like Banford or Mrs. Hepburn—who stands for oppression, morality and disapproval. For the liberation of March to occur, Banford has to be obliterated by a falling tree, cut down of course by March's lover Henry who had earlier said to himself about Banford: 'You're a nasty little thing. I hope you'll be paid back for all the harm you've done me for nothing. I hope you will—you nasty little thing.' She is paid back with interest, and if the tale had ended there, as perhaps it should have, the shocked abruptness of the event might have discouraged questions about its meaning. As written, Lawrence goes on for a few pages in which March envies Banford and Henry wonders if he should have left them to kill each other. Still, 'The Fox' remains a memorable tale whose particularity is richer than its doctrinal reference. It says more than it means. 'The Captain's Doll' is much more the comedy of ideas with the lovers, Hepburn and Hannele, further exploring the proper relationship between man and wife which occupied Birkin and Ursula. For a short novel it seems curiously overextended, disposes of Hepburn's first wife by making her fall out of a window (a joke?) and is burdened by the rather tedious figure of Hepburn himself who spends much time peering solemnly at the stars through his telescope. By itself, without the fact of *Women in Love*, it would excite little interest.

St. Mawr

With *St. Mawr* the 'Lawrence problem' presents itself most fully for inspection. Leavis would have us admire its sardonic 'doing' of rootless London society, of Lou's husband 'being an artist', of the intensity and seriousness of Lawrence-Lou's awareness of modern sterility and her wish to live more deeply and passionately in a harmony of mind-and-blood consciousness. Richard Poirier has seen it as a moving example of the attempt to create a world elsewhere, through Lou's early imaginings of what the horse means and later through her attempt to articulate her feelings about 'wild America' on the farm in New Mexico. But as with the other tales, someone has to be got out of the way so that Lou can have her vision of at least possible liberation: in *St. Mawr* that someone is her husband Rico. Lawrence wastes no time in warming to the task; when Rico is introduced we are told that

> He was anxious for his future, and anxious for his place in the
> world, he was poor, and suddenly wasteful in spite of all his
> tension of economy, and suddenly spiteful in spite of all
> his ingratiating efforts, and suddenly ungrateful in spite of
> his burden of gratitude, and suddenly rude in spite of all his

good manners, and suddenly detestable in spite of all his suave,
courtier-like amiability.

With the exception of Lou's mother, Mrs. Witt, nobody in the tale, not
even Lou herself, finds Rico 'detestable'. But Lawrence's thumb has
tilted the pan at the outset: Rico is a pathetic, or detestable, contradiction; a thwarter of life, a purely social being and an unserious
man. Since nobody in society will punish him, the novelist must
put things to right—this is the sort of burden Lawrence takes on
himself increasingly in his later fictions.

St. Mawr is everything Rico is not, yet is himself thwarted by
Man, unfairly mastered by a race that has lost the capacity for true
mastery. There is no mistaking the depth of Lou-Lawrence's feelings
about St. Mawr; passages in which Lou thinks about or observes the
stallion are expressed with a care and poignancy that deliberately
contradict the slapdash casualness Lawrence affects in relation to the
young people and to English society: 'Since she had really seen St.
Mawr looming fiery and terrible in an outer darkness, she could not
believe the world she lived in. She could not believe it was actually
happening . . . the talk, the eating and drinking, the flirtation, the
endless dancing: it all seemed far more bodiless and, in a strange way,
wraithlike, than any fairy-story.' It is perhaps understandable then
that when Lawrence attempts to embody Lou's feelings in pointed
dialogue with her mother, some strain is felt; as in the following
exchange about St. Mawr's Welsh groom, Lewis, whom Mrs. Witt
has called stupid:

> 'No, mother, he's not stupid. He only doesn't care about our
> sort of things.'
> 'Like an animal! But what a strange look he has in his eyes!
> a strange sort of intelligence! and a confidence in himself. Isn't
> that curious, Louise, in a man with as little mind as he has?' . . .
> 'Why, mother!' said Lou impatiently. 'I think one gets so
> tired of your men with mind, as you call it. There are so many
> of that sort of clever men. And there are lots of men who aren't
> very clever, but are rather nice: and lots are stupid. It seems to
> me there's something else besides mind and cleverness, or
> niceness or cleanness. Perhaps it is the animal. Just think of
> St. Mawr! I've thought so much about him. We call him an
> animal but we never know what it means. He seems a far

greater mystery to me than a clever man. He's a horse. Why
can't one say in the same way, of a man: *he's a man?* There
seems no mystery in being a man. But there's a terrible
mystery in St. Mawr.'

After which Mrs. Witt is given, for her, an incredibly naïve line—
'Man is wonderful because he is able to *think*'—which Lou has no
trouble rounding on in the expected way.

It may be that in criticizing Lawrence here I simply reveal my own
limitations as a clever man. But the exclamatory and thrilled air of
it all is hard to accept. Though in other places Mrs. Witt is revealed
to be a ruthless ironist and relentless wit, she here plays straight-woman
to Lou's vision and is set up with extremely simpleminded lines. In
a similar manner Lawrence sees to it that there is not the least hint
of complication or mystery in the stage-Dean Vyner and his stuffy
wife who preside over the small English parish where Lou and her
mother are temporarily settled, nor in the fashionable young people
who invite Lou and Rico about. With the hills of Wales as backdrop'
one of the young set is allowed to say: 'I think this is the best age
there ever was for a girl to have a good time in. I read all through
H. G. Wells' history, and I shut it up and thanked my stars I live in
nineteen-twenty odd, not in some other beastly date when a woman
had to cringe before mouldy domineering men'. Thus Flora Manby's
declaration, and one knows the response it invites—the lip curled in
knowing contempt for this frivolous jazz-age young woman. Yet Lou
Witt is only twenty-five herself; is there no human speech possible for
a woman which is neither social inanities on one hand or world-weary,
wholly disillusioned knowingness about men and horses on the
other? Not, it seems, in the world of this cut-to-order fable.

The book's climax occurs on that same excursion along the Welsh
border where Flora makes her declaration. St. Mawr rears; Rico,
trying to regain control, pulls the horse over on top of him and injures
his own leg. A recent book in discussing this scene typifies the academic
acceptance of Lawrence which seems to me not only inadequate but
pernicious. One of the young people has been demonstrating his
superficiality by whistling a new dance tune:

> 'That's an awfully attractive tune,' Rico called. 'Do whistle
> it again, Fred. I should like to memorize it.'

Fred began to whistle it again.

At that moment St. Mawr exploded again, shied sideways
as if a bomb had gone off, and kept backing through the
heather.

'Fool!' cried Rico, thoroughly unnerved . . .

after which he pulls the horse over backwards on top of him. The critic
(Keith Sagar) remarks that the real fools are those who whistle dance
tunes—'Triviality in the face of life is what distinguishes them, the
old effort at serious living given up'—and that (as Lou learns later)
since what St. Mawr had reared at was an adder, 'In thwarting him,
Rico has thwarted the deepest impulses. In this context St. Mawr's
destructiveness is healthy.' When the tune-whistler, Fred Edwards,
tries to help Rico by grabbing the reins, St. Mawr convulses again, and
Lawrence says: 'Horror! The young man reeled backwards with his
face in his hands. He had got a kick in the face. Red blood running
down his chin!' About which Mr. Sagar simply comments: 'We cheer
his kick in the face of the young man.'[3]

On the contrary, I should say that 'we cheer' only if we forget that
novels are made out of words, if we see nothing embarrassing and
crude in Lawrence's exclamatory, falsely-naïve rendering of that kick
in the face. Or if, when 'It turned out that Rico had two broken ribs
and a crushed ankle. Poor Rico, he would limp for life', we're quite
willing to accept that fate as the right punishment for 'thwarting the
deepest impulses'. A more ironic reader might ask, what price the
deepest impulses, or how much does one deserve to be punished for
whistling dance tunes once too often? And this is not even to consider
the 'vision of evil' Lou has afterwards in which Lawrence loudly lays
out the allegorical reference of events: 'Mankind, like a horse, ridden
by a stranger, smooth-faced, evil rider. Evil himself, smooth-faced
and pseudo-handsome, riding mankind past the dead snake, to the
last break.' All this without the slightest regard for Lou's presumed
consciousness, as her creator goes on to preach about Germany, Russia,
Judas and various other matters.

The remarkable thing about *St. Mawr*, and about Lawrence
generally as an artist, is that even after nailing down the book in such a
way it goes on to become quite interesting: in conversations between Lou
and Mrs. Witt; in Mrs. Witt's spiriting away of the horse accompanied

by Lewis the groom; most of all in the long finale which relates the history of the ranch Lou buys and the confrontation between mother and daughter, between cynical nihilism and the still-struggling effort to create a new myth of 'wildness' in America. And again, as often in Lawrence, it is in the incidental pleasures, moments when the novelist seems relaxed, not pressing to make his big points, where truly the 'full play of all things' goes on. One should read him then in an uneasy doubleness of response, with a distrustful eye cocked at the doctrine and a disdain for the way it hobbles characters into the narrow confines of an author's will. But also with eyes open as, breathing more freely, he produces a matchless bit of nature or an undeniably strong whiff of despairing, hopeless sadness and impotence. This divided response will assure against assenting to academic readings like the just-instanced one, in which we find ourselves all too effortlessly on the right side, Lawrence's side. Surely he would not want us so easily there, would prefer us to be a bit insouciant, as one of his favorite words has it. Such insouciance characterizes perhaps the two best books he wrote during the years between *Women in Love* and *St. Mawr*— the studies in American literature and *Sea and Sardinia*. My preoccupation here with the novels and stories, and in the necessity of arguing with Lawrence, shouldn't obscure these important evidences that the writer is larger than the novelist.

Post-Mortem Effects

The novelist came back to life twice in the late 'twenties, in *Lady Chatterley's Lover* and at moments in *The Man Who Died*. With these affirmations of the phallic mystery, Lawrence celebrated his real subject once more, freed from doctrinal hagglings about Leader and Follower, wreaking less jeering vengeance on those who stood in the way of passional responses fully expressed. Yet there is a truth in Middleton Murry's review of *Lady Chatterley* (*Adelphi*, June 1929) which he termed 'for all its fiery purity' 'a deeply depressing book'. Murry was depressed because he understood Lawrence to be saying that the *only* sensitive awareness we need, and which is real, is awareness of the sexual mystery. All the eggs are there intensely gathered in one basket and presented to us with fervour and reverence. Do we accept them gratefully?

In addition to defenses of the novel against censorship, its merits as a work of art have recently been argued by Frank Kermode who is concerned to show how, triumphantly in *Women in Love* but often enough in the succeeding books, Lawrence's doctrine is resisted, even contradicted by the stuff of life incorporated in those books. Kermode sees *Lady Chatterley's Lover* as, despite serious lapses, a great achievement, and he calls *The Man Who Died* 'one of the most perfect of Lawrence's shorter fictions'. This is much more generous language than I myself should use about these last works; and Kermode has to work hard to make it stick, especially when discussing what until recently was not shared wisdom about *Lady Chatterley*— that Connie's shame is finally 'burned out' by an act of anal intercourse initiated by the resourceful gamekeeper. Kermode wants us to understand and accept the buggery, along with the initial paralysis of Clifford Chatterley (which readers have always and justly complained about as making things too easy by half) as apocalyptic symbols of the sort that Spenser and Milton used. He argues that

> . . . just as Lawrence himself recognised, when he read his first draft, that Chatterley's lameness symbolised 'the paralysis, the deeper emotional or passional paralysis, of most men of his sort and class today,' so we recognise the symbolism of Connie's rebirth. Both symbolisms belong to a metaphysic which Lawrence had long since internalised, and which the tale had, in its own way, to make objective. If we trust them it is because we trust the tale.

If Lawrence had, as on all evidence seems likely, 'internalised' the metaphysic of which these symbols are part, that seems to me regrettable, since as ideas or beliefs they are not very sturdy ones. More important though, is the 'tale' we are encouraged to trust somehow independent of the worth of these symbols or ideas? One might complain that, compared to tale-tellers like George Eliot, or James, or Arnold Bennett, Lawrence does not tell a very good tale here, that few readers move on breathlessly to find out what happens next—as they should do in Forster's ideal of the good story. Whatever connection there is between the ruined condition of industrial England

and Sir Clifford's paralysis is of that 'symbolic' kind which the novel asserts rather than can possibly demonstrate; thus the lovers' world becomes desperately idyllic, pastoral right down to those famous garlands woven into pubic hair, and, not only from Middleton Murry's perspective, depressing.

It is depressing that Lawrence believes so relentlessly in symbols which exclude so much of life, of history, of friendship, tolerance, sympathy, good-humor, the minor Forsterian virtues Lawrence in *Lady Chatterley* is too busy to practise or imagine. His fervent self-righteousness in the great cause makes us want to pick holes in his vision. He is against both the grey Puritan and the liberated smart youth of the 1920s; for he knows that 'Life is only bearable when the mind and body are in harmony, and there is a natural balance between them, and each has a natural respect for the other.' This sentiment, from 'Apropos *Lady Chatterley's Lover*', might be nodded at soberly, except that it goes along with an exultant kick at Swift, who supposedly was disturbed that 'Celia, Celia, Celia shits': 'A great wit like Swift could not see how ridiculous he made himself!' exclaims Lawrence with a ridiculous disregard for the excellently witty poem in which that refrain is sung by a hapless beau, and in which 'Swift' is not at all the horror-stricken figure Lawrence invents. It is Mellors rather, assuring Connie that 'if tha shits and if tha pisses' he wouldn't have it any other way, who is truly ridiculous and silly-sounding. Katherine Anne Porter was extremely perceptive when she complained in her 1961 *Encounter* essay on the book that the whole attempt to hallow 'dirty words', or to exalt bodily functions as marvelously natural and worthy of respect, was a mistake. In effect Miss Porter was saying that there is a gutter-side to life, a ribald, unsentimental lore that has grown up about certain functions which Swift made use of in his poem, and that there was something obscene about Lawrence trying to elevate and rescue them into natural acceptance, 'to purify and canonise obscenity . . . to take the low comedy out of sex'. Surely this is the most interesting question to ask about *Lady Chatterley's Lover* and one which a reader will answer as temperament directs.

More generally it involves one's attitude towards Romanticism in our century. As late as 1916 Lawrence could write about Swinburne that 'He is a great revealer, very great. I put him with Shelley as our greatest poet. He is the last fiery spirit among us . . .' Not quite the last, it turned out. It may well be that any attempt at 'objective' appraisal of Lawrence's work is doomed to failure. Roy Fuller was not speaking only for himself when in one of his Oxford poetry lectures he pointed out how his own relation to Lawrence began with a blind love affair with the books; after the affair ended and he fell out of love he was never able to look at them with the required dispassion. In late adolescence twenty-five years ago, one hitched one's wagon to Lawrence because he was a leader who knew how things should be revised, knew what was true and what false, what live and what dead. When thereafter one's life did not confirm these truths, one found other writers who talked in quite different ways and who did not even unanimously admire the fiery spirit of D. H. Lawrence. After the adverse criticism directed here against some key books in which the spirit reveals itself, it may seem disingenuous to end with a salute to Lawrence. But there are acceptable terms for this salute in another phrase of John Carey's, with whose remarks about Lawrence's doctrine we began. Speaking of *Paradise Lost* Carey says that it is 'great because it is objectionable. It spurs us to protest. Hence its continued life . . .' At least this kind of greatness the later Lawrence unarguably exhibits.

IV

Some 1920s Fiction:
Ford, Forster, Woolf

The leader for the *Times Literary Supplement*, 10 April 1919, was titled 'Modern Novels' and written, anonymously of course, by Virginia Woolf. A sort of try-out for the longer, more tendentious 'Mr. Bennett and Mrs. Brown', it seeks to clear room for Mrs. Woolf's own kind of fiction, the kind that, after publishing the admirable but old-fashioned *Night and Day* (1919) she would attempt in 'Kew Gardens', *Jacob's Room* and beyond.[1] 'Modern Novels' contains Virginia Woolf's famous metaphor for 'Life' as 'not a series of gig lamps symmetrically arranged; but a luminous halo, a semi-transparent envelope surrounding us from the beginning of consciousness to the end'. The novelist's task is to convey this 'unknown' and 'uncircumscribed' spirit—that is the 'proper stuff of fiction', at least as it looked to be in 1919. She salutes Hardy, Conrad and to a lesser extent W. H. Hudson, for having provided the proper stuff that enlivens their work; while to Wells, Bennett and Galsworthy she gives only the most qualified praise amounting to a not-so-faint damning of their collective enterprise. In one way or another they are all 'materialists' who 'spend immense skill and immense industry making the trivial and the transitory appear the true and the enduring'. In the midst of all this skill and industry, Life escapes. Mrs. Woolf looks to Joyce (*Ulysses* was at that moment appearing in the *Little Review*) and to the Russians (Chekhov is singled out) for providing necessary examples of the 'spiritual' and for disregarding the adventitious, to the extent that their novels and stories do not look like fiction as conventionally understood. She identifies what she calls the 'utmost sadness' found in the conclusions—or the recognition that there are no conclusions—

of the Russian mind; but she also discerns, in the tradition of English
fiction from Sterne to Meredith, an opposite instinct 'to enjoy and
fight rather than to suffer and to understand'. Another name for this
last instinct is Humour, and it will inevitably be present in any novel
that attempts to catch and convey 'everything . . . every feeling,
every thought; every quality of brain and spirit . . .'

This emphasis on the spiritual was to provide Wyndham Lewis
with a target for attack when, fifteen years later in *Men Without Art*,
he criticized Virginia Woolf's 'idealism' as too disembodied. It is certainly true that the Lewis of *Tarr* (which she may or may not have
read by 1919) and even more certainly of *The Apes of God* ten years
later, would not attempt to convey 'every feeling, every thought'
freed from the harshly witty and judgemental voice of the overriding
author. Nor would Huxley in the brittle and controlled entertainments
of his early novels, nor would even Lawrence in the polemical urge
of his later ones, have exactly filled the bill. Although in her essay
Mrs. Woolf stands up for English humor and comedy, she was inclined
to balk, partly on fastidious but also on intellectual grounds, at the
loudly excessive, often indecent satire and parody of Joyce, Lewis or
Huxley which in different ways tended to hold Life at bay (or take it
by the throat) as much as Edwardian novels did. Yet it is wrong to
dismiss Virginia Woolf's demands as merely serving either the interests of her own fiction or the Bloomsbury cause. She was honestly
and accurately pointing to certain possibilities for the novel that are
legitimate, indeed admirable, and which were in fact realized in the
three best 'liberal' novels written in England in the 1920s: Ford
Madox Ford's *Some Do Not*, Forster's *A Passage to India*, and her
own *To the Lighthouse*. The heavily-used adjective 'liberal' is nevertheless the best one for characterizing a permanent attitude toward life:
the aspiration to breathe free, to understand and sympathize more
widely than the codes permit, to make evident at least in one's own
authorial voice, if not in the lives of one's heroes and heroines, the
tolerance, good-humour and sympathy named by Forster as his
humanistic ideals.

These three novels also seem to me to combine more memorably
than any other 'twenties novels the two impulses Virginia Woolf
saluted in her *TLS* speculation about modern fiction. Although her

praise of *Ulysses* is ringed round with qualifications and faint disclaimers (though a work of great originality it doesn't compare with 'high examples' of masterpiece-art like *Youth* or *The Mayor of Casterbridge*), what she singles out for admiration is significant: the 'Hades' sequence where Bloom attends Paddy Dignam's funeral. She alludes to 'its brilliance, its sordidity, its incoherence, its sudden lightening flashes of significance' which on a first reading—and she would have read it in the September 1918 *Little Review*—touch the quick of the mind. Virginia Woolf is surely right to single out the section where *Ulysses* is at its very finest: the sordid comedy of Bloom amongst the Irishmen proceeding to the cemetery, the 'incoherence' yet splendid relevance of Bloom's thoughts as the ceremony proceeds, the lightening flash of significance when he moves away from thoughts of death, 'buried females or even putrefied with running gravesores', and back to life affirmed in his inimitable manner:

> There is another world after death named hell. I do not like that other world she wrote. No more do I. Plenty to see and hear and feel yet. Feel live warm beings near you. Let them sleep in their maggoty beds. They are not going to get me this innings. Warm beds: warm fullblooded life.

Touching the quick of the mind, the passage's power is inseparable from the vitality of its language, so displayed as to allow us to imagine a person. Mrs. Woolf might not have been willing to grant *Ulysses* the utmost sadness she found in the Russians; yet there are many such moments of revelation in which we feel the life revealed as both very sad and richly endowed with the 'humour' that in Joyce is gallowsish, indecent, endlessly inventive in its brilliance.

Of the three novels to be taken up here, only Virginia Woolf's was clearly influenced by Joyce's fictional procedures, and at that less than its predecessor *Mrs. Dalloway*. Ford's advocacy and practice of the 'time-shift' and *progression d'effet* is Flaubertian, Jamesian, Conradian in inspiration: and even Christopher Tietjens's internal monologues, which might superficially recall Bloom's or Stephen's, are something quite other. While Forster's practice as a novelist is fully established by 1905; compared to *Ulysses*, *A Passage to India* is patently conventional in its virtues. Still, the novels share with *Ulysses* the wider and more 'human' qualities admired by Mrs. Woolf. For all their technical ingenuities—and I don't except Forster from this, although his technique is less a matter for exploration than Ford's or Woolf's—they come across as marvelous books because of their human warmths and pleasures, their ability to be very gloomy and very funny about life, almost in the same breath of words. As much as with *Ulysses*, it is a mistake to assess technique in *Some Do Not* or *A Passage to India* or *To the Lighthouse* without asking where it leads to in the human realm; without, that is, talking about the sense of life imparted in such interesting ways by the narrative voice of each book. 'We cannot say where technique begins or ends', said Eliot apropos poetry; but in these novels it goes far enough at least to present us with the essential persons who were their authors.

Ford and *Some Do Not*

> She had moved to a chair close beside the fire-place and now looking at him, leaning interestedly forward, as if at a garden-party she had been finding—*par impossible!*—a pastoral play not so badly produced. Tietjens was a fabulous monster.

Sylvia Tietjens never put it better than in this perception which characterizes in its appropriately impressionistic rendering, the book where Tietjens has his being. One feels the truth of it registered at a point of insight wider than an individual psychology; we don't respond to Sylvia but to the presence of Ford's mind. Nor is the perception expressed with sour, grudging or any other nameable kind of admiration, since it is really beyond the possibilities of being tonally classifiable: in what tone do you tell yourself that you're involved in 'a pastoral play not so badly produced' involving your fabulous monster of a husband? An early reviewer of *Some Do Not* was moved to a related style of admiration in these sentences quoted in Mizener's biography of Ford: 'an England that Englishmen generally will have some difficulty in recognizing. . . . This country and people . . . are made astonishingly real to the reader. . . . It is really a triumph of mind over matter.'[2] What looks 'astonishingly' real is in fact what looks very strange indeed, and what words like 'fabulous' or 'pastoral' might also describe.

To back up for a moment: Ford is well on his way, if he hasn't already got there, to becoming the academic's novelist *par excellence*; this is testified to by the number of essays, explications, definitive 'readings' that over the past fifteen years (and particularly in America) have been devoted to Ford's novels, mainly to *The Good Soldier* and the *Parade's End* tetralogy. Although the effect of this amount of critical explanation on any writer would be to soften or dehumanize his impact, Ford's case is more curious than that. One understands why his novels, especially *The Good Soldier* and the Tietjens saga— *Some Do Not* most prominently—should attract and invite attempts to 'straighten out' the books and help readers get at what's really going on in them. Yet the more ingenuity, often of an intelligent sort, brought to bear on elucidating *progression d'effet*, or illus- trating the beneficial use of the 'time-shift', or assessing the weight and reliability of a narrative voice, the more the books begin to feel like beautifully calculated machines instead of the stranger, more humanly imperfect things they are. The 'triumph of mind over matter' Ford effected in them is astonishing because, first and last, his was a very queer, very attractive mind. Discussions of technique in the novels tend to forget, in the orderly progression of the critic's own sentences, how maddening and disconcerting much of our reading experience of the books feels like. As we scramble about *The Good Soldier* trying to remember (along with its narrator, Dowell, who should know) what came before what and just when; or as we uncertainly wonder whether, at some juncture, Christopher knew that Sylvia knew . . ., we are doing something quite different from marveling at Ford's complicated craftsmanship. That we often feel things to be in a mess as they are in life, says much about what it's like to read Ford.

The critical consensus on him is that *The Good Soldier* and *Parade's End* are his two lasting achievements in the novel: one admires the former for its ingenious revelation of a mind, and through that mind the tragic-comic contradictions of prewar English society—it is 'the best French novel in the language' and a classic of modernist, post-Jamesian composition. The tetralogy on the other hand, for all its time-shiftings and concealments, is a more sprawling and also a more attractively imperfect work: to love the book is to love Christopher Tietjens. But I wish to be more critical than Fordians are about even his best books, having read *The Good Soldier* always with fascination but also held it off at a distance. For all the beautifully incised moments in Dowell's 'saddest story', the story is very much a *tour de force*; and arguments between intelligent critics (like Schorer and Mizener for example) about how much Dowell 'is' Ford, to what extent Ford shares the beliefs, reticences, protestations and *naïvetés* he endows his narrator with, are less crucial than recognizing how grotesquely impossible is the whole 'affair'. No matter how openly receptive and sympathetic we try to be as readers, there still remains our clear-eyed, common-sense self which knows that this saddest story is very much and essentially a *story*. To call it the saddest one immediately precludes responding to it as to a really sad story, like *Anna Karenina* or *Portrait of a Lady* or *The Great Gatsby*. With an art as clever and as in evidence as Ford's, how can things be that sad? Though likely to be contradicted by lovers of the book, I would say that although one finishes it with immense respect for its author, this respect is a result of something different from giving oneself generously and in risky sympathy to the novel's imagined world, its characters and events.

Parade's End asks of us, and achieves at least in part, that risk of sympathy and deeper involvement. In part, for I would break this long novel into three parts, of which only the first, *Some Do Not*, is assuredly a work of greatness. The battle over whether *Last Post* belongs as the true conclusion to the saga at least suggests its uncertain status, while *No More Parades* and *A Man Could Stand Up*, for all their occasionally fine effects, are more simple and at times more tedious than the nearly self-sufficient brilliance of *Some Do Not*. It is right to speak of a reader's sympathetic involvement in Tietjens's affairs, though that involvement is quite other than is suggested by this description of the novel's action, quoted from a dust jacket: 'Inescapably he is caught up in the vicious intrigue and folly let loose by war, and enmeshed in bitter sexual conflict with his faithless vengeful wife; inescapably he is forced to choose between allegiance to an outmoded code of honour and personal survival in a corrupt age.' This sounds like an exciting tale to read, complete with reader quivering to find out what happens next; but in fact *Some Do Not* is a wholly different story, its brilliance being of the sort that diverts admiration from sensational excitements to its behavior as a piece of imaginative writing.

For example, a sensationally exciting occurrence in such a tale as the blurb describes would be to have the 'faithless, vengeful wife' throw something at her patient, suffering husband, as at one point Sylvia Tietjens does, but in the following manner:

> Being near Tietjens, she lifted her plate, which contained two cold cutlets in aspic and several leaves of salad: she wavered a little to one side and, with a circular motion of her hand, let the whole contents fly at Tietjens' head. She placed the plate on the table and drifted slowly towards the enormous mirror over the fire-place.
> 'I'm bored,' she said. 'Bored! Bored!'
> Tietjens had moved slightly as she had thrown: the cutlets and most of the salad leaves had gone over his shoulder. But one, couched, very green leaf was on his shoulder-strap, and the oil and vinegar from the plate—Sylvia *knew* that she took too much of all condiments—had splashed from the revers of his tunic to his green staff-badges.

There may be a piece of 'rendering' in Flaubert or James or Conrad as odd as this one, but surely none more so. When, in Anthony Powell's *A Buyer's Market*, Barbara Goring empties the sugar canister over Widmerpool's head, we are treated to a long, slow-motioned, stunningly verbal performance of the whole process: Powell's art is memorable for its extended fireworks. Ford is more deadpan, or perhaps more ingeniously playful in his pretence that what we really need as a guarantee of art's truth is Sylvia's claim, having tossed the salad, that she knows she uses too much oil and vinegar, alas. Or that it is just 'one, couched, very green leaf' which still perches on Tietjens's shoulder-strap, the cold cutlets evidently having universally landed on the floor.

Ford neglects to inject Dickensian warmth into his comic scene, and thus its total effect is the more strange. It is equally impossible to cheer Sylvia or feel sorry for Tietjens, drenched as he may be with oil and vinegar in this fabulous monstrosity of an occurrence; while it has been *de rigueur* to salute Ford's novelistic capabilities in exploiting the 'time shift', even more central to the feel of his writing is its disinterested and lordly presentation, in language grotesquely precise, of character and event. One longish example of many will serve to present Tietjens, the fabulous monster himself, sauntering along the golf links at Rye:

Although Tietjens hated golf as he hated any occupation that was of a competitive nature, he could engross himself in the mathematics of trajectories when he accompanied Macmaster in one of his expeditions for practice. He accompanied Macmaster because he liked there to be one pursuit at which his friend undisputably excelled himself, for it was a bore always browbeating the fellow. But he stipulated that they should visit three different, and, if possible, unknown courses every week-end when they golfed. He interested himself then in the way the courses were laid out, acquiring thus an extraordinary connoisseurship in golf architecture, and he made abstruse calculations as to the flight of balls off sloped club-faces, as to the foot-poundals of energy exercised by one muscle or the other, and as to theories of spin.

Tietjens has just been consulting his notes on past mashie shots and is about to address his ball with a niblick, when the future love of his life, Valentine Wannop, appears. Of course it's not just golf-architecture and theories of spin which occupy him; Tietjens often palms Macmaster off on another player and sits in the club-house studying race-horse forms, or investigates soft-billed birds' nests ('though he hated natural history and field botany'); or he amuses himself by 'tabulating from memory the errors in the Encyclopaedia Britannica', and writes an article on the subject, though he himself despises reference books. He knows extraordinary things such as that 'there has been nothing worth *reading* written in England since the eighteenth century except by a woman', although of course he doesn't read novels but just knows what's in them. The woman, conveniently, turns out to be Valentine's mother.

The like of such a man was never on sea or land; surely he is a creation of Ford's fantastic imagination. His wife, Sylvia, runs him a close second, seeing through her husband brilliantly: 'I tell you he's so formal he can't do without all the conventions there are and so truthful he can't use half of them.' As a very devil she cannot be bettered: ' "Sylvia would have evil thoughts in any place," ' says her mother to Father Consett, Sylvia's spiritual guide. Yet Tietjens deserves to have nothing less than a first-class tormentor: by the same token his growing love for Valentine Wannop is not independent of the fact that she is, so we are told, the finest Latinist in England.

To common sense all this is improbable beyond any argument. In a book of brilliant chapters, perhaps the most memorable one is of Mrs. Duchemin's breakfast at which are assembled Tietjens, Macmaster (bent on capturing his hostess), Valentine, her mother (eager to cultivate Macmaster since her new book is about to appear and he is a critic), Mr. Horsley (an enormous curate who interjects 'Tee-hee' every 'four or five words'), and for a brief but unforgettable span the Reverend Mr. Duchemin himself ('Breakfast Duchemin of Magdalen') whose madness threatens to collapse the occasion into sexual revelation until, on Macmaster's suggestion, he is deftly punched in the kidneys by his keeper, Parry, 'The Bermondsey light-middle weight'. The chapter has rightly been praised for Ford's wonderful presentation of all these human oddities in dramatic interaction, but it should be emphasized once more how unbelievably perfect everything turns out, whether it is the outburst or the subduing of Duchemin, the triumph of Macmaster, or the reunion of Tietjens and Mrs. Wannop as Valentine begins to flower in his eyes. The commonplace about Ford's memoirs is that they make things up, invent and insist upon as fact his fabulous impressions. Why should Ford the novelist be any less of a liar? The remarkable thing about the personages and scenes of *Some Do Not* is that, invented and inflated to heroical-comic status, they maintain themselves there without becoming creatures of the narrator's satiric shafts, as if Ford, fascinated or appalled by what he's created, has no interest in then attempting to moralize over or deflate their natures.

Sylvia Tietjens refers to her relationship with her husband as constituting 'a pastoral play not so badly produced', and certainly there are many sequences in Tietjen's meditations on the golf links, or later in the trenches in France, that reach toward versions of content and fulfilment in nature or poetry. But if the account of Ford's novel here put forth makes sense, the whole of *Parade's End* in its creation of heightened and simplified characters—fabulous monsters of one sort or another—is a very well-produced pastoral play with an imagination behind it which yearns to breathe freer than life's complex circumstances permit. As Tietjens walks away from the golf links

> He felt himself to be content for the first time in four months. His pulse beat calmly; the heat of the sun all over

him appeared to be a beneficent flood. On the flanks of the older and larger sand-hills he observed the minute herbage mixed with little purple aromatic plants. To these the constant nibbling of sheep had imparted a protective tininess.

Such moments must have been equally excellent and equally rare for Ford himself. As *Parade's End* develops and Tietjens's fortunes worsen, the moments become more insisted upon, while the imagined righting or transcending of them through loving Valentine Wannop or England's past grows in possibility and desperation.

Our admiration for Tietjens and his creator as well demands that they be defeated and broken up by circumstances while we wait with them, viewing from afar 'The King Over the Water'. That phrase is the title of R. P. Blackmur's excellent and little-known analysis of Ford's sensibility as 'an image of devotion to lost causes known to be lost'.[3] In politics or philosophy, Blackmur writes: 'we call this the cultivation of ancestral Utopias; in literature, since we can recognize these cultivations with the pang of actuality, they make a legitimate, though necessarily always subordinate, subject matter.' Blackmur finds Ford a minor writer, his novels not enough able to demonstrate the counterforce of causes *not* lost, by which the devotions and yearnings—the impulse of pastoral—can be measured. Regretfully, since there are such fine moments in them, I would have to agree that the last three volumes of *Parade's End* are agreeable, minor literature; a way of suggesting how this is evidenced would be to examine their increasingly lengthy concentrations on Tietjens's or Valentine's or Sylvia's internal narrative, well-punctuated by ellipses and other breakings-off. But *Some Do Not* is a major work of the imagination because of Ford's evident devotion, in every chapter, paragraph sentence and just word, to the novelist's art. Here everything came together, knowledge and passion and witty absurdity, into an art that is very much a cause *not* lost, though it can't save Tietjens or England or the Modern World. Nor could it of course save Ford himself from Robert Lowell's question:

But master, mammoth mumbler, tell me why,
the bales of your left-over novels buy,
less than a bandage for your gouty foot?

Lines like these save Ford from being placed on a pedestal and made the object of a too-solemn reverence he cannot sustain. Perhaps the best epithet of all for him was Graham Greene's in a posthumous appreciation of Ford's last book *The March of Literature*, in which, Greene concluded: 'this great writer takes his bow—as one of our finest prose writers, as a poet, and—it would have been incomplete else—as one of the scamps of literature.'[4]

Forster and *A Passage to India*

Forster, we remind ourselves, is an Edwardian novelist: *A Passage to India* is untouched by the experiments of *Ulysses* or *Women in Love*, the comic negatives of Huxley or Lewis, the technical and psychological daring of *Some Do Not*. Yet as much as any single novel can do, it breaks away from Forster's *œuvre* and moves beyond all Edwardian novels to establish itself as a distinguished and finished work of modern genius. Of course neither this novel nor Forster's work in general has lacked admirers, to the extent that one views the *Critical Heritage* volume on the novelist, some five hundred pages of it, with shock. Forster lived long enough to become the object of books and essays by critics writing twenty-five to thirty years after the publication of his last novel; *A Passage to India* was acclaimed when it was published and has never fallen very far below the reviewers' original estimate of it. So it is almost refreshing suddenly to come across, in the midst of adulation and enthusiasm, Pete Hamill's irreverence in a 1965 review of *Two Cheers for Democracy*. Hamill was tired of the 'totemization' of Forster, the sense that as the old man lived on it would soon be

> ... time again for still another birthday, another fawning appraisal, another essay entitled '*A Passage to India* After Twenty-Five Years.' Again this prim nanny of a novel will be brought forth as a vigorous champion.

'Prim nanny' indeed! But Hamill was no more brash than Katherine Mansfield in a diary entry of 1917 written upon perusal of *Howards End*:

> ... it's not good enough. E. M. Forster never gets any further than warming the teapot. He's a rare fine hand at that. Feel

this teapot. Is it not beautifully warm? Yes, but there ain't going to be no tea.

And I can never be perfectly certain whether Helen was got with child by Leonard Bast or by his fatal forgotten umbrella. All things considered, I think it must have been the umbrella.[5]

In the language of *A Passage to India*, the echoing walls of Forster's civility drove at least two readers to intemperate rudeness. It is true that Katherine Mansfield died before *A Passage to India* was published, and that when Pete Hamill remarked on its primness he was still waiting, like others, for Forster's novel about homosexuality to appear. When it did, nothing much happened except that one's admiration for *Passage*—and *Howards End* too—increased. Yet how can a 'prim' book keep finding new readers?

It is true though that *A Passage to India*, while relatively free from the coy moralizings, reader-buttonholings and arch whimsy that disfigure Forster's earlier books, is still at moments primly 'literary' in its narrative manner. Aziz and Fielding are dealing with the collar-stud, in a fine scene of embarrassed communication, when Aziz trying to be 'stiff' feels instead the other's 'fundamental good will':

> His own went out to it, and grappled beneath the shifting tides of emotion which can alone bear the voyager to an anchorage but may also carry him across it on to the rocks. He was safe really—as safe as the shore-dweller who can only understand stability and supposes that every ship must be wrecked, and he had sensations the shore-dweller cannot know.

This prose reads as if it were one of Joyce's exhibits from parodies of English prose styles in the 'Oxen of the Sun' chapter of *Ulysses*. Compared to the supple and sensitive dialogue Forster gives Fielding and Aziz, all this metaphorical shifting of tides and voyaging sounds stale and prim enough. There is a related tendency to say too much, when a few pages later the omniscient narrator fills us in on how various characters respond to what Aziz is saying: 'As for Miss Quested, she accepted everything Aziz said as true verbally. In her ignorance, she regarded him as "India", and never surmised that his outlook was limited and his method inaccurate, and that no one is India.' The capping remark especially makes us wince, since that lesson is forcefully being demonstrated elsewhere, with fine and inventive particularity, through incident and scene.

But the book shucks off its infelicities by taking us to the point where we say about a blemish, oh that's just Forster. That this 'Forster' commits infelicities, makes 'mistakes', is imperfectly the subtle artist, guarantees also his active and risk-taking involvement in the tale he tells. Reading *A Passage to India*, one feels that for all the carefully metaphoric or tripartitely symbolic organization of 'Mosque', 'Caves', 'Temple' (plus innumerable subsidiary and contributory threads of continuity) the book has not been all made up in advance; it could go on in one way, but it could well go another. It is, as often advertised, an ironic novel, but one in which the author does not become a manipulator in comfortable control of drawing out the ironies. Middleton Murry saw this most astutely in his incisive though not always fully comprehensible *Adelphi* review of 1924. The appearance of this 'very fine' novel after fourteen years (*Howards End* was published in 1910) should be termed a 'miracle'; Forster had decided, though only *just*, that there was still something worth writing a novel about, and thus 'the silence was interrupted'. But, Murry continues

> I scarcely think it will be interrupted again. The planning of Mr. Forster's next novel should carry him well on to the unfamilar side of the grave. It will take him, I imagine, a good deal more than fourteen years to find the word which will evoke a different echo from the primeval cave of Marabar: and I fancy (such is my faith in his intellectual honesty) that he will not speak again without the assurance of a different reply.

The prophesy was astonishingly correct, although Murry tended to make them rather too glibly, having five years previously ingloriously predicted that Yeats was singing his swan-song as a poet. Outwardly, says Murry, the book declares that 'I am revealing a strange and unknown continent—India—as it has never been revealed before.' But inwardly it 'whispers: "I am obeying the word: Command that these stones be made bread." ' And that not even Forster can do.

I think that Murry means that Forster is suffering from that 'twilight of the double vision' which his elderly heroine, Mrs. Moore, experiences at the Marabar caves. Like her he can neither act nor refrain from action; and the outward tale—what will happen to Aziz, Adela, the trial, its aftermath, even the later meeting of Fielding and Aziz years later—is no more than an engaging story to keep us entertained while the book's real tribulations go on underneath. These tribulations— Murry would perhaps not agree—surface at several moments after the trial, most memorably in regard to Fielding who, having walked out on his fellow Anglo-Indians at the club, stands gazing from the upper verandah at the Marabar Hills, feels 'dubious and discontented suddenly' and wonders about his success as a man:

> After forty years' experience, he had learnt to manage his life and make the best of it on advanced European lines, had developed his personality, explored his limitations, controlled his passions—and he had done it all without becoming either pedantic or worldly. A creditable achievement, but as the moment passed, he felt he ought to have been working at something else the whole time,—he didn't know at what, never would know, never could know, and that was why he felt sad.

Ou-boum, bou-oum. The sadness Fielding experiences here is spread over the remaining pages of 'Caves' where the primary emotions are weariness, nameless regret, wistful inadequacy as Matthew Arnold's 'buried life' rises to the surface in waves of reluctant admission. Mrs. Moore dies, Adela and Ronny break it off, everybody says goodbye to one another and drifts off here or there; while Fielding's earlier advice to Aziz about the virtues of traveling light now echoes plaintively. Forster has already reminded us that a man can only presume to 'travel light' when he has no wife and children; Fielding is headed back to England and will acquire just those new burdens.

Forster's liberal imagination can imagine these things and they make him—like Fielding, a man in his forties when the book was written—feel sad. Fielding and Adela experience 'a friendliness' but it is as if dwarfs are shaking hands, 'assuring each other that they stood on the same footing of insight'. Earlier Fielding had entertained the epistemological possibility 'that we exist not in ourselves, but in terms of each others' minds'; now this seems to be the depressing conclusion to the 'horrible, senseless picnic' which precipitated everything. And perhaps other readers have experienced something similar to my own feelings about the final 'Temple' section of the novel; that brilliantly assured as it is—Forster now playing the detached and rather amused observer of 'muddle' at the Mau festival—it has less than an inevitable relation to the previous two hundred pages. One can put the book down at the end of 'Caves' and say, now there remains a Coda which will ingeniously work itself out. But the painful immediacy and increasingly grey atmosphere which the main part of the book expressed so truthfully are now absent as 'many years later' two of the principals meet once more, while India goes about her inscrutable ways.

A Passage to India is one of the finest modern novels, not a 'prim nanny' of one, because its art is so fully and powerfully put in the Jamesian service of rendering felt life ambitiously and intensively, scanting the claims of neither but putting art and life into creative relation. The recent publication of *Maurice*, Forster's suppressed novel of homosexuality completed in 1914, doesn't add to the novelist's reputation but does perhaps make *Passage* even more interesting and remarkable. In reviewing *Maurice* George Steiner pointed out plausibly that the choice and treatment of theme in the Indian novel 'it now seems likely, represents an act of sublimation, a "second go" at commitments and insights he had been forced to suppress in their original form'. Steiner's notion is that the confrontation between society and the homosexual in the suppressed book was projected into the encounters between whites and natives, 'emancipated rulers and "advanced" Indians' in *Passage*; and that whatever did or didn't happen in the Marabar caves is uncompromisingly expressive of the force of sexual suggestion. It's certainly true that Forster feels the relationship between Fielding and Aziz to be most poignant and valuable. That one can't travel light with wife and children is underlined, rather too crudely, in a narrative comment about Fielding's marriage after Aziz questions him about it. Forster tells us that Fielding 'was not quite happy about his marriage', that he was 'passionately physical again' in 'the final flare-up before the clinkers of middle age', and that Fielding knows 'his wife did not love him as much as he loved her, and he was ashamed of pestering her.' That word 'pestering' is an indication of how worked-up Forster is at this point, to the final extent of the final page of having Aziz ride his horse 'furiously' against Fielding '— "and then," he concluded, half kissing him, "you and I shall be friends." ' Fielding, holding him affectionately, wonders why they can't be friends now, at which point the horses swerve and the sky says, ' "No, not there." ' It is a wonderful culminating moment, its poised sadness so beautifully concluded by the storyteller at his most compelling: and beyond discussion in any terms, like irony or symbolism, that are more fixed than the modulating complications of Forster's speaking voice.

Among many rewarding perceptions which dot Forster's Clark Lectures in the spring of 1927, published that same year as *Aspects of the Novel*, is one which occurs towards the close of his discussion of 'Story' where he is considering it as 'the repository of a voice'. Forster says that 'It is this aspect of the novelist's work which asks to be read out loud, which appeals not to the eye, like most prose, but to the ear; having indeed this much in common with oratory.' He then pulls back and claims perhaps too little for this voice ('It does not give us anything as important as the author's personality') since so much of what we hear in *A Passage to India*, from the ironic sophistication of its opening paragraphs to the regretful but inevitable fall with which it ends, reveals the many-sided personality named Forster as nothing else can. This personality is distinguished from its contemporaries because expressed through a voice that succeeds in being both vulnerable and powerful. It confesses to human imperfections but manages, when Forster is writing at his best, to turn these limitations into virtuous strengths. At his best Forster is very much *in* the novel just considered; or in *Aspects of the Novel*, probably as clever a collection of remarks about fiction as has been made; or in his acute writings about music, the concert in *Howards End* or his 1947 Harvard talk, 'The Raison d'Être of Criticism in the Arts'. With the exception of Bernard Shaw, no English literary man of this century is a better critic of music.

Finally, what Forster stands for is important beyond the question of whether or not he wrote great novels. That 'something' may be suggested by recalling his response to Eliot after D. H. Lawrence had died—not just calling it but listening to the voice as it delivers the response. It will be remembered that Forster had written a letter to the *Nation and Athenaeum* about the general ignoring of Lawrence's death, in which he says that all we can do is 'to say straight out that he was the greatest imaginative novelist of our generation'. Next week came a letter from Eliot, not wishing to 'disparage' Lawrence's genius or 'disapprove' when an eminent writer like Forster speaks straight out (Eliot puts the words in quotation marks). But, Eliot submits, the judgement is meaningless unless we know 'exactly what Mr. Forster means by *greatest, imaginative*, and *novelist*', and he submits also that there are at least three other novelists for whom a similar claim might be made. Forster replied as follows:

> Sir,—Mr. T. S. Eliot duly entangles me in his web. He asks what exactly I mean by 'greatest,' 'imaginative' and 'novelist', and I cannot say. Worse still, I cannot even say what 'exactly' means—only that there are some occasions when I would rather feel like a fly than a spider, and that the death of D. H. Lawrence is one of them.

Forster has the last word here, and one's sympathies are instinctively with him—the little fellow who has been sent to the bottom of the class suddenly shows he's a pretty big fellow after all. But Eliot had a point; he heard or intuited the sentimental appeal in the invitation to speak 'straight out' and realized that Forster's own caginess and appeal as a writer consisted in a good deal more and less than 'speaking straight out'. Yet how briefly, masterfully, and indirectly does Forster answer him and climb to the top! Here his voice magically transforms us from readers into listeners; whether Lawrence was unjustly ignored or Eliot was right becomes of little moment by comparison with our delighted assent to something vibrantly heard, at the moment.

Virginia Woolf and *To the Lighthouse*

Since I believe that Virginia Woolf's fictional achievement consists mainly of *To the Lighthouse*, then perhaps only the critic's own exclusiveness is revealed. Yet it seems to me such a distinguished and endlessly rewarding book, especially in its long first section 'The Window', as to dwarf the rest of her novels. The criticism and polemic contained in her *Collected Essays*, in the feminist books—particularly *A Room of One's Own*—and in *A Writer's Diary*, plus much further material available in Quentin Bell's biography, is enough in itself to constitute a formidable contribution to modern letters, and to make her a figure (like the Wyndham Lewis who satirized her) whose

significance can't be measured as a novelist's merely. In proposing to
direct my remarks wholly at the *Lighthouse* I should explain briefly,
if dogmatically, why my sympathies aren't much engaged by her
other novels. If we except *Orlando* from the fictional list and agree
to take it instead as a 'sport' with lively moments, then the consensus
would place *Mrs. Dalloway* and *The Waves* as the two other most considerable novels. Yet *The Waves*, so frequently acclaimed as a 'masterpiece' and sometimes by reputable critics, seems to me quite intolerable:
precious, pretentious, 'feminine' in the worst oh-so-delicate way, and
a terrible bore to read, let alone read through:

> But who am I, who lean on this gate and watch my setter
> nose in a circle? I think sometimes (I am not twenty yet) I am
> not a woman, but the light that falls on this gate, on this
> ground. I am the seasons, I think sometimes, January, May,
> November; the mud, the mist, the dawn. I cannot be tossed
> about, or float gently, or mix with other people.

Thus Susan, in *The Waves*, and the reader is invited to abandon
himself to preposterous though sympathetically rendered musings.
Great amounts of labour can be expended on elucidating 'technique'
in *The Waves*, but that such elucidation can make the novel's various
voices more palatable is to be doubted. Leonard Woolf told Virginia
it was the best of her books, but added that its first hundred pages
were extremely difficult and that it was 'doubtful how far any common
reader will follow'. The difficulty in my view is that of taking the
'prose-poem' seriously enough to keep on listening throughout those
pages. *Mrs. Dalloway* is by contrast a quite different matter, a remarkable piece of work, but one whose limitations are seen when compared
with *To the Lighthouse*.

Let us enlist Forster's help immediately, since no better critic of
Virginia Woolf's books is likely to appear. In his 1925 review of *Mrs.
Dalloway* Forster took the occasion to survey the novelist's work up
to that point, and when he came to consider the new, distinctively
Woolfian impressionistic style, he quoted a long passage from 'Kew
Gardens', then said that 'The objection (or apparent objection) to this
sort of writing is that it cannot say much or be sure of saying anything.
It is an inspired breathlessness, a beautiful droning or gasping which
trusts to luck, and can never express human relationships or the

structure of society.' This, said by the writer who had just published
a novel which expressed both human relationships and the structure
of society, had its point and still has it as the essential criticism to be
made not only of a tentative experiment like 'Kew Gardens', but also
and more so of *The Waves*, of the early *Jacob's Room* (which Forster
thinks succeeds) and the unfinished *Between the Acts*. The 'inspired
breathlessness', the 'beautiful droning' manages, in her two best books
to root itself in a female character whose presence one can take seriously
while breathless inspiration is set off against less hectic, more earthly
breathings.

In his second appreciation of her work, written after Virginia
Woolf's death, Forster gave a name to the quality which saved her
from just beautiful droning. He admits that the great risk such a
novelist took was that of constructing the Palace of Art, a rarefied
aesthetic building of utterly refined, exquisite sensation. She escaped
this, Forster goes on to say, partly because of her sense of humour and
because 'she liked writing for fun': 'Literature was her merry-go-
round as well as her study': and he adds that if you stay outside the
Palace of Art you may at times be tempted to play the fool. Had
critics taken this suggestion of Forster's more seriously, they might
have spent less time pursuing patterns or designs in Woolf's novels
and paid more heed to the humanizing force of her excellent sense of
fun. In his survey of the novels, Forster rates her second one (*Night
and Day*) rather low, since as an exercise in 'classical realism' it goes
against the very principles of modern fiction she put forth in 'Mr.
Bennett and Mrs. Brown'. Yet although that novel is long, conventional and too devoted to its own plot, it often shows the developing
firmness of Virginia Woolf's judgement in its humorous exposures
of human affectations and blindnesses. *Night and Day* can still be read
with attention and interest and is noteworthy as a warning about what
the novelist gave up in order to carry out her new experiment. Its old-
fashioned refusal to bow down before Time as the new God of novelists
is not automatically to be patronized as benighted.

But *Mrs. Dalloway* is something else: sprightly and incisive
moment by moment; well-balanced and well-placed as a whole. Its
narrator, rooted in no particular time or place but always on the move
keeping us off-balance and on our toes, renders with a few strokes the

public servant Hugh Whitbread, inspecting a shopfront window in Harley Street, whose very clocks 'nibbled at the June day, counselled submission, upheld authority, and pointed out in chorus the supreme advantage of a sense of proportion. . .' By which we are invited to be superior to timepieces, insofar as we participate in the pretense of controlling them through clever fantasies about what they 'say'. Then Hugh himself, the human representative of such authority and proportion is introduced:

> . . . one or two humble reforms stood to his credit; an improvement in public shelters was one; the protection of owls in Norfolk another: servant girls had reason to be grateful to him; and his name at the end of letters to *The Times*, asking for funds, appealing to the public to protect, to preserve, to clear up litter, to abate smoke, and stamp out immorality in parks, commanded respect.

And we look critically, humorously at him 'pausing for a moment (as the sound of the half-hour died away) to look critically, magisterially, at socks and shoes'. This externally chirpy wit can of course wear out its welcome—and it is surely not overly daring of the novelist to reduce Public Service to the protection of owls in Norfolk. Virginia Woolf's faith is that the book's serious weight will be felt in Clarissa Dalloway's final identification with the mad and now dead Septimus Warren-Smith; as the clock strikes and the words 'Fear no more the heat of the sun' come to her she knows that 'Death was an attempt to communicate, people feeling the impossibility of reaching the centre which, mystically, evaded them; closeness drew apart; rapture faded, one was alone.'

Mrs. Dalloway's romantic, Keatsian identification of extreme happiness and the idea of death is certainly shared by her creator, indeed is the idea lurking not very far behind everything that occurs in Virginia Woolf's novels. The wordless moment at the end of 'The Window' section of *To the Lighthouse* comes when Mrs. Ramsay knows that her husband wants her to tell him she loves him:

> But she could not do it; she could not say it. Then, knowing that he was watching her, instead of saying anything she turned, holding her stocking, and looked at him. And as she looked at him she began to smile, for though she had not said a

word, he knew, of course he knew, that she loved him. He
could not deny it. And smiling she looked out of the window
and said (thinking to herself, Nothing on earth can equal this
happiness)—

And she proceeds not to say her inexpressible feelings, but looks at her
husband and smiles: 'For she had triumphed again. She had not said
it: yet he knew.' As we know from reading the novel, and from
Virginia Woolf's fiction generally, this is less an insight into the
character of Mrs. Ramsay than into the human condition in which the
impulse to 'say' one's feelings, to make structures of orderly verbal
arrangements, contends with and eventually submits to the waves, or
tides, or 'sea' of what's outside the organizing mind. Or inside it,
surging beneath the surface order, 'So that the monotonous fall of the
waves on the beach . . . made one think of the destruction of the island
and its engulfment in the sea, and warned her whose day had slipped
past in one quick doing after another that it was all ephemeral as a
rainbow . . .' So it is fitting that after the moment of happiness,
the 'triumph', the communication-beyond-saying with Mr. Ramsay,
there is a blank space. Time passes, but without Mrs. Ramsay there
to register its passing; death is the fullest communication: 'If it were
now to die, T'were now to be most happy.'

These designs and concerns have been adequately remarked on,
indeed could hardly be missed by readers of Virginia Woolf. But it is
her appetite for fun that makes *To the Lighthouse* invigorating rather
than lugubrious. This is true also of *Mrs. Dalloway*, yet compared to
the fullness with which Mrs. Ramsay and her husband are imagined
there is something a shade literary and made-up about the miseries of
Septimus Warren-Smith in the earlier book, even though his madness
was animated in part by the creator's fears about her own sanity. But
Mrs. Ramsay is given a more sensitive, somewhat less breathless,
range of feeling than Clarissa Dalloway; and she has her extraordinary
children and her husband over which reflection can play. The truth
to feeling behind, say, her momentary wish that her children never
grow up depends less upon experimental prose to convey it than upon
a bold 'saying', on the novelist's part, of the human commonplace.
And there is a similar boldness in the presentation of Mr. Ramsay,
seen not only through his wife's eyes and those of other characters,

but perhaps most memorably (in the sequence beginning 'It was a splendid mind') through the narrator's conceit of Ramsay as Alpine explorer, or leader of a Polar expedition, or embattled ship's captain, attempting to get from Q to R ('Very few people in the whole of England ever reach Q') but unable to do it. The heroic similes, the alphabetical conceit by which human intellectual striving is expressed may be called mock-heroic so long as we see that the poise and humor with which Virginia Woolf conceives of Ramsay is not mockery:

> Who will not secretly rejoice when the hero puts his armour off, and halts by the window and gazes at his wife and son, who, very distant at first, gradually come closer and closer, till lips and book and head are clearly before him, though still lovely and unfamiliar from the intensity of his isolation and the waste of ages and the perishing of the stars, and finally putting his pipe in his pocket and bending his magnificent head before her—who will blame him if he does homage to the beauty of the world?

No one, certainly not Virginia Woolf; and in such a passage the writer manages to express both her own yearnings and temporal anxieties, her sense of the vague and unutterable sadness permeating life, by making a distinct literary creation out of them that can be delighted in, not wept over or pitied.

This discussion of Virginia Woolf has made no use of the term 'Bloomsbury', but surely the term points to an exploitation of and fondness for the mock-heroic, a literary attitude towards life which informs the great dinner-party scene in *To the Lighthouse*. In his demonstration of how the novelist writes both in seriousness and in fun, Forster asks us to look out for passages in the books where food is described, then after a pained glance at the prunes and custard served her at the women's college which figures in *A Room of One's Own* he heads directly for the *Boeuf en Daube*. Like most readers, Forster loves the 'great dish' and invites us to 'peer down the shiny walls of the great casserole and get one of the best bits . . . Food with her was not a literary device put in to make the book seem real. She put it in because she tasted it. . . because her senses were both exquisite and catholic. . .' This is eloquent and charming, and no decent person would of course want to convert the casserole into a literary device. But the *Boeuf en Daube*, like everything else at Mrs. Ramsay's dinner-party, becomes more than itself, is transformed momentarily into a portion of eternity; like James Ramsay's picture of the refrigerator he lovingly cuts out of the catalogue, it becomes fringed with joy.

If 'mock-heroic' recalls perhaps too limitingly 'The Rape of the Lock', still, remembering the eventual apotheosis of that bit of hair, we see what magical transformations the mode admits of. At the climax of the dinner-party old Augustus Carmichael suddenly rises, 'holding his table napkin so that it looked like a long white robe', and begins to chant the 'Luriana Lurilee' verses that have begun to resound about the table, then bows to Mrs. Ramsay as if in homage. We know the poem to be the most vapid of chocolate-cream sentiment ('The China rose is all abloom and buzzing with the yellow bee') but suddenly it, like the *Boeuf en Daube*, partakes of eternity. Or does so if by now we've acceded to high Bloomsbury play; how frail all these pleasures and poetries are in a world of pain without God; how necessary and civilized then to raise them to an imaginative level of playful contemplation. But Virginia Woolf always goes a step further, brings us back into the world of time passing where pain and death are real and *Boeuf en Daube* but a dream. After the previously quoted, extended comparison of Mr. Ramsay to the heroic explorer, ending with the final 'who will blame him', there is a space and a new paragraph beginning with the words 'But his son hated him'. So here, after Mrs. Ramsay returns the bow to Carmichael and passes through the door he holds open before her

> It was necessary now to carry everything a step further. With her foot on the threshold she waited a moment longer in a scene which was vanishing even as she looked, and then, as she moved and took Minta's arm and left the room, it changed, it shaped itself differently; it had become, she knew, giving one last look at it over her shoulder, already the past.

This is wonderful writing and the book never quite recovers from it. Or rather, once Mrs. Ramsay leaves the scene the symbolic coordinates become both more insistent amd more fuzzed up, so when Mr. Ramsay finally reaches the Lighthouse 'he might be thinking, We perished, each alone, or he might be thinking, I have reached it.

I have found it, but he said nothing.' Take your choice, and we are left (rather palely, I think) with 'ambiguity', with Lily Briscoe, her finished painting and her 'vision'. But it doesn't detract from the richness of the book's first two hundred pages. We must reconcile ourselves to a season of failures and fragments, said Virginia Woolf in the essay which she ended by warning us never to forget Mrs. Brown. *To the Lighthouse* is a homage to a very un-Mrs. Brown-like heroine, but it fulfils the creator's advice, presenting human life in neither materialistic nor purely spiritual, ideal terms; neither as predominately a candidate for satiric guffaw or for lyric tears. It was Virginia Woolf's most rewarding discovery of the proper stuff of fiction.

V

English Poetry in the 1920s: Graves and Lawrence

The case for treating English poetry written in the 1920s as if it were a subject exhibiting an orderly progression of major and minor practitioners duly to be distinguished, is shakier even than such cases usually are. And in confining my own treatment of it to the work of Robert Graves and D. H. Lawrence I probably give up at the outset any claim to do more than remark on some poems by writers of a different generation, one beginning his long and productive career, the other one ending his brilliant and too-short one. But there are good reasons why the postwar years were not the easiest ones to be a poet in. The surge given to writing poetry by the fact of World War I may be admitted, along with the knowledge that naturally most of the poems thus written were bad ones. The most significant 'War Poets'—Owen, Sassoon and Rosenberg—either died in the war or ceased to develop interestingly after it, while a finer poet than any of those three—Edward Thomas—was presented to the public through a posthumous collection of his poems in 1920. But Thomas, like the War Poets, needs to be appreciated and criticized in the context of English and American reactions to Swinburnian and Tennysonian mellifluousness; needs to be seen in relation to Frost, Pound and Yeats, and compared with the Georgian poets. That last-named group appeared in *Georgian Poetry 1920–22* for what was to be its last stand as (in Eliot's clever-cruel gibe) 'the annual scourge' of the Georgian anthology. It is a not very exciting collection in which Lawrence's poem 'Snake' stands out vividly.

Two valuable books of criticism published in 1926 give some support to one's sense of the elusiveness of 1920s English poetry: Edwin Muir's

Transition, a collection of essays on contemporary writers, and
I. A. Richards's *Science and Poetry*. Muir had himself just published
a first book of poems, although his most distinctive poetry was written
in the 1940s and beyond. In *Transition*, Muir was able to put forward
an impressive group of novelists for his investigation: first Joyce, then
Lawrence, then Virginia Woolf; followed, more surprisingly, by
Stephen Hudson, with Strachey and Huxley bringing up the rear.[1]
But when he came to the poets Muir had less to show: a chapter on
Eliot, one on Robert Graves—just then on the verge of collecting his
verse written between 1914 and 1926; finally, and unconvincingly, a
look at Edith Sitwell in which she is dignified by being placed in the
company of Blake and Rimbaud. One feels that, unlike his dealings
with the novelists, Muir is uneasy with the poets, perhaps as a con-
sequence of being one himself and thus in competition. Yet something
more is involved, and this something Muir tries to account for by
claiming that his difficulties with contemporary poetry are partly a
matter of there not being much of it around: 'There is very little
poetry being written to-day, and it is legitimate criticism to note that
by its nature it is not poetry that could be produced in great quantity.'
For, Muir goes on to argue, it is an age of poetic debility because
Science is in command, making us look coldly at the things poets are
used to contemplate with passion. It is thus right for poetry to be
'colder, more intellectualized, more sceptical than it used to be' since
that is the nature of the modern world: impersonal, rapid-
changing, demanding that a tentative, ironic and cold eye be cast
on it.

Muir is at least in part echoing Eliot's line about how modern
poetry had to be difficult in an age of great complexity; I. A. Richards
responded to that age by attempting, in *Science and Poetry*, to give
poetry a good name again, make it respectable and necessary as
'pseudo-statement' in a century characterized by, as he termed it, 'The
Neutralization of Nature'. If it is hard to see quite why the issue was
so worrying to Richards, at least the conclusion put forth in his little
book (recently revised and reissued as *Poetries and Sciences*) seems less
than startling—that poetry should be regarded as the custodian of
'supra-scientific myths'. More interesting are his too brief remarks on
the four poets from a reading of whom Richards claimed he was moved

to reflect about science and poetry: Hardy, de la Mare, Yeats and
Lawrence. Hardy comes first and is praised for his refusal to be con-
soled in the face of a neutralized nature; but the other three were
not so forthright, and dodged rather than faced the difficulties:
'Mr. de la Mare takes shelter in the dream-world of the child,
Mr. Yeats retired for a season into black velvet curtains and the
visions of the Hermetist', while Lawrence's effort is described as 'a
magnificent attempt to reconstruct in himself the mentality of the
Bushman'. I shall return to Richards's further remarks about Lawrence; but in general his penchant for the striking phrase about each
of these poets doesn't lead towards criticism of them nor even provide
useful clues as to how they might be approached. De la Mare and
Hardy wrote nothing after the war which would necessitate altering
what one had said about them previous to it. Yeats's development is
of course complicated beyond any attempt to treat of it here, though
it is odd that Richards should trot out the 'black velvet curtains' charge
when poems like 'Easter 1916' and 'Meditations in Time of Civil
War' had been around for years. But Lawrence's postwar work differs
significantly and boldly from his earlier 'Rhyming Poems' and deserves consideration as something more than an appendix to his
novels. And then, after paying respects to worthy minor figures,
such as Edgell Rickword and Roy Campbell, we are left, it seems to
me, with Robert Graves as the most interesting new poet of the
1920s.

If this constitutes a relative dearth one might blame in part the
example of Eliot. William Carlos Williams's bitter and melodramatic
comment in a letter about how *The Waste Land* exploded like a bomb
and sent his generation back to the classroom, is a colorful way of
pointing to what must have been an increased reticence, at least on
the part of some, to rush quickly into print on this or that subject.[2]
The strings are pulled tight for a few years, then loosened up again
by the facility of Auden and those associated with him. In the meantime the 'twenties decade turned into a remarkable age for the
criticism of poetry. Its three major documents, all of them still
eminently rereadable and useful, each of them still not as absorbed or
current as they deserve to be, are arguably as follows: *A Survey of
Modernist Poetry* (1927) by Laura Riding and Robert Graves;

Practical Criticism (1929) by Richards; and in the next year Empson's *Seven Types of Ambiguity*—these of course in addition to Eliot's essays, and with Leavis's *New Bearings* and *Revaluation* in the near future. But the Riding–Graves–Richards–Empson sequence is particularly and closely related through their common interest in exploring poetic ambiguity, in trying to demonstrate to the Plain Reader that Shakespeare's poems are at least as hard as E. E. Cummings's; and that late-Victorian assumptions about how poems had to communicate an easily understandable lesson about something out there called Life, needed to be junked in the face of both traditional and what they hoped would be—was beginning to be—current poetic practice.

Furthermore Riding–Graves, Richards and Empson brought to their practical criticism highly developed gifts of irony. Richards's wry commentary on his students' protocols, Empson's deadpan, hilarious time-bombs strewn through *Seven Types*, the hardboiled and amusing scorn which animates the Riding–Graves *Survey* and their *Pamphlet Against Anthologies* (1928), are of a piece with their authors' rejection of the highfalutin and the solemn in dead poems and dead literary movements. (Riding and Graves title one of their chapters, approvingly, 'The Humorous Element in Modernist Poetry'.) While critics like Muir and Richards (in *Science and Poetry*) were mainly content to point at Science as the power which had made uncertain the purpose and behavior of contemporary poets, it was Riding and Graves who first anatomized poetry's recent past and defined what it was now to be engaged in. The fifth chapter of *A Survey of Modernist Poetry* is titled 'Modernist Poetry and Dead Movements', and smartly clears away Imagism, the Georgians, and the War Poetry which they rightly saw as an extension—or second wind—of Georgian poetry.

These dead movements had focused on manner, on how to *present* a subject; modernist poetry on the other hand was concerned with nothing less than the reorganization of the whole matter of poetic thought. Riding and Graves put it this way:

> The ideal modernist poem is its own clearest, fullest and most accurate meaning . . . the poem does not give a rendering of a poetical picture or idea existing outside the poem, but presents

the literal substance of poetry, a newly created thought-
activity: the poem has the character of a creature by itself.

Their book is made up of splendidly analyzed examples of some of
these new creatures and the ways in which they discomfit the Plain
Reader. These examples are taken predominantly from contemporary
poems by American writers—from Cummings, John Crowe Ransom,
Marianne Moore and Eliot—suggesting that there was some difficulty
in finding specimens from the home country of bona fide modernist
poems. Sparing in their praise, they are ruthless in their denigration,
as in these sentences about H.D.:

> The only excuse to be made for those who once found H.D.
> 'incomprehensible' is that her work was so thin, so poor, that
> its emptiness seemed 'perfection,' its insipidity to be con-
> cealing a 'secret,' its superficiality so 'glacial' that it created a
> false 'classical' atmosphere. She was never able, in her tem-
> porary immortality, to reach a real climax in any of her
> poems.

Harshly amusing, and what one was waiting to have said about all
those tiny gems tendered by H.D. But a serious point has been made:
Riding and Graves wanted poems to be both detached from their
creator—as an interesting child should be from its parents—yet
infused with intelligent responsiveness to things, rather than, as in
H.D.'s poems, with loftily or glacially detached superiority. The poem
would feel relevant, in the broadest sense, to one's concerns, but would
not be 'relevant' (in the recently cheapened sense of that word) to
the latest timely issue:

> *Modernist*, indeed, should describe a quality in poetry which
> has nothing to do with the date or with responding to civiliza-
> tion ... It would not, however, ignore its contemporaneous
> universe, for the reason that it would not be stupid and that it
> would have a sense of humour—the most intelligent attitude
> toward history is not to take one's own date too seriously.
> There would occur evidences of time in such poetry; but
> always its modernism would lie in its independence, in its
> relying on none of the traditional devices of poetry-making in
> the past nor on any of the artificial effects to be got by using
> the atmosphere of contemporary life and knowledge to startle

and give reality. . . . Most of all, such poetry would be
characterized by a lack of strain, by an intelligent ease.

Graves's Poetry

Unless Riding and Graves meant something less than it sounds when
they cast out 'the traditional devices of poetry-making in the past' as
anathema to the modernist poem, one would have to charge Graves
with writing poems that rhymed, scanned and did other traditional
things. Otherwise, though, the description of 'modernist' quality
accurately characterizes many of the poems he had already written
by 1927, for example 'The Cool Web':[3]

> Children are dumb to say how hot the day is,
> How hot the scent is of the summer rose,
> How dreadful the black wastes of evening sky,
> How dreadful the tall soldiers drumming by.
>
> But we have speech, to chill the angry day,
> And speech, to dull the rose's cruel scent.
> We spell away the overhanging night,
> We spell away the soldiers and the fright.
>
> There's a cool web of language winds us in,
> Retreat from too much joy or too much fear:
> We grow sea-green at last and coldly die
> In brininess and volubility.
>
> But if we let our tongues lose self-possession,
> Throwing off language and its watery clasp
> Before our death, instead of when death comes,
> Facing the wide glare of the children's day,
> Facing the rose, the dark sky and the drums,
> We shall go mad no doubt and die that way.

Innumerable poems written over the last fifty years about and in
praise of language, must not keep us from appreciating how fine and
original a poem is this one of Graves's. As is usual, his work disdains
imagistic richness in favor of a sparer and un-dense exploiting of
images; still the words come alive—'spell' and 'self-possession' are
vigorously double-minded in their possibilities. And there is as well

the splendid musical pacing of the final six lines which both draw together and extend the poem's attitude: the long sentence, winding its enjambed way in contrast to earlier end-stopped lines and strong closing couplets, suspends us on the repeated 'Facing', as the soldiers, children and sky enter into the madness or death which comes of letting 'our tongues lose self-possession'.

In an earlier, slightly different form 'The Cool Web' was the final poem in Graves's collection of *Poems 1914–26* published when he was collaborating with Laura Riding on the modernist poetry book. He had then written poems as distinctive and various as 'Rocky Acres', 'Ghost Raddled' (later 'The Haunted House'), 'The Pier-Glass', 'Lost Love', 'The Ridge-Top' (later 'Love in Barrenness'), 'Love Without Hope', and an early version of 'Pure Death'. *A Survey of Modernist Poetry* showed that Graves had read and assimilated Eliot (there is a long analysis of 'Burbank with a Baedeker') but his own practice is not in bondage to *The Waste Land*, nor to Pound; *Survey* cocks an eye at Pound's poem about the lady in Kensington Gardens for having too much of 'short-story material' in it, not being as 'independent' as modernist poems should be. While uninfluenced by Eliot and Pound, Graves's best poems still show him miles away from and ahead of the Georgians with whom he appeared in the anthology of 1920–22; *Survey*'s remarks on Georgianism as another 'dead movement' are sharp and just. Surely anybody who could tell jokes as cruelly funny as the ones which fill *Goodbye to All That*, Graves's 1929 autobiography, was too lively and unsolemn to be surrounded by the pieties, sincerities and archness of Gibson and Davies and Abercrombie.

In future collections Graves was to prune away the sometimes amusing, leisurely, longer satiric pieces of his—often with contemporary names named—so as to leave only shorter, more austere and gallows-humoured lyrics. One can't argue with Graves's rightful choice, but it's well to remember that a reader of his 1914–26 collection would have been able to complement 'The Cool Web' and other such impersonal poems with free-swinging personal epistles like 'The College Debate' (addressed to Edith Sitwell) or 'The Marmosite's Miscellany'. Graves's humour then would not look quite so chilly, embattled or last-ditch as it does, say, in the fifty-poem collection (*No More Ghosts*) he published with Faber in 1940. But even in terms of that collection, or the severely and intelligently selected editions we have read him out of since, it is wrong to see Graves's poetry as depressed or depressing, 'coldly' engineered work operating through logic and devoid of the imagery which supposedly cheers us up. If Kenneth Burke's useful definition in *Attitudes Toward History* of 'grotesque' as 'The cult of incongruity without the laughter' is accepted, then Graves's best lyrics, grim as they sometimes feel, are not grotesques, but morally passionate, elegant and humorous instances of poems that help us live our lives.

One understands why he so much admired John Crowe Ransom and Robert Frost: both of whom, like Graves, were committed to rhyme in poetry, though able also to blend blank verse in rhythms of speech against the limits of meter. But to an even greater degree than exists in either of their poetries, there is already fully formed in Graves's work of the 1920s an intensity of concern that poems should, in Wallace Stevens's phrase, press back against the pressure of reality—that reality which eventually defeats us.

> We looked, we loved, and therewith instantly
> Death became terrible to you and me.

begins 'Pure Death'; and many of the poems turn around Stevens's chant in 'Sunday Morning' by making beauty, as experienced through love, the mother of death. In 'Pure Death' the lovers give each other everything until they have nothing left but death to give, a present which is duly unwrapped 'with such bewilderment/As greeted our love's first accomplishment.' By itself this poem might read as little more than a metaphysically ingenious exercise; in context with Graves's other poems about death and love, it turns out to be fully meant. 'In Procession' has the poet awake from a fabulous dream in which he has been railing in strange tongues, and he cries

> Oh, then, when I wake,
> Could I courage take
> To renew my speech,
> Could I stretch and reach
> The flowers and the ripe fruit
> Laid out at the ladder's foot,

but instead, 'cowardly', he tells of 'This Town of Hell/Where between sleep and sleep I dwell.'

Yet the impulse towards the renewal of speech and towards song
is a courageous way of pressing back against reality's pressure, a way
of not dwelling wholly in the Town of Hell. Love in Graves's poetry
may be 'Sick Love', as one of his very best poems has it, but—or
therefore—the invitation to momentary song, glimpsed and celebrated beauty, is powerfully meant and at the root of his poetic impulse:

> Be warm, enjoy the season, lift your head,
> Exquisite in the pulse of tainted blood,
> That shivering glory not to be despised.
>
> Take your delight in momentariness,
> Walk between dark and dark—a shining space
> With the grave's narrowness, though not its peace.

So ends the poem, and it may by an accident of language remind us
of a tendency, even among admirers, to speak of Graves's narrowness
as a poet, his goodness only to be appreciated within severe limits.
Though it may be narrowness, it goes deep; such depths as are
intuited from poems like this one where even though its last line can
be foretold from the beginning, there is still the sense of discovery, of
something achieved as if for the first time. The wonderful moments
in Graves's poems occur when something suddenly bursts in front of
us; and although we look back, reread the poem and see how everything led up to this moment, it still seems a miracle.

Such fullness within momentariness is what goes deep and makes it
wrong to talk about Graves's presence in the poems as a brittle,
gloomy, death-obsessed one. In the fashion of postwar Huxley and
Lewis, Graves sees through everything, but sees through so thoroughly
that something on the other side becomes visible—no mystic truth
(at least not in the 1920 poems) but one that comes from viewing our
human experience as common, inevitable, poignant:

> Below the ridge a raven flew
> And we heard the lost curlew
> Mourning out of sight below.
> Mountain tops were touched with snow;
> Even the long dividing plain
> Showed no wealth of sheep or grain,

But fields of boulders lay like corn
And raven's croak was shepherd's horn
Where slow cloud-shadow strayed across
A pasture of thin heath and moss.

The North Wind rose: I saw him press
With lusty force against your dress,
Moulding your body's inward grace
And streaming off from your set face;
So now no longer flesh and blood
But poised in marble flight you stood.
O wingless Victory, loved of men,
Who could withstand your beauty then?

'Love in Barrenness', the poem's eventual title, would, like Graves's narrowness, be a way to think about the terrain of his poetry. Published in the early 1920s it has Hardy behind it (perhaps 'I Found Her Out There') but typically as in Graves without the oddly distinguishing human touch: this could be any girl, turned suddenly into the goddess lovers turn their loves into. Another emblem there of Graves's superiority to any Georgian effort along these lines; the certainty and flexibility of verse movement, the accuracy and clear, informing economy of its statement, the disdain for any winningly personal gesture, any coy nudge in the reader's ribs. And so the final question has sophisticated dignity, is made in a tone we can't find exactly the right words to describe. But the authority and grace of the compliment is its own answer.

Lawrence's Poetry

'The only native English poet of any importance to survive the First World War was D. H. Lawrence': A. Alvarez's claim in his still influential essay on Lawrence's poetry is a fair starting-point for discussion.[4] Graves survived the war—just—but his significant work as a poet did not begin until after it. Edward Thomas did not survive, and his death was perhaps English poetry's most grievous loss to it. Edith Sitwell had at the time, and still has, her admirers; but though she made up the third poet in Edwin Muir's chosen group of Eliot, Graves and Sitwell, her poetry seems to call for neither enthusiastic analysis nor stern denigration. If one finds charming such pieces as 'Trio for Two Cats and a Trombone' ('Long steel grass—/The white soldiers pass—/The light is braying like an ass') from *Façade*, or the 'Aubade' to 'Jane, Jane,/Tall as a crane,/The morning light creaks down again', then her poems written in the 'twenties offer ample opportunities for delight, fancy sound-effects and 'striking' word-juxtapositions. Nobody I think would say they have anything to do with life; as art they seem sterile and pretty quickly boring. At the opposite extreme from Edith Sitwell there would then be Lawrence, whose poems have of course everything to do with life.

Yet Lawrence is at the opposite extreme from just about any poet one might produce. He is at least as moral and judgemental as Graves; yet is a taste for the poems of one compatible with liking the other's? If Alvarez is right, if Lawrence is the 'foremost emotional realist of the century', and if even his bad poems have the 'badness of genius', then Graves can be appreciated as only a very minor talent. And indeed Alvarez treated Graves rather uneasily in *The Shaping Spirit* as someone whose poems he admired but who produced 'drawing-room art' and who was judged not to have survived the war. My own judgement about Lawrence will come as no surprise, considering my previous remarks about his 'twenties fiction: it is that the poems from this decade are largely disasters—shrill and embarrassing outbreaks of uncontrolled feeling; that they are about 'life' usually in crude, often hysterically 'moral' ways which make the morality offered a bad one. I also think it probably impossible, or at least even more a tightrope act than with most poetry, to 'look at words on the page' and demonstrate convincingly that here is a good, there is a bad use of them. Alvarez much admires the poems and also finds it extra-ordinarily difficult to come up with an articulate way of praising them. Although his essay must have had R. P. Blackmur's earlier and adverse criticism of the poems in mind (Alvarez keeps insisting that the good poems just *look* careless but are really organized in a new and original way), I think the careless-careful argument is but a mask for one's deeper attraction to or repulsion from the poems and Lawrence's personality.

Alvarez is briefly dismissive of any influence Georgian or Imagist styles had on Lawrence's early poetry, claiming that they have no part in his best work. He ignores the *Rhyming Poems* except for some discriminating praise of 'End of Another Home Holiday'; yet if I were not here concerned with the Lawrence who survived the war, but rather with the poetry he wrote between 1910 and 1915, I would want to single out a number of these early rhyming poems for admiration. Even when the rhymes are forced, when he is writing poems more conventionally finished than the 'poetry of the present' he later gave allegiance to, many of them are memorably filled with thoughtful responses to the life he was living: with exultation at nature, depression at end of holiday or the teaching school-day, the imminent breakup of a romance, nostalgia for home and mother, insouciance towards unfaithfulness in a relationship. A list of the most returnable to and attractive of the *Rhyming Poems* would begin with the first one in *Collected Poems*, 'The Wild Common', and go on to include the two 'Letter from Town' poems, 'End of Another Home Holiday', 'Corot', the school poems—particularly 'Last Lesson of the Afternoon'—, 'A Winter's Tale', 'Last Words to Miriam', the poems occasioned by his mother's death, 'Piano', and 'Hymn to Priapus' (included in *Unrhyming Poems* though it rhymes). This list may be too long or too short, depending on how stern are one's standards, but it is put forth in a similar spirit to the one provided by Richards's discussion of Lawrence in *Science and Poetry*. Richards ambiguously saluted Lawrence for reconstructing in himself the Bushman's mentality; then in considering *Fantasia of the Unconscious* he spoke of most of Lawrence's verse as interesting jottings 'from a psychologist's notebook, with a commentary interspersed'. And he allowed himself to wonder at how 'the poet who wrote the "Ballad of Another Ophelia" and "Aware", some pages of *Birds, Beasts and Flowers*, and *The White Peacock*, should have wandered, through his own zeal misdirected, so far from the paths which once appeared to be his alone to open'.[5]

If *Sons and Lovers* were to replace *The White Peacock* and my own list substituted for Richards's favorite poems, I sympathize with the wonder, or the lament. Lawrence refers deprecatingly, in the 1928 preface to his poems, to the 'young man' who back in the days of *Rhyming Poems* used sometimes to put his hand over the mouth of the demon that was trying to speak in those poems. We are supposed

to approve of the liberated demon—liberated at least since the exul-
tations of *Look! We Have Come Through!* in 1917. But it may be
instead—clearly I believe it to be so—that the young man was finally
a more interesting human being, for all his unresolved perplexities,
than the demon who spoke as if he knew what was right for himself,
poetry, and mankind. Even more than in the novels, cruelty and
self-pity break into and mar Lawrence's later poems in ways no
amount of careful revision or additional craft could expunge. So it is
often embarrassing to hear the demon who seems patently to be poking
us in the ribs, saying look, what a demon am I!

But a really outstanding poem of Lawrence's, like 'The Elephant
is Slow to Mate' (published in *Pansies*, 1929), provides standards
for measuring other ones:

> The elephant, the huge old beast,
>   is slow to mate;
> he finds a female, they show no haste
>   they wait
>
> for the sympathy in their vast shy hearts
>   slowly, slowly to rouse
> as they loiter along the river-beds
>   and drink and browse
>
> and dash in panic through the brake
>   of forest with the herd,
> and sleep in massive silence, and wake
>   together, without a word.
>
> So slowly the great hot elephant hearts
>   grow full of desire
> and the great beasts mate in secret at last,
>   hiding their fire.
>
> Oldest they are and the wisest of beasts
>   so they know at last
> how to wait for the loneliest of feasts
>   for the full repast.
>
> They do not snatch, they do not tear;
>   their massive blood
> moves as the moon-tides, near, more near,
>   till they touch in flood.

Although in his Foreword to *Pansies* Lawrence asked that these poems
be taken as 'thoughts rather than anything else', there is no need
to call 'The Elephant' anything else or less than a poem, and if I am
not mistaken a very good one. It is of course only posing as an unrhyming poem, since it rhymes and does so artfully to provide a
continuity of sweep that is assisted by enjambment, stanzaic organization and syntactical pausings or movings ahead.

Even if it is unfair to bind the whole of the *Unrhyming Poems*
volume with the 'Poetry of the Present' essay Lawrence wrote to
introduce the American Edition of *New Poems* ten years before in
1918, the language of that essay may be recalled, since it is usually
referred to as a mature statement of his poetic principles. It contains
much rapturous appreciation of the ever-presentness of life, of flux,
mud, 'the still, white seething, the incandescence and the coldness
of the incarnate moment . . . the quick of all change and haste and
opposition . . . the Now'. This 'instant poetry' (Lawrence's all-too-apt
term) written in praise of the Now is talked about in orgasmic terms
as 'the very jetting source of all will-be and has-been'; as 'like a spasm,
naked contact with all influences at once. It does not want to get
anywhere. It just takes place.' Free verse then qualifies as the only
verse where one can experience the 'insurgent naked throb of the
instant moment'. But a poem like 'The Elephant' simply makes
irrelevant such insistence on the moment, the Now, the naked throb.
Not, surely, because it lacks powerful immediacy; the poem never
dissolves into ruminative meandering or moralistic speculation, as do
so many of Lawrence's supposedly freer, nakedly-throbbing ones.
'The Elephant' is both strongly immediate and extremely considered;
it is as slow to achieve its poetic consummation, as delicate and as
inevitable, as the beasts themselves who 'do not snatch, do not tear'
but eventually and massively 'touch in flood'. And if not exactly a
humorous poem, it exhibits witty ability to decide that elephant
hearts are 'shy', or that 'he' and 'she' elephant wake in the morning
without a word to one another.

It would, though, be mistaken, or at least misleading, to claim
that 'The Elephant' is an example of Lawrence's sympathetic perception into the 'otherness' of birds, beasts or flowers, and to praise it
for dispassionately rendering the unhuman world. Clearly we are to

128 ENGLISH POETRY IN THE 1920S:

admire these beasts in their mating because it is so unlike the way human beings behave in comparable circumstances. There is the 'thought' that our triviality, our nervous and pushy verbality, is made insignificant, perhaps contemptible by such massive consummation, analogous in its shock to Hardy's Titanic meeting the Iceberg. But Lawrence doesn't press too hard, doesn't buttonhole the reader to harangue him about his inadequacies; instead he gives him an interesting action to contemplate, carefully and thoughtfully rendered in words that sparkle with energy and accuracy. The poem is thus in one sense truly 'impersonal', released from whatever motives impelled the poet to write it. Lawrence's thumb is not so much in the pan that we are prevented from saying, well, those elephants certainly do have a time of it. We need not then immediately decide that our own life is incredibly shabby, no longer worth living.

If Lawrence had often written this way there would be no need to struggle for some special, 'life' vocabulary with which to appreciate his later poetry. To read and enjoy 'The Elephant', that is, one need not speak the way Alvarez does here:

> The stuff of Lawrence's poetry, the 'lifeline,' are those essential experiences in which he registers his full humanity. His poems are the inner flow of a man in the act of becoming aware— aware not only of his feelings and their cause, but of their full implications. By the flexibility of his verse-forms he can catch this flow in all its immediacy and with peculiarly little fuss.

Alvarez has just finished discussing and admiring 'Snake', perhaps the most anthologized of the later poems and generally taken to be one of Lawrence's best, perhaps one of the pages from *Birds, Beasts, and Flowers* that Richards liked. Despite some good writing about the snake the poem represents for me exactly what is embarrassing and unpleasant about the later Lawrence; and no formal talk (as Alvarez provides) of how short lines alternate with longer lines and movements play off against each other can make the poem's morality more satisfactory. Recall that in 'Snake', too long to quote in full here, the 'I' is anticipated at the water-trough by an 'earth-golden' snake come to drink. He looks at the man and continues to drink. The man hears voices of his 'education' telling him that the snake is poisonous and should be killed, but in fact the man likes the snake, feels honoured

that he has visited him and lets him drink his fill. As the snake prepares
to depart, the man finally tosses a log at him, doesn't hit him but makes
him writhe quickly back into his hole in the wall. At which point the
poem concludes:

> And immediately I regretted it.
> I thought how paltry, how vulgar, what a mean act!
> I despised myself and the voices of my accursed human
>   education.
>
> And I thought of the albatross,
> And I wished he would come back, my snake.
>
> For he seemed to me again like a king
> Like a king in exile, uncrowned in the underworld,
> Now due to be crowned again.
>
> And so, I missed my chance with one of the lords
> Of life.
> And I have something to expiate;
> A pettiness.

This would seem exactly to fill Alvarez's bill—'the inner flow of a
man in the act of becoming aware—aware not only of his feelings and
their cause, but of their full implication'. Yet consider the moral
style of 'Snake', and in comparison with Coleridge's poem since the
albatross is invoked. The ancient mariner really shoots the bird and
suffers for it: 'Instead of the cross, the Albatross/About my neck was
hung.' The 'I' in 'Snake', on the other hand, is unchanged, his voice
unaffected from beginning to end. Early in the poem he confesses that
he likes the snake, that he feels honoured to be so visited, and that he
is careful to take seriously the viper's drinking privileges. He also
invites us to grimace with him at 'the voices of my education'—the
later adjective 'accursed' is already fully implied in the scorn with
which these voices are invoked. When he finally tosses a log at the
snake, not even hitting him at that, the act seems something less than
worthy of doing heroic penance for. At any rate consider how crudely
and abstractly Alvarez's 'act of becoming aware' of feelings is rendered: 'I thought how paltry, how vulgar, what a mean act!/I despised

myself and the voices of my accursed human education.' In fact the
despising seems turned outwards rather than in on the self, since the
speaker's voice never changes, is as self-righteously assured in its
repentance as it was before:

> And so, I missed my chance with one of the lords
> Of life.
> And I have something to expiate;
> A pettiness.

A pious hush falls over the scene, as 'a pettiness' shamefully rever-
berates in our consciousness. Or supposedly it does, unless one becomes
aware of D. H. Lawrence peeping through sentimentally and arrogantly, assuring us that really he is a fine and noble spirit, that he
is constantly inspecting and criticizing his feelings, is alert to the
smallest betrayal or insult offered toward 'life'. That log *couldn't* just
have been playfully tossed at the animal; it had to be an occasion for
promised expiation. And only morally superior persons can perform
that sort of act.

In other words, rather than the poem registering Alvarez's 'full
humanity' with 'peculiarly little fuss', it seems to me typical of many
of Lawrence's later poems in that it makes a great and portentous
fuss about 'a pettiness' that someone in his full humanity might handle
with an attitude more flexible than dead solemnity. Lawrence railed
at Proust and other novelists of sensibility for worrying whether the
twinge was in their right toe or not; the moral analogue of this can be
found in 'Snake'. But the worry seems hoked-up and put-on, the 'I'
merely a convenient pretext, since the mind behind the poem is quite
clear about things and triumphantly secure throughout. To repeat,
my criticism is not a formalistic one, *à la* Blackmur; rather it sees
the poem as perfectly finished, a made object that is what it is, except that what it is—its manner of performance—is self-righteously
unpleasant.

Having said as much we should acknowledge that Alvarez speaks
for many readers and anthologists who single out 'Snake' as one of the
best of Lawrence's later poems. It is also true that some readers take
more pleasure in the fluidities of his free verse style than I do, or than
Hugh Kingsmill did when he wrote the following:

Lawrence's verse, which became progressively more spasmodic and broken-backed, tallied with his philosophy that the real way of living is to answer to one's wants. . . . If he wanted a line of thirty to forty syllables, he wrote, 'Hence he uncovers his big ass-teeth and howls in that agony that is half insatiable desire and half unquenchable humiliation.' If a line of one syllable, he wrote 'Bats!'

More recently an essay by Barbara Hardy praises the free verse of the *Look! We Have Come Through!* sequence and finds that in those poems 'irony and comedy are happily absent since Lawrence is not at his best in either'.[6] The remark could as well be made about *Birds, Beasts and Flowers*; yet it is strange to welcome the absence of what one would have thought were almost indispensable virtues. They are not absent, happily, in Hardy, in Eliot, or in Robert Graves: what is so special about Lawrence that he can be praised for getting along well without them? Even in the later *Pansies* volume where there is much heavy sarcasm, the sometime absence of irony and comedy leaves a poem vulnerable to exactly those qualities, turned against it and wielded by reader rather than author. In another often-anthologized poem, 'We Are Transmitters', the following lines occur:

As we live, we are transmitters of life.
And when we fail to transmit life, life fails to flow through us.
That is part of the mystery of sex, it is a flow onwards.
Sexless people transmit nothing.

How unmysterious 'sex' sounds with the 'that' and 'it' clauses limply spliced together by an all-purpose comma. How arrogantly complacent is the remark about 'Sexless people'. Who wants to be a 'transmitter' anyway, one might wonder, especially when illustrative instances of good transmitting follow:

Even if it is a woman making an apple dumpling, or a man a
    stool,
if life goes into the pudding, good is the pudding
good is the stool,
content is the woman, with fresh life rippling in to her,
content is the man.

Thus the contented cook and carpenter, blessed by the poet with inverted word order and a particularly infelicitous use of 'the stool'.

Feelings of embarrassment and annoyance at being so lectured at
contend in the reader; and even if the poem is taken as just a 'thought'
it becomes no more compelling.

There are 'thoughts' from *Pansies* that do remain in the mind,
detaching themselves from their unmemorable poetic garments.
Perhaps it is not only my own experience that Lawrence is a good
tonic for restless young men inclined to self-pity:

> Mournful young man in your twenties
> who think the only way out of your mournfulness is through a
>   woman
> yet you fail to find the woman, when there are so many
>   women about—
>
> Why don't you realize
> that you're not desirable?
> that no woman will ever desire you, as you are, . . .

or the following amusingly prophetic lines:

> It's no good, the women are in eruption,
> and those that have been good so far
> now begin to steam ominously,
> and if they're over forty-five, hurl great stones into the air
> which are very like to hit you on the head as you sit
> on the very slopes of the matrimonial mountain
> where you've sat peacefully all these years.
>
> Vengeance is mine, saith the Lord,
> but the women are my favourite vessels of wrath.

In both these poems the teasing is done not without humor, the
animus doesn't feel simply bitter and nagging, the 'thought' about
women being in eruption is given nice embodiment through these
over-forty-fives hurling great stones into the air. More than that need
not be claimed for them, but it is enough to make them poems you
remember with pleasure even without returning to read them.

My case that the good poems from Lawrence's later work do not
hold irony and comedy in abeyance means that I am more or less
speechless in front of *Last Poems*. As poems which call on us to
prepare for death ('Have you built your ship of death, oh have you?')
they ask to be delivered in incantatory ways which seek to overpower

us through a universal and toneless appeal to common experience. At times, and with 'Bavarian Gentians' especially, they achieve mythological resonance as well. But they seem to me in little need of criticism, indeed should remain private communications between a dying man and the individual reader depending on his taste and inclination for this sort of communication. They have to be read with the weight of Lawrence's previous life and work behind them; read as such, they seem both hopelessly sad and nobly dignified:

> Not every man has gentians in his house
> in soft September, at slow, sad Michaelmas . . .

> Reach me a gentian, give me a torch!
> let me guide myself with the blue, forked torch of this flower
> down the darker and darker stairs, where blue is darkened on
> blueness . . .

Yet admired or not they don't much affect the overall judgement on Lawrence's later poems: that the theory under which they were written, as put forth in the 1918 preface, was a disastrous one, and that most of the poetry which resulted does not succeed, in another phrase from Wallace Stevens, in helping us to live our lives. Like the novels, they are very much worth arguing about in a way more insulated and self-concealing poetry (de la Mare's would be a prime example) cannot be. My own feeling is, though, that after a certain point of attraction, reaction and lively argument, one simply passes beyond the terms these poems provide for understanding human life—the world will no longer submit to being carved up in these Lawrentian ways, the carver becomes too lonely to endure himself.

VI

The Literature of Criticism

Eliot's publication of *The Sacred Wood* in 1920 gave rise, though not immediately, to a number of controversial literary issues and arguments which were explored and conducted in some of the most imaginative writing of the period between the wars. Partly because The Age of Criticism began in the 'twenties and continued unabated at least into the 'sixties, the contemporary reader is placed in a special relationship to the Age's inaugurators. We don't now pick up Eliot on the Metaphysicals or Marvell or Dryden to find out how to approach these writers; Leavis on Swift is not now to be consulted as our guide to Swift-reading. The terms for discussion of Swift and Dryden have complicated themselves—with those essays by Eliot and Leavis heavily responsible for the complication. But we now read the Eliot and Leavis essays for other reasons, ones I should term 'literary', since their criticism has become literature and the pleasures it affords are comparable to those experienced in reading poetry or novels. This by no means precludes our responding with vigorous assent or equally vigorous denial; but, as with reading poet and novelist, we don't exult in having proved the critic right or wrong. Criticism, like art, never improves; one moves on from a significant critic but doesn't surpass him. Hence this discussion of some English writers and magazines, 1925–35, who produced some unsurpassable literary criticism and much instructive quarreling.

In a 1926 *Criterion* note, Eliot made mention of Wyndham Lewis's just-published *Art of Being Ruled*, along with an essay by I. A. Richards on contemporary poetry, also fresh in the *Criterion*. Eliot recognized a preoccupation in both Lewis and Richards with examining, and inviting artists to examine, the grounds of their endeavour. What did they think they were up to, what difference did it make that the year was 1926; why should a 'modern' writer feel the necessity to educate himself in the nature of his enterprise any more than any other post-Homeric writer did? In the following year, Lewis's own essay 'The Values of the Doctrine behind "Subjective" Art' (*Criterion*, July 1927) made, with customary dark admonition, the following analysis of the contemporary's situation:

> In the arts of formal expression, a 'dark night of the soul' is settling down. A kind of mental language is in process of invention, flouting and overriding the larynx and the tongue. Yet an art that is 'subjective' and can look to no common factors of knowledge or feeling, and lean on no tradition, is exposed to the necessity, first of all, of instructing itself far more profoundly as to the origins of its impulses and the nature and history of the formulas with which it works; or else it is committed to becoming a zealous parrot of systems and judgments that reach it from the unknown.

Lewis spent a good portion of his imaginative energy in the instruction of his 'subjective' contemporaries, but his activity is distinguished only by its higher voltage and extravagance from that of other significant contemporary critics. It is this polemical concern—instruction can be kindly and measured, it can also be brutally annihilating—that gives the criticism of Eliot, of Lewis, of D. H. Lawrence, Pound, the *Calendar* group, Richards, and finally Leavis and the early Scrutineers, its life today.

These polemics take on a special character, become 'literature' with appropriate plot and characters, when their authors begin to argue with each other or (as often) attack the other without receiving any response. To be interested in such matters purely from an aesthetic-appreciative viewpoint admittedly smacks of frivolity. But the attacks and arguings weren't made frivolously, were made in fact with much seriousness and are notable for their pungency and wit. I shall consider some situations where, in Eliot's phrase, the artist as critic is moved to examine what he and his contemporaries think they are doing. Did such critical examination have any consequences for the actual performances of writers in the late 1920s and subsequent decade? Or more realistically, since writers are good at ignoring critics, what difference did such criticism make in the ways we have been instructed to think about these writers?

This task is made easier, perhaps even superfluous, since the terrain has been covered so well by John Gross's *Rise and Fall of the Man of Letters*. In fifty pages of concentrated exposition and criticism, Gross surveys the main contributions of English critics and periodicals between the wars, summing up and valuing disinterestedly the virtues and limitations of each contribution. With Leavis in particular the account is a harsh but I think a just one. My own attempt will not be to summarize and judge in such a manner, but rather to focus on the critics only as what they say directly concerns standards and attitudes towards the literature their contemporaries and they themselves were producing. Certain exclusions are made in the following spirit: Lawrence's criticism has been considered in the earlier discussion of his writings; Geoffrey Grigson's *New Verse* will be touched on in relation to Auden; Middleton Murry and Herbert Read now seem relatively unnecessary to read; the Riding/Graves collaboration has been dealt with earlier. Finally there is Empson's criticism, which is simply not able to be at all taken in by the net I've cast, and which also has fewer polemical concerns with the status of contemporary literature.[1] Let us then proceed to some cases and skirmishes.

Eliot and 'The Inner Voice'

Eliot's major campaign was undertaken against the primacy of 'self', against the cultivation and exalting of originality, against the individual talent proclaiming itself free from the bondage of history, of tradition—of order, in one form or another. Anglican, Classicist, and Royalist as he was eventually to proclaim himself in the preface to *For Lancelot Andrewes* (1928), he had already in 'Tradition and the Individual Talent' defined poetry as an escape from emotion and as distinct from the suffering man who created it. If it were a worthy poem it would know itself only in relation to all past poems— 'the existing works of art'—which formed an ideal order among themselves. In the ten years or so after *The Waste Land* was published,

Eliot's disdain, sometimes teasing, often contemptuous, for the self's pretensions became even bolder, finding more colorfully excessive modes of expression. His essay 'The Function of Criticism' (1923) saw itself as the successor to Arnold's appointed task of 'cleaning up the whole country', as Eliot had referred to it in *The Sacred Wood*, and that country evidently was filled with devotees of something called 'the inner voice'. Middleton Murry had tried to construct a homemade tradition to compete with Catholicism or Classicism—both of which accepted the principle of 'unquestioned spiritual authority outside the individual'—by claiming that in the last resort English writers, statesmen and divines, inherited from their forbears only a dependence on the inner voice. In reply, Eliot scoffed at the business of any 'last resort':

> My belief is that those who possess this inner voice are ready
> enough to hearken to it, and will hear no other. The inner
> voice, in fact, sounds remarkably like an old principle which
> has been formulated by an elder critic in the now familiar
> phrase of 'doing as one likes'. The possessors of the inner voice
> ride ten in a compartment to a football match at Swansea,
> listening to the inner voice, which breathes the eternal mess-
> age of vanity, fear and lust.

Not only vanity, fear and lust, but ten to a compartment, with football and Swansea thrown in for an authentic shiver of disgust. Nowhere does Eliot sound more like Matthew Arnold, the 'elder critic' here so coyly referred to. Its snobbery and illiberalism virtually invite us to rebuke it from all our impulses of democratic decency; at the same time it is explosively witty, Old Possum reading the riot act to an accompaniment of cheers and other approbations.

Such castigation was to culminate in the American lectures published ten years later as *After Strange Gods* and not since reprinted. Here the major figure brought to court on charges of heresy—a blatant attention to and advocacy of the inner voice—was D. H. Lawrence; but the paragraphs on Lawrence in those lectures were only the last trump in Eliot's efforts to excommunicate him. Mention has already been made of the *Nation and Athenaeum* letter wondering what Forster could have meant by calling Lawrence 'the greatest imaginative novelist of our generation'. Before that, in a 1922 *Dial*

letter written after reading *Aaron's Rod*, Eliot allowed that Lawrence
hadn't really done anything as good as *Sons and Lovers*, partly because
'he theorizes at times when he should merely see'. But in one scene
from the new novel is revealed 'the terrifying disinterestedness of the
true creator', and for that, Eliot says, Lawrence can perhaps be for-
given his subsequent lapse into theory. Nine years later in his *Criterion*
review of Murry's *Son of Woman* (July, 1931) he was much less
ready to forgive Lawrence: Murry's is praised as a great book, and the
infamous passage about Lawrence's 'ignorance', the injurious consequences which might have ensued had he become a Cambridge don
—'rotten and rotting others'—are deplored by Eliot even in their
absence. Lawrence's hungering for 'a greater intimacy than is possible between human beings' is noted, his Oedipal sufferings lamented,
and various spiritual unpleasantnesses which disturb Eliot are pointed
to. The shocking thing about the review, apart from its loosely written
(for Eliot) character and its length, is his admission—in adducing a
passage from *Lady Chatterley's Lover* as an example of Lawrence's
cruelty—that he had not in fact read that novel. Nor had he read
Fantasia of the Unconscious, published ten years before, although he
tells us it is an important book. Finally, in *After Strange Gods*,
Lawrence's lack of a sense of humour and incapacity for 'thinking'
are named, at the same time as his great powers for heretical statement are acknowledged.

Years later F. R. Leavis defended Lawrence against Eliot's criticism by attacking the Impersonal Theory itself which, from the time
of its original formulation in the 'Tradition' essay, was radically
unable to account for the presence of an author in his work.[2] But
surely it was not the Impersonal Theory which led Eliot to become, as
Christopher Ricks put it recently, 'Lawrence's greatest antagonist,'
but the dramatic challenge Lawrence provided to Eliot's deepest
personal style of life. He might and did publish Lawrence's work in
the *Criterion*; all the more reason then why it must be made clear
how different were the objects of their respective allegiances. Whether
or not, as Leavis charges, Eliot absurdly overvalued Virginia Woolf—
in contrast to his devaluing Lawrence—one can understand why with
Mrs. Woolf he felt safe: no one was liable to think of her art as somehow challenging and countering the emphases of *The Waste Land* or

'The Hollow Men'. Lawrence was another matter; not because he was more 'personal' than Virginia Woolf, rather that Eliot had conceived him as a more considerable, significant and troublesome affair. This can be generalized further: Leavis, in that same essay, refers to Eliot's judgements (or lack of them) of his contemporaries as more or less disastrously wrong, and he charges the *Criterion* with signally failing to perform a sufficiently critical function in regard to such contemporaries as Auden, Spender, Virginia Woolf, David Garnett and others—so implicated with 'Bloomsbury' coterie values was Eliot. On the other hand, in respect to Donne or Dryden or Marlowe, he is allowed to have contributed insights of revolutionary importance.

Leavis never asks himself whether an artist of Eliot's stature can function as a disinterested 'objective' analyzer and valuer of the contemporaries with whom he is in competition as well as cooperation. One could counter positively by saying that though (to Leavis) they are not admirable writers as D. H. Lawrence is, Joyce, Pound, and Lewis were all valued (overvalued Leavis would say) and to some extent analyzed by Eliot's criticism. But perhaps Leavis really believes that only he himself can truly and disinterestedly perform the function of criticizing his contemporaries. In fact his own criticism looks as excitingly, sometimes as maddeningly 'personal', interested in certain writers and values to the exclusion of other ones, as ever Eliot's did. Leavis's adverse judgements on the *Criterion* cannot be wholly separated from the fact that S*crutiny* was set up to perform that function of criticism which the older magazine supposedly wasn't performing. Yet anybody who reads through the *Criterion* is likely to find all sorts of interesting and varied journalism, unScrutinyish though most of it is.[3] We are beginning to appreciate both magazines in the terms of art rather than of truth, that art being one of lively and memorable performance.

Wyndham Lewis, 'Personal-Appearance Artist'

My assertion, in correction of Leavis, that the *Criterion* did in fact present a respectable amount of still-readable articles and reviews by a wide-ranging group of writers may be just, but it is not a very

interesting way to talk about the magazine. When Leavis, in his essay
on Eliot as critic, says the following we sit up and take notice:

> It seems to me that there was nothing more adequate behind
> the *Criterion* than the general idea of a great European re-
> view; the idea as it might have been formed in (say) Irving
> Babbitt's lecture room. What Eliot learnt from Ezra Pound
> or Wyndham Lewis or the social-literary world in which he
> formed his notion of England didn't help him to anything
> better.

The magazine can thus be understood and dismissed by naming the
malign influences behind Eliot's mind; that Pound, Lewis, Babbitt,
and the social-literary world known to Leavis as 'Bloomsbury' can be
put together in a horrified sentence is surely stunning, even if it tells
us more about who Leavis dislikes than who formed Eliot's mind.
But the naming of Lewis as one of the forces behind the *Criterion* is
unfortunate, not only in suggesting that Lewis might consort with
Bloomsbury, or in failing to mention that he criticized Pound's historical snobbery in the strongest of terms, but in ignoring Lewis's
trenchant and hilarious criticisms of Eliot, the Impersonal Theory
and its consequences. Here is Lewis's way of describing the *Criterion*
(in *Men Without Art*):

> As to the *Criterion*, that is a very 'catholic' canon: it is a very
> broad, and indeed loose-minded affair, where the politics of
> *la vieille France* jostle the disintegrating tenets of 'super-real'
> psychoanalysis . . . [Eliot] exhibited himself as 'a royalist' to
> an indignant whig public—he called them a lot of naughty
> whigs and wagged his finger—and supplied *just so much* of that
> comedy as was welcome to brighten up a scene, but not a scrap
> more than was safe and comfortable.

Lewis doesn't accuse Eliot of humbuggery, merely of being—and the
word is taken from Richards's *Science and Poetry*—'pseudo-everything'. So, Lewis goes on, Eliot can surround himself with 'shady'
figures like Herbert Read ('psychoanalyser and dutifully sex-dissector
of William Wordsworth—how this scandalized Babbitt!') or can publish Lawrence's short stories

> . . . and so long as his colleagues do not blow the gaff, or over-
> conscientiously drag out all these damaging contradictions into

the light of common day, all is well, and Mr. Eliot, sardonic but decorous, goes peacefully his *pseudo* way! Indeed, stretched out in a comfortable deck-chair under his poop-awning (the latest *Crime Club* romance upon his knee), he is perfectly ready that his first mate should head the good ship *Cri* for *any* old port—the most *liberal* in the world, or the *reddest*, for that matter, in the universe . . . providing only the boatswain *pipes* at the right time, in the true traditional fashion, and as long as the royal colours continue to float aloft and the crew touch their forelocks and say *sir* when addressing an officer!

This excellent comedy is also an incisive creation of the *Criterion*'s style; beyond that it is made in the service of a serious and complicated point about Eliot's whole relation to 'personality', to what Lewis calls Eliot's 'disgust' at that mysterious entity.

Years before, according to Ford Madox Ford's account in *Portraits from Life*, Lewis had burst into Ford's rooms and announced that artists like Ford, Conrad, W. H. Hudson—all that 'old gang'—were finished. What the public now wanted was personality, fireworks, lively individual performances in which the artist should be under no pains to conceal himself. All the labor of trying to make a book so like life that it would hardly feel like a book, all the elaborate time-shiftings and point-of-view manipulations with which post-Jamesian artists had spun out their tales, were old hat. Now nothing was to count except the vigorous impact of a splendidly live user-of-words like Wyndham Lewis, 'personal-appearance artist' as he was later to be dubbed. Since Ford was the essentially dedicated novelist of impersonal craft, Lewis no doubt chose those particular tactics to reveal to him that the game was up. With Joyce or Pound or Eliot the tactics had to be changed: Joyce and Pound are considered (in *Time and Western Man*, 1927) as expressers of the fashionable 'time-philosophy' in the service of which 'personality' becomes broken up and down into a series of rapidly-changing, momentary events with no central self to hold them together. But the criticism of *Ulysses* Lewis makes in that book is often wonderfully perceptive, thoroughly entertaining, and mainly independent of the big idea Joyce is supposed to be an example of. With Pound, Lewis hones in on him as 'a man in love with the past', marvelous as a tour-guide and translator, but captivated by the Spirit of Romance to the extent where he

is an extremely untrustworthy guide to the present, prone to sentimentality, snobbery and hysteria.

Readers of 'The Revolutionary Simpleton' section from *Time and
Western Man* will observe that Lewis is not purely a destructive
critic, that his admiration for Pound and Joyce is substantial and that
he is willing to give credit where it's due (no credit, however, is
given to Gertrude Stein, Anita Loos, nor, regrettably, to Charlie
Chaplin—who also figure in the section). But the praise is surely
dwarfed by the blame; thus Lewis might be dismissed as the jealous
denigrator of others' successes and his criticisms discounted, if it
weren't for their superb energy as comic performances. The two paragraphs quoted from his attack on Eliot as 'pseudo-everything' may
suggest how this energy operates, particularly in the extended fantasy of Eliot as skipper of the 'good ship *Cri*', stretched out under the
awning with a Crime Club volume on his knees. Such writing disarms
a reader who might under other circumstances—say under circumstances of the onslaught by an outraged, grim Leavis—be prepared
to defend Eliot.

When Lewis attacks a figure or issue, he also takes care to charm
and entertain his reader; as when he discusses Eliot's separation of
poem from poet, of an utterance like *The Waste Land* from the poet
who uttered it ten years ago (it is now 1934). I. A. Richards is treated
throughout *Men Without Art* as Eliot's sidekick and helpful theor-
etician of what Lewis calls the 'disbelief' theory: that poetry is really
pseudo-statement. But when this sidekick made his remark about
The Waste Land having effected a 'complete severance between
poetry and *all* beliefs', Eliot (though of course he could say no better
than the next man just what the poem meant, since poet and critic
were separate) has to admit he thinks Richards—for once— may be
wrong. Lewis speaks of this 'disintegration into a multiplicity of
chronologic selves' as exempting Eliot from giving any answers 'on
the grounds that he is no longer the *same* Mr. Eliot, but another, so
cannot possibly know what *The Waste Land* Tom planned or intended'.
And since, in the just-published *The Use of Poetry and the Use of
Criticism* (1933) he had spoken of the poem as 'an outburst of words,
which we hardly recognize as our own', Lewis is provoked to the
following fantasy about Eliot's automatism:

Something touches a button, and out it comes. So, if you marched up to him five minutes after he had 'released' some 'outburst of words' in this manner, and exclaimed, 'Ha, ha! Got you this time my fine fellow! What did you mean when you wrote *that*—and *that*!' he would be quite capable of replying with the utmost detachment '*Who* wrote *what*? I am sorry, I am entirely unable to answer you. I have not the least idea! It is not to *me* you must address such questions. Go rather and address yourself to my partner Mr. I. A. Richards! He is not very reliable, but he probably knows more about it than I do.'

Or he might say it was incubated a twelvemonth beforehand, and that so much had happened in the meantime.

What it boils down to is that Lewis does not believe in the 'anonymous, "impersonal" catalytic' because he is sure that the artist's personality (Eliot's for example) is, however thoroughly disguised, very much there in the poem; and Lewis would prefer it, think it more honest that a man, a personality 'should exaggerate, a little artificially perhaps, his beliefs. . . .' Though the literary challenge represented by Eliot is distinguishable from that of Ford Madox Ford's, in each case Lewis counters their penchant for anonymous art with an exaggerated statement of belief expressed through a fantasy, ironically controlled to expose his opponents as less sensible and truthful than is he himself.

Eliot never replied to the attack. Perhaps he thought it a good hit; certainly it did not put a halt to his admiration for Lewis's work. Joyce got back at Lewis in *Finnegans Wake* (with a joke about 'Spice and West End Women'); Pound was unwoundable; Lawrence seems not to have been aware of the sardonic shafts aimed at his romantic primitivism (in *Paleface*, 1929). Perhaps it was difficult to be outraged by a personality which exaggerated itself into the role of 'The Enemy', the name Lewis adopted for the magazine he edited and most of whose three issues he wrote. Knowing how much Virginia Woolf dreaded the hostile review, it is pleasant to observe that even though she suffered from Lewis's attack on her (mainly on the 'Mr. Bennett and Mrs. Brown' essay) in *Men Without Art*, she referred to it in her diary in these terms:

> This morning I've taken the arrow of W. L. to my heart: he makes tremendous and delightful fun of B. and B.: calls me a peeper, not a looker, a fundamental prude: but one of the four or five living so it seems who is an artist . . .

Lewis had in fact written quite insultingly of Virginia Woolf's 'insignificance' as a novelist—'she is taken seriously by no one any longer today, except perhaps by Mr. and Mrs. Leavis'—though he allows her symbolic significance as 'a sort of party-lighthouse'. Lewis pretends he is surrounded by people who tell him Mrs. Woolf is a 'purely feminist phenomenon'; still he has chosen her 'back' to 'transport himself across the thorny region of feminism'. But this region is never traversed by the essay, which is preoccupied instead with exposing Woolf's claim that because 'materialists' like Bennett, Wells and Galsworthy—the 'three Edwardian bullies'—ignored life, the 'soul' of Mrs. Brown, therefore Virginia Woolf and the other post-Edwardians (Joyce, Lawrence, Forster, Strachey and herself being the ones who mattered) had to reconcile themselves to 'a season of failures and fragments'. Her skilful attempt thus to apologize for the fragmentary character of modernist work is ridiculed by Lewis: what, he asks, is fragmentary about *Ulysses* or the novels of Lawrence? Virginia Woolf's desire to be adequate to the soul of Mrs. Brown is turned roughly on its head by a comic portrait of Mrs. Woolf and her fellow modernists 'longing to "bag" the old girl, and yet completely impotent to do so, because no one was there to show them how, and they could not, poor dears, be expected to do it themselves!' So, he has Mrs. Woolf say: 'You will never get anything out of us except a little good stuff by fits and starts.' Of course Virginia Woolf would precisely not use the phrase 'good stuff'; it is unfair criticism and yet, as Lewis constantly maintained, satire *is* unfair. In this case it opens up to new perspectives an essay which, like *Ulysses*, is still regarded too reverently.

Lewis's critical effort, most energetically apparent in the years 1927–34 in reference to the literature of his contemporaries, is a permanently valuable contribution to literature. His artful attempt to break down divisions between literature and life, criticism and creation, words and reality, is made always through performances which are meant to provide us with the 'tremendous and delightful fun' Virginia Woolf speaks of. He was perhaps the only writer in England who could equal Eliot in his union of a wild and mischievous wit with immense stylistic, verbal powers. His appearance of rationality, common sense, the 'classical' virtues, is acceptable only if a reader senses the violent, fantastic dislocations of 'reality' effected by his intuitive nose for trouble, the absurd or the false-hearted. The few literary polemics pointed at here form only a small part of large and varied campaigns he waged on wider fronts throughout his career.

The *Calendar of Modern Letters*

Since Lewis was so good at seeing through others it is fitting that he was also seen through, as in the following sentences:

> Without Lewis contemporary literature would be very much less alive, and in a less promising condition, probably, than it is. He has been a great ice-breaker, and his ridicule has scorched up many pretentious shams. But latterly his energy has been spent in a reckless way; one is reminded of a powerful man tormented by gnats. The apostolic fervour which the campaign for their extermination develops as it grows is a sign of a weakening of the sense of reality . . .

The author, Edgell Rickword, wrote them as the conclusion to his evaluation of Lewis, one of a number contained in the second volume of *Scrutinies* published in 1931. Although the unavailability of Rickword's periodical, the *Calendar of Modern Letters* (1925–7) and the essays contained in the two *Scrutinies* volumes—now out of print and generally unknown—means that it is only a pretence that they are now or ever will be read as 'literature of criticism', they are nonetheless a remarkable phenomenon.

We are indebted to Leavis for the *Calendar*'s being known as well as it is. He brought out, in 1933 and with his own magazine well launched, a selection of essays and reviews titled, appropriately, *Towards Standards of Criticism*, while making it clear that his own *Scrutiny* was likewise devoted to furthering those standards. The *Calendar* had criticized Eliot's *Criterion* for its pretensions to philosophic rightness contrasted with its 'many blunders with regard to the actual works of poetry or literature before it'. It now looks on balance as if the *Calendar* was remarkably free of such blunders. As for its own 'philosophic rightness', this was wisely left undefined beyond the invoking of 'standards of criticism'; the point being that if you have to ask what these are, as with Louis Armstrong's remark about jazz, you can't be expected to recognize them. But to say that the *Calendar* avoided blunders is faint praise; in its generally excellent reviewing the treatment of new novels especially stands out: Douglas Garman's judicious appreciation and questioning of Huxley on the publication of *Those Barren Leaves*; J. F. Holms on *Mrs. Dalloway*, and Bertram Higgins generally (another editor of the magazine, along with Garman and the Rickword cousins). But most of all it is C. H. Rickword who time and again says the right thing with regard to T. F. Powys, Dreiser's *An American Tragedy*, David Garnett, or *Lolly Willowes*. Rickword's review of Lawrence's *The Plumed Serpent* speaks of its 'continuous falsification of reality', of his metaphysics as 'a sentimental vulgarization of the ordinary dualism of subject and object, togged up in the tawdry finery of emotive (often erotic) symbolism'; but also directs itself to the particularities of style as they are felt in a succession of quoted sentences about a Mexican town, a typical one of which reads: 'The strange emptiness, everything empty of life!' Rickword says that

> Here, the insistence on the subjective epithets, the hypnotic drumming on the note of death and its harmonies betray the inauthenticity of the response. Contact with the thing observed is not immediate, but dissipated and confused by the echoing, emotive overtones. The necessity for constant interpretation of this sort suggests that the experience to be conveyed had not its roots in actuality, that Mr. Lawrence's hortatory remarks owe much of their fervour to their being primarily addressed to himself.

These observations were an example of Rickword's attempt to talk about 'the progressive rhythm' manifested by a novel; and in his 'A Note on Fiction', beginning as a review of Elizabeth Drew's book on the novel but becoming much more, he conducted a brilliant investigation of the concepts of 'plot' and 'character' through which fiction is customarily and crudely discussed. If taken seriously, this essay alone would put out of business most of the writing about novels that has occurred in the fifty years since Rickword published it.

Leavis remarks upon the relative liveliness and critical superiority of the *Calendar* to the *Criterion*. But what most sets off the *Calendar* from Leavis's own *Scrutiny* is the earlier magazine's lack of favorites, its refusal to hold back adverse criticism from anyone. We shall consider this charge in relation to *Scrutiny*, but it appears that the *Calendar*'s alliance with 'standards of criticism' was a purer, more disinterested one than Leavis's was to be, perhaps because Leavis committed himself so wholeheartedly to Lawrence, that overwhelmer of critical standards. The *Calendar*, like the *Criterion*, published work by both Lawrence and Lewis and was evidently able to hold both of them in its collective mind without being torn apart. And when Edgell Rickword wrote an essay on Lewis after the *Calendar* had folded, his admiration of the vitality and 'ice-breaking' aspects of Lewis didn't make it impossible—in fact made it perhaps all the more necessary—to complain when something went wrong. With reference to Lewis's own magazine: '*The Enemy* is too much like a Sunday school where it is preached that sensation and various other things are a sin; as soon as Lewis leaves off flogging the hostile idea, the preacher supervenes, and the pulpit-tones roll out loud and deep—'The noble exactitude and harmonious proportion of the European, scientific ideal, the specifically Western heaven is one example of what might be plentifully illustrated.' Rickword points out how un-disinterested is Lewis's own criticism, how he seems always to need an idea to agree with or condemn before he can respond to a work of literature. Lewis's 'witch-hunts' are mentioned: 'His reaction to a writer of the scale of Proust is remarkably thin and doctrinaire'—which is precisely so when we recall Lewis's guilt-by-association condemnation of Proust as another adherent to the 'time-philosophy'. It is good to have Lewis attack primitivism in Sherwood Anderson and Lawrence, but 'There is too great a demand for orthodoxy, a tendency to nip experiments in the bud, say, the *surréaliste;* a grandmotherly solicitude for our infant stomachs, threatened by the hard tack of the New Diabolism'. This is criticism at its best because it understands that you cannot appreciate a writer's achievement fully until you have probed and exposed his weak spots and failures. It is stylistically as well as intellectually adequate to its subject; it is even amusing to read. And it does not leave us with the sense that some other writer, or viewpoint, or truth is to be recommended and preferred. The writers considered in the second volume of *Scrutinies*—Eliot, Huxley, Joyce

Lawrence, Strachey, Woolf and the Sitwells—were all there was; Rickword and his associates had no different list to propose, nor did the age stand in need of condemnation for throwing up these figures as representatives of creativity in literature. They were simply worthy of having standards of criticism applied to them—which is what these *Calendar* critics did so well for such a short time.

F. R. Leavis and *Scrutiny*

In his introduction to *Towards Standards of Criticism*, Leavis quotes approvingly C. H. Rickword's contention from 'A Note on Fiction' that 'the main thing to be noted about the new "subjective" novelists is their increasing tendency to rely for their effects not on set pieces of character-drawing, but directly on the poetic properties of words'. There is perhaps an echo here of Eliot's conclusion to his *Sacred Wood* essay on Swinburne in which he turns away from that poet to 'Mr. James Joyce and the earlier Conrad', each of whose prose is attempting to express 'new objects, new groups of objects'. Leavis's feeling was that in *Principles of Literary Criticism* (1925) and *Practical Criticism* (1929), I. A. Richards had provided much useful help for the student concerned with how writers of verse used the poetic resources of words; but as for fiction, he says in the same preface to the *Calendar* selection, there are only Henry James's prefaces and C. H. Rickword's essay. An overstatement, yes, but it is about as fruitless to search out 'over-statements' in Leavis's writing as it is in Lewis's or Eliot's. What primarily distinguishes his work and, for all its divergences, shows his debt to the books by Richards mentioned above, is that Leavis was a teacher with a mission.

In *How to Teach Reading*, the title of his 1932 pamphlet-reply to Ezra Pound's *How to Read*, there is a moment revealing for what it shows about Leavis's vision of possibility in the early 1930s. Under the title 'Positive Suggestions', he insists that what he calls 'The Training of Sensibility' should be where everything starts from as far as the student is concerned: 'It should, by continual insistence and varied exercise in analysis, be enforced that literature is made of words, and that everything worth saying in criticism of verse and prose can be related to judgements concerning particular arrangements of words on the page.' The teacher would develop his own technique of analysis and would go to Richards for what theoretical help he needed— particularly to his account of terms like 'rhythm', 'meaning', 'senti- mentality', as indispensable ones for dealing with poems. With this 'apparatus', as Leavis calls it, and 'a good sensibility trained in con- stant analytic practice' the teacher will be able to teach—what?

> . . . he will be able to learn, and to teach, how to discuss pro-
> fitably the differences between particular poems, to explain in
> detail and with precision why *this* is to be judged sentimental,
> *that* genuinely poignant; how the unrealized imagery of *this*
> betrays that it was 'faked' while the concreteness and associ-
> ative subtlety of *that* comes from below and could not have
> been excogitated; and so on.

He goes on to recommend *Seven Types of Ambiguity* as a further education in analysis for those who can learn from it.

What is staggering about this statement, with its this/that polarity, is how the promise is held forth without significant reservation; one sits down sensibly, reads Richards, reads poetry and considers how the terms do or don't apply, then education *can* work, the heaped-up junk from years of non-critical misrule will be swept aside, a new, brighter, clear-sighted response is just around the corner. The un- ironic promise is of a piece with Leavis's sharp oppositions between 'poignant' and 'sentimental', 'faked' and 'from below'. And of course by exercising this kind of trained capacity towards literature one will also carry that awareness over into life, will be as little the dupe of advertising or political sloganeering as of the cheap poem. Richards in *Practical Criticism* produced different responses to the unidentified poem, set them in some sort of order and proceeded to make his own remarks about what they revealed of human responsiveness and its lack. Leavis speaks as if, having gathered up the data, it turns out that readers need to be better educated, and that by taking themselves in hand, with the aid of Richards or other teachers like Leavis himself, they will no longer fall prey to such demonstrably human imper- fections.

The great thing about Leavis's criticism has been and is still the challenge it puts to inert valuations of books and writers, the way it

makes you ask yourself whether what he sees and hears is what you
have seen and heard. The poor thing about it, or about its unwary
reader (and I remember myself as a most devoted one of them) is the
temptations it offers towards accepting a judgement about X's essential triviality or cheapness when in fact one has never read a word of
X's work. One fatefully remembers, for example, phrases about
Sterne's 'irresponsible (and nasty) trifling' or 'the brutal and boring
Wyndham Lewis', when in fact one's reading of Sterne or Lewis may
well have been infrequent or non-existent. On the other hand there
is something ignoble about complaining that one can't withstand the
forcefulness of Leavis's judgements—except that by setting up as a
teacher one incurs special responsibilities towards the young that a
non-educator artist like Eliot or Lewis does not. At any rate, around
1930 he attempted, and continued the attempt throughout the twenty-
year career of *Scrutiny* (1932–53) to impose a standard of 'seriousness'
on English letters, midway between the wars, by which most well-
known works and established artists would be severely judged and
found wanting. As is well known, the major contemporary writer
he invoked as an instance of seriousness, as standing for 'health', as
exhibiting the 'religious' sense in relation to sex, creativity and the
natural world, was D. H. Lawrence. But to put forth Lawrence as
the supremely intelligent novelist and critic, occupied in all his
works with nothing less than helping us get into a new relation with
ourselves and with the universe, Leavis came smack up against the
other modern figure to whom, confessedly, he was most indebted:
T. S. Eliot.

That 'certain critic and poet', scrupulously but also cryptically
acknowledged (as John Gross points out) in the preface to Leavis's
New Bearings in English Poetry, was writing about Lawrence in
terms quite opposed to the ones Leavis had chosen; so although Eliot's
views on poetry could be saluted, on life and morality he was not so
sound. Leavis's review of *After Strange Gods* is his most interesting
attempt to sort out attitudes towards Lawrence and Eliot: he branded
'uncritical' Eliot's charge that Lawrence lacked a sense of humour,
was guilty of 'a certain snobbery', showed an 'incapacity for what we
ordinarily call thinking'—as if Eliot's complicated distaste and terror
with respect to Lawrence's writings could be definitively placed by

such a word, or could then be understood as a mere failing on Eliot's part. Fortunately for Leavis's case, Eliot had invoked Lewis's criticism of Lawrence as an authoritative one: thus Leavis could and did eagerly tear into Lewis as absolutely unqualified to criticize Lawrence in any way. As we noted earlier, Leavis's disgust at Eliot's Impersonal Theory grew with the years, but rather than cleverly and good-humouredly pointing out its inconsistencies (as Lewis had done) he railed against it many years later with the grandest condemnation—the 'Tradition' essay is 'a most significant defeat of intelligence'. At the same time Leavis's admiration for Eliot's poems, particularly those written in the 1930s and beyond—'Ash-Wednesday', 'Marina' and *Four Quartets*—increased to the point where he has devoted much recent attention to praising their 'astonishing sincerity'. It is as if he were paying into Eliot's poetic account while withdrawing liberally from the critical one.

Probably any critic with a wholehearted devotion to a single modern figure, as was Leavis's for Lawrence, and who is not himself an artist in active competition with his contemporaries—as were Eliot, Lewis or Lawrence—runs the risk of drawing the lines in an impossibly exclusive manner. On the positive side, Leavis's achievement was a two-headed one; he explored and practised new ways of talking about English literature of the past: the 'revaluations' of Donne, Marvell, Dryden, Pope, 18th Century poetry, Johnson, Wordsworth, Keats, Shelley, and of George Eliot and Henry James, are permanently valuable essays, not the less so for their ability to be argued with, the way they stimulate a teacher and student to see whether Leavis's observations about a passage are in fact true. We can test them on our pulses; for example, the essay on Swift's irony makes a very strong and oversimplified case about the way Swift uses words, but it is a case that needs to be met if one is to go further in understanding and appreciating Swift. And Leavis is often superb at the exposure of pretentiousness, of second-rate talent masquerading as something else: here the *Scrutiny* association with sympathetic colleagues, and particularly with Queenie Leavis—whose contributions to the magazine are outstanding—was a life-giving one.

But as a critic of modern literature, of immediate predecessors and contemporaries and of those writers who would emerge in the 1930s and beyond, Leavis reveals the gravest limitations, ones of a sort that make him less intelligently open to new voices than were American critics like Edmund Wilson, R. P. Blackmur or, later on, Randall Jarrell. Let us recall what Leavis's sense of the admirable and the less-than-admirable writers looked like at the time he formed *Scrutiny*. There was Lawrence. There was Eliot's poetry, and his distinctive though flawed contributions as a critic. There was Yeats, notably the Yeats of the recently published *Tower* and *Winding Stair* volumes, though Yeats revealed grave disabilities. There was Pound—or rather there was the Pound of *Hugh Selwyn Mauberley* and of some stimulating though wrong-headed and injudicious critical practice. There was Hopkins, extravagantly celebrated as a modern poet in *New Bearings*. There was promise to be found in Auden's *Paid on Both Sides* and others of his early poems; there were touches of virtue in recent poems by Empson and Richard Eberhart; there was substantial value in the work of Ronald Bottrall. Apart from Eliot, none of these writers, possibly excepting Bottrall, went on in the 1930s or beyond to produce anything Leavis admired or could see in other terms than as a falling-off, a failure to 'develop'.

As for novelists: besides Lawrence, and decidedly in secondary spots, was the Forster of *A Passage to India*, though not the Forster of *Aspects of the Novel*. There was the work of T. F. Powys, particularly *Mr. Weston's Good Wine*, and already one begins to ask who else was there? Leavis later praised L. H. Myers's *The Root and the Flower*; he had already found some interest in Dos Passos, less in Faulkner, little or none in Hemingway. There was the Joyce of *Ulysses*, but that writer had already become obscured in the dissolution of the word which *Work in Progress* was revealing; and anyway if you cared for Lawrence you could hardly take a sustained interest in Joyce, as Leavis was eventually to formulate it. Huxley seems to have been of interest mainly because he wrote the preface to Lawrence's letters and admired Lawrence. Virginia Woolf achieved something with *To the Lighthouse*, but her subsequent work and her criticism in general were unsatisfactory.

One can, making one's own adjustments in emphasis when necessary, say that Leavis was a hard taskmaster, occupied only with making sure that the very best literature got the hearing it deserved. One can hold him up as the scourge of indiscriminate discoverers of genius under every bush. I don't produce the list in the spirit of a triumphant indication of his narrow taste; but it does appear that very early in his career he made his choices, selected a few poems and novels written in the years 1915–30, and then with very few exceptions judged all subsequent work by other artists, and often by ones who had done good work in the 'twenties, to be inferior or not worthy of attention. Partly this is a matter of what happened in English writing during the 1930s: one group of writers—the 'gang' as Spender called them—was 'political' and breezily colloquial in ways Leavis couldn't stand; another group (even less of a group than the first one) produced satirical art in novels which paid no reverence to Lawrentian life and which turned men and women into very strange shapes indeed. One wants to say that there was at least *one* novel written in the 1930s Leavis should have admired, namely Lewis's *The Revenge for Love*. But Lewis ceased to be mentioned in *Scrutiny* after about 1934, and Leavis's own references to him grew ever more contemptuous.

Still, it would be a mistake to explain what happened to Leavis by pointing to English imaginative writing in the 1930s as somehow the culprit. He created himself as the embattled hero, and an embattled hero simply can't let himself go round liking, even in qualified ways, very many of the novels and poems which the age was demanding. 'An accelerated grimace' was Pound's phrase for what the age demanded; and Leavis deeply revered the poem from which it was taken. But we might also remember that Lewis, discussing Pound as 'A Man in Love with the Past' also called him 'an exceedingly untrustworthy guide to the present'. Leavis was no man in love with the past, in the romantic sense Lewis ascribes rightly to Pound; but he was, in his very different way, an untrustworthy guide to the new work of the present as it appeared. The American critics mentioned earlier, without academic commitment, 'teaching' if they did so at all without much ideology, not likely to write a book called *Education and the University*, could afford to be more open and eclectic in their welcomings of new writing. That is one of the reasons why they can still be read for critical help on particular modern authors, whereas Leavis—like his creative contemporaries Eliot and Lewis—survives as literature.

VII

Auden & Co.

Lewis began his chapter on Eliot in *Men Without Art* by remarking on the 'salutary *fear of speech*' the master had instilled in his youthful followers and imitators. Such seriousness and trepidation about the act of writing must, Lewis speculates, have impressed and scared them to the extent where some 'after endless painful deliberation, have scribbled a half a dozen lines and then fled away for good and all from composition upon such austere terms'. Now it is 1934, and things are very different:

> But at last the spell has been broken. And Mr. Auden has done it. . . . It is he who has really given the *coup de grâce* to Mr. Eliot's spell. Mr. Auden abounds in speech—words have no sinister terror for him! So once more the ink is flowing freely and the paper manufacturers are taking on a few more hands . . . it will take some time for the emancipatory effect of Mr. Auden's volubility to get things flowing easily again.

Oddly enough, Auden's volubility and literary success seem to have held no terrors for Lewis; neither here nor in other references does he show any interest in adversely scrutinizing the Auden phenomenon —as he was scrutinizing the phenomena of other successful contemporaries. Perhaps Auden presented himself as of a new generation, as a young fellow not to be discouraged; or it may be that Lewis was charmed by the jaunty insouciance of Auden's manner. Perhaps it occurred to him that he and Auden were working in part towards similar satirical ends—attempting through brilliant verbal combinations to expose the external absurdities of mankind, rather than sincerely spilling out the insides of their own consciousnesses. Perhaps

Auden would be the leader of 1930s verse-writers, while Lewis would take charge of the novel and any other prose forms which happened to need leadership. Auden's own references to Lewis ('that lonely old Volcano of the Right', he calls him in *Letters From Iceland*) are also affectionate and mainly respectful, though both writers very much went their own and separate ways.

Lewis's account of Auden-volubility taking over from Eliot-reticence—the climate of 'thirties poetry replacing that of a more austere age—has not been contradicted. What is more remarkable is that this takeover had the active cooperation of the editor of the *Criterion* himself, who published *Paid on Both Sides* and other poems by Auden and Stephen Spender, and whose friend John Hayward reviewed *The Orators* in glowing terms. Neither Eliot's own authority as a literary judge nor his distinction as a poet was diminished by Auden's success; this was no matter of a revolution overturning the established order. 'Ash-Wednesday' appeared in 1930; there could be no question of the wholly individual style of such a queer poem (to say nothing of its sentiments) setting itself up as a model or guiding beacon for aspiring young poets. The aged eagle hardly needed to stretch his wings. He covered everybody and could afford the admiration he freely and no doubt sincerely gave to the younger Auden.

In fact, Auden had strong support early in his career: on the one hand the blessings of Bloomsbury, also Eliot and the *Criterion*; on the other hand the scourge of Bloomsbury—Lewis—along with the critic who both championed and criticized Auden better than anyone else in the decade—Geoffrey Grigson and his magazine *New Verse*. Even *Scrutiny* and Leavis himself had measured praise for *Poems 1930* and *The Orators*, though it soon turned around and consistently belaboured Auden for his 'undergraduate' failure to 'develop'. Various figures were drawn along, justly or unjustly, in the wake of Auden's success, as Spender's account in his autobiography *World Within World* reminds us:

> In 1932, Michael Roberts edited an anthology of poems called *New Signatures*, published by the Hogarth Press. This he followed a year later with a second volume, containing prose as well as poetry, called *New Country*. These two

anthologies revealed the existence of a new, for the most part socially conscious, group of young writers. Of these, W. H. Auden, William Empson, Cecil Day Lewis, Rex Warner, William Plomer, A. J. S. Tessimond, John Lehmann, Julian Bell and myself made the greatest impression. These writers wrote with a near-unanimity, surprising when one considers that most of them were strangers to one another, of a society coming to an end and of revolutionary change.

Spender then goes on to distinguish among Auden, Day Lewis and himself, and to acknowledge, rather vaguely, Auden's influence on them. And looking back on the 1920s he characterizes the writing of that decade as consisting variously of 'despair, cynicism, self-conscious aestheticism, and the prevalence of French influences'. It was anti-political, while the new generation no longer considered politics alien to literature; on the contrary, they would speak to the condition of England and of mankind. Nothing in Spender's account contradicts the one given by Orwell in 'Inside the Whale' twelve years earlier, though Orwell's tone is sharper and less reverent towards the whole matter. Orwell throws in some different names, most prominently that of Louis MacNeice (whom Spender mentions only once and briefly in his autobiography), and caustically describes the literary climate of the 1930s as 'a sort of Boy Scout atmosphere of bare knees and community singing', with the typical literary man as 'an eager-minded schoolboy with a yearning toward Communism'. 'Serious purpose' has replaced the 'twenties 'tragic sense of life'.

Spender and Orwell are as well qualified to speak about English poetry in the 1930s as anyone imaginable; yet the gap between their sensible generalisations and the particular experience of reading Auden's work during that decade is immense, in a way it is not when the work of Day Lewis or of Spender himself is in question. Consider some familiar and representative lines from Day Lewis's long poem *The Magnetic Mountain* (1933):

> You who go out alone, on tandem or on pillion,
> Down arterial roads riding in April
> Or sad beside lakes where hill-slopes are reflected
> Making fires of leaves, your high hopes fallen:
> Cyclists and hikers in company, day excursionists,
> Refugees from cursed towns and devastated areas;

Know you seek a new world, a saviour to establish
Long-lost kinship and restore the blood's fulfillment.

The poem is dedicated to Auden and filled with injunctions: 'Wystan,
Rex, all of you that have not fled,/This is our world . . .', or 'Look
west, Wystan, lone flyer, birdman, my bully boy!', and less personally
—'You'll be leaving soon and it's up to you, boys,/Which shall it
be? You must make your choice./There's a war on you know . . .'
Day Lewis is quite unembarrassed by his own eager gestures; he
may have got the tandems and arterial roads out of Auden, but the
'influence' is wholly superficial; there is nothing the least bit problematic about either the tone, syntax or development of these lines
hopefully gathering together all cyclists and hikers. It sounds and
looks like poetry, but in fact brings no surprises, no metaphorical or
tonal disturbances of accepted ways of putting things together. Day
Lewis undoubtedly thought his poetry was filled with serious purpose.
It now feels to us strictly inert, of interest only in filling out the Spirit
of the Age.

Auden

By contrast, even the most rhetorically purposeful of Auden's
addresses, when listened to carefully, sends out mixed signals. His
most ambitious early attempt at a publicly serious voice is to be
found in the long poem now called '1929' ('It was Easter as I walked
in the public garden') which ends with a proposed remedy for the
general ill ('It is time for the destruction of error') and this recipe for
love:

      We know it, know that love
      Needs more than the admiring excitement of union,
      More than the abrupt self-confident farewell,
      The heel on the finishing blade of grass,
      The self-confidence of the falling root,
      Needs death, death of the grain, our death,
      Death of the old gang; would leave them
      In sullen valley where is made no friend,
      The old gang to be forgotten in the spring,
      The hard bitch and the riding-master,

Stiff underground; deep in clear lake
The lolling bridegroom, beautiful, there.

John Fuller's remark about these lines, in his *Reader's Guide to W. H. Auden*, seems to me interestingly misdirected:

> Though 'death of the old gang' (i.e., the die-hard Tories) seems merely to be thrown in for good measure, the poem ends by prophesying the burial of these beautifully selected representatives of their social class, 'The hard bitch and the riding-master.'

Fuller then goes on to suggest tentatively that the 'lolling bridegroom' is really a healing figure, perhaps a 'periphrasis for the dead Christ'. At any rate, he concludes: 'The accumulation of images here, however obscure, is none the less marvellously convincing.'

If this poetry is 'convincing' it is indeed difficult to say what it convinces us of, other than that Auden has a way with words; this granted, then Fuller's nonetheless-convincing-though-obscure is the wrong way to put it. There is absolutely nothing obscure about Day Lewis's images, in the passage quoted above which so perfectly fits Orwell's charge of Boy Scoutism and school-boy yearning toward Communism or some related form of salvation. The reader is invited to cheer as the passage draws to its close. With Auden it's hard to know what to do. John Fuller speaks as if the 'old gang' reference were just thrown in as a dig at die-hard Tories; but nobody forgets this moment in the poem, perhaps because it is more 'obscure' than the 'i.e.' explanation Fuller accords it. Then there is the very manner of saying what we, what 'love' needs: '. . . would leave them/In sullen valley where is made no friend,/The old gang to be forgotten.' This sudden movement into what may be termed Norse Saga Telegraphese, a well-known characteristic of Auden's early poetry, has the effect of making the address less direct, more magically spellcasting and, if you will, obscure. Why are 'the hard bitch and the riding-master', in Fuller's terms, 'beautifully selected representatives of their social class'? Because they somehow sound good together in the lines, or because putting them together 'stiff underground' sounds nastily necrophilic? As for the lolling bridegroom: can one really without embarrassment think of Christ after the obscure unease produced by the invocation of such an ambiguous figure? What most surely does sound convincing here is the rhythmic assurance

that binds the last twelve lines of the poem into a coiled single
sentence, suggestive, but not at all clear in what it asserts. Or the
way a 'sullen valley' can be called up into what seems an inevitable
rightness simply by the saying of the words.

I am suggesting that Auden's early poetry presents to reader and
critic a problem which hasn't been but should be faced up to. Fuller's
valuable guide to the poems is also a cautionary example of how deter-
mination to explicate their obscurities can sometimes over-determine
them. Take the beginning of 'The Letter' which now occupies pride
of place as the first of *Collected Shorter Poems 1927—57*:

> From the very first coming down
> Into a new valley with a frown
> Because of the sun and a lost way,
> You certainly remain: to-day
> I, crouching behind a sheep-pen, heard
> Travel across a sudden bird,
> Cry out against the storm, and found
> The year's arc a completed round
> And love's worn circuit re-begun,
> Endless with no dissenting turn.

Fuller says about these opening lines that 'the new valley is a new
love, the season Spring, the sun unaccustomed, making the poet
frown. But already the year has passed, and he finds himself sheltered
behind a sheep-pen during a storm, reflecting on love's restlessness,
its endless cycle of erotic desire.' How sensible the paraphrase makes
it sound: yet looking back at the lines themselves we might well ask
why or how the 'new valley is a new love', why the sun is 'unaccustomed', or even why it is the poet who frowns? Fuller's explanation
that this poet has taken shelter from a storm behind a sheep-pen,
again seems more matter-of-factly sensible than the telegraphic non-
committal staccato accent of

> . . . to-day
> I, crouching behind a sheep pen, heard
> Travel across a sudden bird
> Cry out against the storm. . .

In other words the narration is both more obscure and more disturb-
ingly memorable than Fuller makes it sound.

Another intelligent critic of Auden, John Bayley, distinguishes him from Eliot by claiming that Eliot's later poetry aims at creating an atmosphere of sincerity, while Auden's ironical gestures are undermining of sincerity—we don't know just how or where to have him. But Bayley also claims that 'The Auden irony and urbanity we follow gladly for their own sake and can be persuaded of their final seriousness by external means, i.e., by the subject matter—refugees, war, etc.—which the poet puts before us.' This remark might make sense applied to a poem like 'September 1, 1939', though its tone is quite unambiguously 'sincere'. But as an account of earlier Auden poetry it won't do. Consider 'Consider', an arresting poem filled with portentous and fantastic directives with which it is impossible to know exactly how to deal. Here we are presumably to view a diseased society—'as the hawk sees it or the helmeted airman'. What hawk or airman might see is a 'cigarette-end smouldering on a border'; 'the view of the massif/Through plate-glass windows of the Sport Hotel'; the 'insufficient units'

> Dangerous, easy, in furs, in uniform
> And constellated at reserved tables,
> Supplied with feelings by an efficient band,
> Relayed elsewhere to farmers and their dogs
> Sitting in kitchens in the stormy fens.

Is it merely churlish to ask why constellated units in furs or uniforms are any sicker than farmers in the stormy fens? And if everybody is sick, it's easy enough to look on here, admire there, consider this or that, without the slightest cost to our own self-confidence. All we need do is to submit to the efficient voice that carries us along and will not stay for any questions we might wish to ask.

After a space the 'insufficient units' are swiftly dropped, and we hear of a mysterious 'supreme Antagonist' who seems to be 'More powerful than the great northern whale', and who is

> Ancient and sorry at life's limiting defect,
> In Cornwall, Mendip, or the Pennine moor
> Your comments on the highborn mining-captains,
> Found they no answer made them wish to die.

To analyze the Antagonist as 'really' Satan, as (in Fuller's term) the 'Censor, responsible for repressing man's natural instincts and bringing about that self-consciousness which separates him from the rest of the animal kingdom' may be well and good, indeed necessary to 'explain' the poem. But it takes no account of the grand, vague and threatening gesture towards Cornwall, Mendip and the Pennine Moor. For this is a theatrical poetry which makes bold flourishes toward meaning; the only external means which could make it 'serious' are not wars and refugees, but Lawrence, Homer Lane, the psychological healers and theories we are told lie behind Auden's early poems. Stopping short of importing these theories to explain obscurities leaves us with much to take pleasure in; an authoritative, hectoring voice, come back from somewhere to tell us all before it's too late:

> Seekers after happiness, all who follow
> The convolutions of your simple wish,
> It is later than you think; nearer the day
> Far other than that distant afternoon
> Amid rustle of frocks and stamping feet
> They gave the prizes to the ruined boys.
> You cannot be away, then, no
> Not though you pack to leave within an hour,
> Escape drumming down arterial road:

This is meant to be thrilling—who would *want* to be away when such a threatened action occurred? How comfortably scary it is to think about that 'distant afternoon' when the 'ruined boys' received their prizes! As diagnostic, let alone curative poetry, operating out of a firm criticism of society, 'Consider' is of no value at all. But listened to as a performing voice with a hundred tricks up its sleeve, always a new one to follow, it is riveting.

I would argue then, *contra* John Bayley, that the Auden of *Poems 1930*, *The Orators* and the revised *Poems* of 1933 has in truth no 'subject matter' at all, but that we 'follow gladly' for its own sake—as best we can and often confusedly—an arresting, highly resourceful voice. That voice may conduct itself in the it's-later-than-you-think mood of 'Consider', the conclusion to '1929' or 'The Watershed' ('Go home, now, stranger, proud of your young stock'), or the now suppressed 'Get there if you can and see the land you once were proud to own'. Or it may operate through the telegraphic Hopkins-influenced song of 'This Lunar Beauty' or 'Missing' ('From scars where kestrels hover'). In any case the appeal is to the musical ear which thrills and warms to the pleasures of an exquisitely tuned voice. 'Taller to-day' may gesture at bringing in 'The Adversary' (as it once did 'Captain Ferguson' before he was cut out) but the intellectual point of the poem is no more complicated or difficult than what can be taken away from the handsomely poised final two stanzas:

> But happy now, though no nearer each other,
> We see the farms lighted all along the valley;
> Down at the mill-shed the hammering stops
> And men go home.
>
> Noises at dawn will bring
> Freedom for some, but not this peace
> No bird can contradict: passing but here, sufficient now
> For something fulfilled this hour, loved or endured.

Leavis's complaint, which turned soon into the official *Scrutiny* line on Auden—that the early promise of *Poems 1930* was not fulfilled in the poet's subsequent work—is an odd one to understand. Admittedly the whole question of 'development' is a vexed one when applied to poets like Auden, Graves or Eliot himself (who liked to use the word) all of whom produced highly accomplished poems early in their careers. But if 'development' means at least our increased sense of the poet's presence in his poem, more resonant firmness of speech expressive of a passionate and caring human being, and of the musical resources of verse employed in the service of 'ideas', concerns held seriously, then Auden's *Look, Stranger!* (1936) qualifies as a significant development of his work. That argument could be made on the basis alone of the first three poems in the book, the now-suppressed 'Prologue' ('O love the interest itself in thoughtless heaven'), 'A Summer Night' and 'Our Hunting Fathers'. Each of them, in demonstrably and impressively varied styles, proposes a more secure, less coyly elusive relationship between poet and reader than could be found in most of the poems he had written thus far—even though 'Our Hunting Fathers' is anything but straightforward. Perhaps as a corollary of this, Auden seems less to fall into the thrilling scare-tactics of blowing the apocalyptic whistle to gather all good scouts together.

'Prologue' invokes England with something other than sardonic

distaste. It may be the island of the volume's title poem itself; it most
assuredly is invoked in the prologue's prayer to love, and very movingly
so:

> Here too on our little reef display your power,
> This fortress perched on the edge of the Atlantic scarp,
> The mole between all Europe and the exile-crowded sea;
> And make us as Newton was, who in his garden watching
> The apple falling towards England, became aware
> Between himself and her of an eternal tie.

This verse takes on amplitude of great leisure and delicacy, displaying
a voice neither impervious nor nervously self-conscious:

> For now that dream which so long has contented our will,
> I mean, of uniting the dead into a splendid empire,
> Under whose fertilising flood the Lancashire moss
>
> Sprouted up chimneys, and Glamorgan hid a life
> Grim as a tidal rock pool's in its glove shaped valleys,
> Is already retreating into her maternal shadow;
>
> Leaving the furnaces gasping in the impossible air,
> The flotsam at which Dumbarton gapes and hungers;
> While upon wind-loved Rowley no hammer shakes
>
> The cluster of mounds like a midget golf course. . .

One sometimes understands, though less often sympathizes with the
impulses which led Auden to exclude a poem from his canon, but I
think his exclusion of this one is most unaccountable of them all.

'Prologue' is followed by 'A Summer Night', a poem of sixteen
stanzas whose affinities with light verse don't negate its larger
seriousness. More than any poem Auden had written up to that time
it reveals a generous poise of manners, wit that it is absurd to discount
as 'undergraduate', and a confidence that the poem can be 'about'
something other than itself, can acknowledge that it occurs at a time
and a place, and has reference to larger rhythms like the moon's:

> She climbs the European sky,
> Churches and power-stations lie
>   Alike among earth's fixtures;

> Into the galleries she peers
> And blankly as an orphan stares
> Upon the marvellous pictures.

The conceit about the pictures is full Auden, gives the appearance
of having effortlessly come unforeseen to the poet as he went along.
In his review of *Look, Stranger!* and in his other reviews of Auden's
work, Leavis complained that all these *trouvailles* were never inte-
grated into poems that had organization. But the organization of 'A
Summer Night', as with the 'Prologue' preceding it, is wholly and
triumphantly the sense of listening to a wonderful talker, developing
and extending an original moment of well-being ('Out on the lawn I
lie in bed,/Vega conspicuous overhead/In the windless nights of
June') into the intimations of approaching disaster and possible renewal thereafter:

> Soon through the dykes of our content
> The crumpling flood will force a rent,
>   And, taller than a tree,
> Hold sudden death before our eyes
> Whose river-dreams long hid the size
>   And vigours of the sea.
>
> But when the waters make retreat
> And through the black mud first the wheat
>   In shy green stalks appears;
> When stranded monsters gasping lie,
> And sounds of riveting terrify
>   Their whorled unsubtle ears:
>
> May this for which we dread to lose
> Our privacy, need no excuse
>   But to that strength belong;
> As through a child's rash happy cries
> The drowned voice of his parents rise
>   In unlamenting song.

Perfectly lucid, handsomely disposed, the language of this poem keeps
up English as Keats said it must be kept up.

So it is kept up in the more difficult and concentratedly explosive
lyric that follows:

> Our hunting fathers told the story
>   Of the sadness of the creatures,

Pitied the limits and the lack
　　Set in their finished features;
Saw in the lion's intolerant look,
Behind the quarry's dying glare,
Love raging for the personal glory
　　That reason's gift would add,
The liberal appetite and power,
　　The rightness of a god.

Who nurtured in that fine tradition
　　Predicted the result,
Guessed love by nature suited to
　　The intricate ways of guilt?
That human ligaments could so
His southern gestures modify,
And make it his mature ambition
　　To think no thought but ours,
To hunger, work illegally,
　　And be anonymous?

The poem contrasts two views of love, first putting forth the possibilities seen for it by 'our hunting fathers', then in the second stanza
developing a modern view. The problem is just how to paraphrase
this 'modern view': Richard Hoggart holds that it makes a comment
on 'what, at this time, Auden held to be a moral necessity for him and
people like him—that they had to reject even the ''decent'' bourgeois
values for the sake of a greater value'—that, presumably, of Marxism;
while John Fuller takes the second stanza to say

> That love is . . . not a noble force at all, but one to be denied
> because it inevitably leads to the guilt of individualism and
> self-regard. 'His southern gestures modify' means to sub-
> limate love's genital impulses into not a selfish love, but a
> universal, social love.

And Fuller points out that the last two lines are a quotation from
Lenin.

Yet the poem's voice is more evasive than any knowing, Marxist
one would be: 'Who nurtured in that fine tradition . . . Guessed love
by nature suited to/The intricate ways of guilt?' Both Hoggart and
Fuller, in the interests of making clear what Auden is 'saying',
attempt to translate those intricate ways and southern gestures into

intellectually complex and coherent meanings. It appears to me that such coherence is gained only by ignoring the ambiguous tone through which Auden's sly and detached presence is most felt. This presence is not to be taken in by any single view of love, believes in nothing absolutely but the artful development of an extremely knotted sentence woven over each stanza. It is a presence that takes care not to reveal itself except through song, that will not be understood too quickly by the intellect, even as it employs the vocabulary of *Civilization and its Discontents*. It is a poem written as if to undermine the paraphraser, and it will be noticed that I have myself shirked such paraphrase. Like his American contemporary and sometime antagonist Robert Frost, Auden believes that in poetry 'the play's the thing'. And while 'Our Hunting Fathers' may remind us of Yeats, there would be behind the comparable Yeats poem a more diagrammatic notion of the point to be made, while Yeat's tone would be relatively unmistakeable. The poem is wholly deserving of Wyndham Lewis's appraisal of Auden in *Blasting and Bombardiering* as a 'new guy' who is 'all ice and woodenfaced acrobatics'. Perhaps, to use one of the poet's favorite images, only woodenfaced poets can perform their acrobatics on the frontier and get away with it.

The few poems pointed to here are but the barest suggestion of Auden's immense output in the 1930s, to say nothing of successive decades. Along with three considerable books of lyrics (*Poems, Look, Stranger!* and *Another Time*) there is also *The Orators* with its elaborate stunts, and the remarkable collaboration with MacNeice, *Letters From Iceland*, particularly distinguished by Auden's 'Letter to Lord Byron'. The collaborations with Isherwood seem less interesting today, but there is little point in making overmuch of what one prefers or is disappointed in. Geoffrey Grigson wrote the best 1930s' appreciation of Auden in his own excellent little magazine *New Verse* and concluded with this caveat:

> Auden does not obey the codes. But when a monster who writes so much is so fidgety and inquisitive, so interested in things and ideas, so human and generous, and so rude to the infinite, it does not matter at all if the lines of his development are twisted and obscure, if he writes plenty of verse which is slack, ordinary, dull or silly. . .

Grigson knew also, and said so boldly on the cover in defense of his salute, that Auden's 'broad power of raising ordinary speech into strong and strange incantation' was the central reason for listening to him. The incantation, noted here in the opening poems from *Look, Stranger!* was due to become less strange in the volume to come. At least *Another Time*, published just after he went to America, represents a relaxing into satirical light-versish ease (the easy virtues of 'As I Walked Out One Evening' or the easy viciousness of 'Miss Gee' and 'Victor') or into the noble plangency of his most anthologized lyric, 'Lay Your Sleeping Head My Love'. That lyric steps back from the frontier, not altogether to its credit; at least the attempt to replace icy and woodenfaced slyness with a more tender and compassionately human speech, I find embarrassing—the glib knowingness about how of course we betray each other ('Human on my faithless arm') is really more self-congratulatory than anything in 'Our Hunting Fathers'. But like his modernist predecessors, and particularly Eliot, Auden modified though never repudiated entirely his own brilliance as a 'difficult' poet who spoke in riddles. His humanity and generosity, of which Grigson speaks, and which on the evidence of many 1930s poems one might query, is to be found not in the sentiments of 'Lay Your Sleeping Head' or even the self-consciously liberal utterances to Yeats or Freud, but in the rich and unceasing variety of poems long and short in which he continued to speak. In this best sense he never quite subordinated the monster, but managed to enter into a good working arrangement with it:

> I lived with crooks but seldom was molested;
> The Pure-in-Heart can never be arrested.

Spender

'Auden, Spender, Day Lewis and MacNeice' seems to be the usual lineup in which 'the gang' presents itself for inspection. Day Lewis's 'thirties poetry is of historical interest merely, a lesson—if we need one—in how the simplifications of an enthusiast in poetry and in politics announced themselves. Stephen Spender presents a more interesting challenge for the criticism of poetry, although for me he

does not as a poet matter much more than Day Lewis. Yet several of
of his lyrics have become anthology pieces '(The Landscape near an
Aerodrome', 'The Express', 'Ultima Ratio Regum', and one of them
is still to be encountered on all sides—'I think continually of those
who were truly great.' Confining my remarks about Spender to that
single poem is abrupt, but unfair only if the poem falls obviously below
the level of his other work; to me it seems fairly to represent Spender's
procedure and presence, and it has had many warm admirers, one of
them Day Lewis in 1934: '. . . it is one of Spender's greatest merits
that, when he tells us he thinks continually of those who were truly
great, we are in no doubt that he does do so.' I quote the first stanza:

> I think continually of those who were truly great.
> Who, from the womb, remembered the soul's history
> Through corridors of light where the hours are suns
> Endless and singing, whose lovely ambition
> Was that their lips, still touched with fire,
> Should tell of the Spirit clothed from head to foot in song.
> And who hoarded from the Spring branches
> The desires falling across their bodies like blossoms.

Without saddling Spender with the praise, it is worth quoting.
Day Lewis's sentences about the poem from *A Hope for Poetry*:

> There are certain obvious and superficial defects in this poem.
> The transition from image to image is sometimes a little
> blurred, and there is a tendency for the image sequence to be
> stretched rather too far for coherence. But merit easily out-
> weighs defect. We are aware at once of that gravity and in-
> ward illumination—passion glowing through a crystal sin-
> cerity—which makes the best of Spender's verse so appealing.
> The Great War tore away our youth from its roots. I see in
> this poem a successful attempt to re-establish communication
> with the past, a minor miracle of healing.

That this should have been written fifteen years after *The Sacred
Wood* is in itself a minor miracle. Yet Day Lewis's gushing admiration
is relevant to the kind of response Spender's poetry invites. Since
everyone agrees that his poems lack humor and guile, it falls to
'sincerity' to make up for that lack. Clearly Day Lewis believes that
the poem's defects are superficial or 'technical' ones—images a bit
blurred here, too stretched-out there, and that—just as clearly—they

become of little import in relation to 'passion glowing through a crystal sincerity'. Rather than fussing about whether the images work out or not, one might instead ask whether the poem's awkwardness of speech doesn't constitute a defect: 'What is precious is never to forget' or 'Never to allow gradually the traffic to smother'. In fact, 'I think continually' doesn't present 'speech' at all, in the sense that we hear speech in Auden's '1929' or 'Consider', since Spender operates through an elevated monotone which booms out inspiring adjectives and substantives: 'lovely ambition', 'Spirit', 'song', 'Spring branches' 'Blossoms', 'Ageless springs' and so forth. With no discernible changes of pitch or tone and with no challenges placed before the reader; only the invitation to remember, revere, not to forget light and love be it morning or night. 'In Flanders field the poppies grow/Between the crosses row on row'—one can either remain silent before Spender's poem or impute to it sincerity, which as I. A. Richards reminds us in *Practical Criticism* is 'a word much used in criticism, but not often with any precise definition of its meaning'.

A later poet, Thom Gunn, was moved to write a poem which begins: 'I think of all the toughs through history/And thank heaven they lived, continually.' The allusion is an understandable one since Spender's first line, without the protections of irony, leaves the poet open to being asked whether he thinks from morn to night about the truly great, or perhaps thinks not so much about the merely great as the *truly* great. On the other hand, some readers whose appreciation of 'the poetic' bulks larger than the demand to be entertained or disturbed will find 'I think continually' and Spender's work in general satisfying enough.

MacNeice

When Louis MacNeice died suddenly in 1963, Eliot wrote a eulogy for *The Times* stating his belief that MacNeice was a great poet. Even if words need less to be weighed at such a moment, the praise is extreme for Eliot to have given. It may be that, as G. S. Fraser has suggested, Eliot felt a greater personal affinity for MacNeice than for any of the other 'thirties poets he had assisted and published.[1] Yet one wants immediately to protest that however charming and attractive MacNeice's poetry may be, 'great' is exactly what it's not and what no reader is likely to call it. Conrad Aiken struck the right note, reviewing MacNeice in 1941:

> For sheer readability, for speed, lightness, and easy intellectual range, Mr. MacNeice's verse is in a class by itself. Open it anywhere, whether in narrative, eclogue, or lyric, and at once you are swept away by the tireless and effortless enumerative pace, the bright rush of nominal images, the gay prodigality of scene, the so easily caught tune and sound. Yes, this is the world we know, all right, and this too is a fellow we can like.[2]

Aiken then went on to enumerate some of the things—Freud and pubs and football and economic muddles and political ideologies and love affairs—that the fellow's poetry is filled with. Still, for all its momentary magic it was too topical, and Aiken doubted whether it possessed the 'residual magic' to make us return and study how the things were said.

MacNeice himself tended to put the case for poetry, by implication his own, rather too simply. At least in *Modern Poetry* (1938) he drew the line between substance and style over-confidently, saying that 'Words are essentially a vehicle of communication', so word-aesthetes were misguided; that Arnold was right in plumping for 'subject', Pater wrong in doing so for 'style', and that 'the poet's first business is *mentioning* things. Whatever musical or other harmonies he may incidentally evoke, the fact will remain that such and such things— and not others—have been mentioned in his poems.' The italicizing of 'mentioning' seems a deliberately flaunting of this seemingly unpoetic activity, and looks to be a justification for a poem like 'Birmingham':

> Smoke from the train-gulf hid by hoardings blunders up-
>   ward, the brakes of cars
> Pipe as the policeman pivoting round raises his flat hand,
>   bars
> With his figure of a monolith Pharaoh the queue of fidgety
>   machines
> (Chromium dogs on the bonnet, faces behind the triplex
>   screens).

> Behind him the streets run away between the proud glass
>   of shops
> Cubical scent-bottles artificial legs artic foxes and electric
>   mops,

Yet something more subtle is being done with words here than using them as 'vehicles of communication'; our pleasure and surprise come from following a voice as it threads its way over the long lines and just manages to get everything in and make it come out right. Not the poetry of an aesthete perhaps, but certainly not the poetry of an engaged communicator trying to give us just the facts and all the facts.

At the same time MacNeice's relationship to 'ideas', the 'easy intellectual range' of his poetry which Aiken speaks of, is a very easy one indeed. We know that he studied philosophy at Oxford, but the 'philosophy' behind the lyrics and *Autumn Journal* is certainly not complex; nor is it convincing, I think, to say as G. S. Fraser does that MacNeice and Eliot are comparable because they were both interested in the problem of the One and the Many. 'Turf-stacks' is a fair enough example of how a MacNeice poem goes about its business of mentioning things and communicating an idea.

> Among these turf-stacks graze no iron horses
> Such as stalk, such as champ in towns and the soul of
>   crowds,
> Here is no mass-production of neat thoughts
> No canvas shrouds for the mind nor any black hearses:
> The peasant shambles on his boots like hooves
> Without thinking at all or wanting to run in grooves.
>
> But those who lack the peasant's conspirators,
> The tawny mountain, the unregarded buttress,
> Will feel the need of a fortress against ideas and against the
> Shuddering insidious shock of the theory-vendors,
> The little sardine men crammed in a monster toy
> Who tilt their aggregate beast against our crumbling Troy.
>
> For we are obsolete who like the lesser things
> Who play in corners with looking-glass and beads;
> It is better we should go quickly, go into Asia
> Or any other tunnel where the world recedes,

> Or turn blind wantons like the gulls who scream
> And rip the edge off any ideal or dream.

This version of pastoral is artfully arranged in its vigorous rhythmic insistence ('Such as stalk, such as champ in towns. . .'), its elaborate, internal off-rhyming, and its air of syllogistic progress—'Here. . . But . . . For. . .' But when the idea is inspected, held up for consideration, it doesn't amount to much; merely that 'we' are the victims of 'they' (the theory-vendors, mass-idea men) and generally to be commiserated with. Which is to say that the poem, for all its no-nonsense air, is really quite soft at the center, melting into a lament (at one moment reminiscent of Hart Crane's 'Chaplinesque') that 'we' are obsolete and had better dispense with our human aspirations, becoming wanton like the gulls or receding into darkest Asia. One might compare Orwell's related hatred and fear of the 'smelly little orthodoxies contending for our souls'; 'Turf-stacks' should have been a poem after his own heart.

If it isn't the theory-vendors who will get us, it is Time, in one appearance or another:

> The sunlight on the garden
> Hardens and grows cold,
> We cannot cage the minute
> Within its nets of gold,
> When all is not told
> We cannot beg for pardon.

In the title of MacNeice's third book of poems, *The Earth Compels*:

> . . . upon it
> Sonnets and birds descend;
> And soon, my friend,
> We shall have no time for dances.

Even when MacNeice is upset by Communist or Fascist threats to the individual his protest is never just political, is always deeply colored by the melancholy knowledge that time, change and death are at work. The sad 'Epilogue' to *Letters from Iceland* mentions things like the fall of Seville and the Olympic Games, pretends (in Grigson's phrase) to take 'note of the universe of objects and events', but is really a poem about being lonely in Hampstead late at night among one's

books and without a woman: 'Nights which no one shares and wait/
For the 'phone to ring or for/Unknown angels at the door.' Addressed
to Auden, the poem celebrates his triumph over the death-wish
MacNeice feels so strongly: 'But your lust for life prevails—/Drinking
coffee, telling tales.' Even so

> Our prerogatives as men
> Will be cancelled who knows when;
> Still I drink your health before
> The gun-butt raps upon the door.

Robert Frost's notion, in his poem 'Carpe Diem', that we can't seize
the present because we're too busy living in the past and the future
seems more truly documented by MacNeice's depressed attempt to
celebrate that present, to mention those things which are always receding from him.

It is right to say, as Julian Symons said in his review of *The Earth
Compels* (*Twentieth Century Verse*, July 1938) that MacNeice speaks
for the ordinary Man and that the pleasures and virtues of the poems
stem from his ability to convince us that we see and feel what he does.
But it might also be added that this Ordinary Man, without ideology,
religion, truth of any overwhelming sort except the truth of change,
is a gloomy fellow who relieves his gloom in outbursts of singing about
it. MacNeice's appeal may well be to that which is the weakest part
in all of us and what his poems most candidly confront. The lines from
Autumn Journal contain seductive knowledge that constitutes a
warning:

> None of our hearts are pure, we always have mixed motives,
> Are self deceivers, but the worst of all
> Deceits is to murmur 'Lord, I am not worthy'
> And, lying easy, turn your face to the wall.

Issuing out of muddle, depression and deceit, the poet asks that he
may kick the habit of self-abasement, and hopes 'with luck and time—
to dance'. But the dance is taking place before our eyes at that very
moment; any appreciation of MacNeice should end where it begins,
with acknowledging that it's not merely the mentioning of things,
the presence of subject which keeps his best poems in touch with life,

but the ring of a voice which now moves towards speech, now towards song:

> The Junes were free and full, driving through tiny
>   Roads, the mudguards brushing the cowparsley,
> Through fields of mustard and under boldly embattled
>   Mays and chestnuts

That was then; but now

> . . . the curtains in my room blow suddenly inward,
> The shrubbery rustles, birds fly heavily homeward,
> The white flowers fade to nothing on the trees and rain comes
>   Down like a dropscene.

('June Thunder')

English sapphics which manage to accommodate the speech of a reflector.

Symons also hoped that MacNeice would become a guide for action rather than merely 'the only real index we have to a contemporary nostalgia'. Yet it was nostalgia that gave its distinctive flavor to the poet's song and may still provide enough 'residual magic' to answer Conrad Aiken's doubts. At any rate much of the long poem, *Autumn Journal*, sounds as fresh as if we were hearing it for the first time—especially when read aloud so that the voice's musical development over a sequence of lines can come out. One example must do to illustrate this impulsion and also to remind us that MacNeice is the poet of London when London suddenly became the frontier:

> In Tottenham Court Road the tarts and negroes
>   Loiter beneath the lights
> And the breeze gets colder as on so many other
>   September nights.
> A smell of French bread in Charlotte Street, a rustle
>   Of leaves in Regent's Park
> And suddenly from the Zoo I hear a sea-lion
>   Confidently bark.
> And so to my flat with the trees outside the window
>   And the dahlia shapes of the light on Primrose Hill
> Whose summit was once used as a gun emplacement
>   And very likely will
> Be used that way again. . .

Here as throughout his work the crowding confusing Present becomes the Past, as it is imagined; the voice, seizing on its appropriate music, manages to create just enough luck and time to dance. Eliot called MacNeice a great poet, but a truer eulogy was probably Philip Larkin's when he said about MacNeice that 'He could have written the lyrics of "These Foolish Things" ' (*New Statesman*, 6 September 1943).

Conclusion

In a special 'American' number of his magazine *Twentieth Century Verse* Julian Symons in 1938 concluded a provocative article titled 'How Wide is the Atlantic, or Do You Believe in America' by observing that, in response to a questionnaire sent out to various American poets, Conrad Aiken had replied by saying he preferred to side-step the inquiry opining that 'The melancholy truth is that in the past quarter century the best English poetry—perhaps the *only* important English poetry—has been American.' After which Symons adds, rather surprisingly for the editor of a little magazine devoted to publishing new English poets, 'That is just about true.' The past quarter-century dating from 1938 would take us back to the war and include 'thirties poetry. Symons avoids comparative judgements of contemporary Englishmen with Americans, though he does consider that over the past ten years America hasn't produced as important a poet as Auden nor as valuable a 'group' as 'the Auden-Spender-Mac-Neice trio'. But with reference to the feebleness of English poetry in the 1920s he produces the following non-feeble list of American ones: 'Aiken, John Peale Bishop, Crane, Eliot, Miss Moore, Pound, Ransom, Miss Riding and Wallace Stevens'. Give or take a few names: let us add William Carlos Williams (whom Symons was infuriated by) and Frost (whom he may have overlooked). Of this list, Crane was dead and Ransom not productive as a poet in the 1930s; the other names on it were actively publishing, in many cases some of their best work. Looking back on the poetry written in England, roughly 1928–39, I would extend Aiken's remark and Symons's virtual agreement with it, to cover the years of Auden and company, while excepting the work of Auden and MacNeice. For the poetry of the 1930s in England doesn't seem to me exceptional either in its lyric beauties or satiric powers; while as political and public statement it is but a curiosity—

Auden's 'Spain' even with its embarrassing moments is in a different
and superior class from anything else written on the subject.

   This evaluation will sound particularly grotesque and ungenerous-
minded if one holds that Dylan Thomas is a great poet or William
Empson a very considerable one. At some point in my life I held both
these opinions, in adolescence about Thomas, in later university-
wit days about Empson; and I have no wish now to compile a catalogue
of faults or to lament the absence of virtues in either of these two
distinctive writers. Grigson's account of Thomas's poetry titled 'How
Much Me Now Your Acrobatics Amaze' (in *The Harp of Aeolus*)
seems to me still a definitive one in its description of Thomas as the
child-bard of dreams and death, Christ and sex, tricked out in a symbolism to be explored by professors of literature and vocally blared out
through a megaphone which seldom removes itself from the bard's
lips. A handful of arresting first lines, at times a compelling rhythm
('The force that through the green fuse drives the flower') are all that
I take away from Thomas's work in the 'thirties. And the situation
does not significantly alter later on, although he was capable of writing
such modulated and subtle lyrics as 'In My Craft or Sullen Art' and
'The Conversation of Prayer'. Perhaps it all depends on whether you
think 'Fern Hill' is a magnificent poem or (as I do) a childish poem
about childhood, broadcast at too high a fidelity.

   With Empson the really formidable difficulties of almost every
poem bid fair to convict the unpersuaded reader of sheer laziness or
simply not being clever enough.[3] And with poems as fine throughout
as 'To an Old Lady' or 'Missing Dates', or parts of 'This Last Pain'
('Imagine then by miracle with me/Ambiguous gifts as what gods give
must be/What could not possibly be there/And learn a style from a
despair.') or as teasingly stimulating—though I can't put it together—
as 'Aubade', one might well argue that Empson had done enough to
justify himself thoroughly as a poet. Yet there is the terrible monotone that drones through the poems, the poker-faced playing at inscrut-
ability, the annoying pretense in the notes that really we can be
sensible about all this and help the reader clear things up by just saying
a bit more here and there. The incredible narrowing of tonal possibilities in both Empson and Dylan Thomas must be seen as an im-
poverishment of the lyric; and certainly they take less note of

'the universe of objects and events' than most names which occur to one.

What remains beyond this is up to the individual as he reads through, say, Robin Skelton's *Poetry of the Thirties* anthology: intelligent short bits by Norman Cameron, Bernard Spencer or Grigson himself; some amusing mockery from Gavin Ewart ('Audenesque for an Invitation'); some promises of things to come from John Betjeman and Roy Fuller; but remarkably little that compares, in its technical interest or in its human reference, with the best poems written by American contemporaries, or in my view with ones to come—in 1950 and beyond—from Larkin, Davie, Tomlinson, Amis, or the same Roy Fuller. If what seems to me a critical fact calls for an explanation, one thinks of possible rationalizations: the attempt to get out from under Eliot's austerity produced overcompensatory reactions, and in too many cases the reactors fell into solemnity and sentimentality. Political anxieties, the search for a Big Subject that would put poetry back into touch with wider public life, produced the spectacle of engaged, committed poems and their attendant simplicities when looked back on. John Cornford's 'Raise the red flag triumphantly/For Communism and for liberty' is justly remembered as a warning. And almost before the possibilities for a supple syntactical voice to develop itself were made use of—and here the examples of Frost or Graves or Yeats could have helped—the new apocalyptics were in the field with wild and whirling word: George Barker, David Gascoyne, Thomas himself. Still, what is, is more interesting than what might have been: English poetry in the 1930s at least represents a challenge to intelligence and discrimination, makes us consider the fact that poetry may try to be other things than, in Eliot's phrase, a mug's game. And perhaps if we count Eliot as by then English, remember that Graves wrote many good poems in the decade, produce Auden and MacNeice and add whatever poets or poems individual taste decides are in their class, then an estimate of 'thirties poetry needn't be so low after all.

VIII

Satire and Fiction:

Examples from the 1930s

> But to come back to the satirist, whose case seemed at first
> sight a particularly difficult one. . . . It will be his task . . .
> like science, to bring human life more into contempt each day.
> Upon the side of the ascetic, in the interests of other-worldliness
> it [satire] will carry on the good work of such pioneers as
> Swift. It will, by illustrating the discoveries of science, demon-
> strate the futility and absurdity of human life. That will be
> its ostensible function. And a very tolerable one it is.
>
> (Lewis: *Men Without Art*)

Extracted from a chapter titled 'The Materialism of the Artist', these
sentences put the case, in terms extreme as Lewis could find, for the
novelist who would operate effectively in the 1930s. Lewis equates
satire and fiction by arguing that any 'fictionist' of intelligence, con-
templating the disasters of the peace as viewed from England *circa*
1934, had no choice but to write satire. As with other writers, perhaps more than most, Lewis to an extent generalized his principles
from what he found himself producing in his fiction, and after producing *The Apes of God* was not likely to turn around and devote his
attention to the bright side of human endeavours. But looking back
on the 1930s in England, it now seems plain, or at least plausibly
arguable, that its best novels did indeed demonstrate the futility and
absurdity of human life. And that the novelists who provided this
demonstration found their task 'a very tolerable one', rather than one
which drove them to drink, despair and early graves. They endured,
and vigorously, not only the disaster to come of World War II, but
went on to write some of their best books in the 1950s and beyond.

The particular novelist-satirists I have in mind are, besides Lewis himself, Evelyn Waugh, Anthony Powell, Graham Greene, Henry Green and Ivy Compton-Burnett. And although he was dead by 1950 and will not mainly be remembered as novelist or satirist, George Orwell clearly belongs with the group of writers here mentioned.[1]

At first glance the books implied suggest a radical dislocation of or severance from the 'liberal' novels of Ford, Forster and Virginia Woolf considered earlier, the masterpiece or blockbuster category bid for by *Ulysses*, Lewis's *Childermass* and *The Apes of God*, or the ambitious visions of Lawrence. Certainly a typical novel by one of the above 'thirties writers—say *Vile Bodies* or *Afternoon Men* or *Living* or *A Gun for Sale*—is short, cool or opaque in its tone, suspicious of eloquence, committed to terse conversations among characters, neither genial nor 'sincere' in its overall manner. Looked at for very long, each writer becomes individual; but they can be contemplated together just long enough to say that they constitute a brilliant embarrassment for the reader who likes to have his art hold up a mirror to troubled times and 'reflect' those times in that art. The 1930s in England were troubled enough; Auden's line about them being 'a low, dishonest decade' doesn't clinch anything, but seems accurate when we raise our heads from the pages of a novelistic entertainment to look out at the world. This looking up and out is what the Auden group has been praised for: they were interested in politics, enthusiastic and passionate about social issues (if often naively so) and had no time for mere art. For example, a nearly contemptuous review of Empson's poetry by Louis MacNeice has as its message that the poems are clever enough, but can't be afforded at the present time (*New Verse*, August–September 1935).

As was evident from earlier remarks about Auden and MacNeice, I do not claim that their work can be understood and appreciated mainly as social or political responses to pressures thrown up by the low dishonest decade; although most of the poems ask to be heard against some larger world of disorder, threat or promise. But when one turns to English novelists in the 1930s, any relation between the 'world' of their books and The Real World is even more problematic. Evelyn Waugh may be spoken of, as Robert Graves does in

The Long Weekend, as 'the Oxford and Mayfair arch-playboy and most gifted novelist of the new Disillusion'; but it will be of scant help in dealing with the novels to look out at the world in hopes of grasping some 'disillusion' that might explain them. In this respect these 'thirties satirists, and particularly Evelyn Waugh (who has often been bracketed with him) can be distinguished from their satirical predecessor, Huxley. *Antic Hay* and *Point Counter Point* bear a critical relation to the society on which they comment with disillusioned point, and even the more fantastic *Crome Yellow* and *Those Barren Leaves* often operate through the clash of recognizably social intellectual positions: here is a Bohemian artist talking, here a nihilist, there a hypocrite, vintage 1920. Admittedly Waugh's early novels make gestures towards a real world out there—university or run-down public school or prison (in *Decline and Fall*); the social whirl of The Bright Young Things (in *Vile Bodies*); London clubs and dances and country-house *longueurs* (in *A Handful of Dust*). But their violently humorous way of dealing with these institutions and ways of life transforms them into the stuff of extravagant art; the artist's stylistic performance virtually obliterates their 'real-world' truth.

This is to argue that his novels are more like *The Waste Land* in the magical transformations they effect, than like the rationally witty art of Huxley or Strachey, or the ideological satire found in much of Lawrence's short fiction. If the argument were kept abstract enough, one could say that *St. Mawr* and *Vile Bodies*, insofar as they both portray rootless, bright young people engaged in their parties, dances and affairs, deal with the same world: liberated postwar youth without stable values and significant work. But in fact the books are nothing like each other, the responses they ask from a reader utterly different. And, again like *The Waste Land*, to speak about Waugh's attitudes or beliefs without minutely considering what it's like to read him on the page, results in a severely truncated and boring view of the writer. Since by now the terrain of Waugh's books—as with those of the other writers dealt with here—has been pretty thoroughly charted, with themes and characters set forth and classified, we will eschew comprehensiveness, electing instead a few memorable moments from them in order to inspect the nature of a complicated art that it is fatally easy to be pedestrian about.

Waugh's Early Novels

One of Waugh's travel books has the author being chauffeured about
Haifa as follows:

> The driver of our motor car was a restless and unhappy man.
> He smoked 'Lucky Strike' cigarettes continuously, one after the
> other. When he lit a new one he took both hands off the wheel;
> often he did this at corners; he drove very fast and soon out-
> distanced all the other cars. When we most nearly had acci-
> dents he gave a savage laugh. He spoke almost perfect English
> with an American accent. He said he could never eat or drink
> when he was out with the car; he smoked instead; last month
> he had driven a German gentleman to Baghdad and back; he
> had felt ill after that. He never smiled except at the corners,
> or when, as we swept through a village, some little child, its
> mother wailing her alarm, darted in front of us. Then he
> would stamp on the accelerator and lean forward eagerly in his
> seat. As the child skipped clear of our wheels, he would give a
> little whistle of disappointment through his teeth and resume
> his despondent but polite flow of anecdote.
>
> (*When the Going was Good*, 1946)

The driver, seen wholly from the outside, might pass for one of
Wyndham Lewis's 'wild bodies' except that Waugh's prose is so unag-
gressively quiet and noncommittal. Still, it contains a number of
discreet time-bombs, as the semi-colons pile up their innocent recital
of what the driver does. A 'restless and unhappy man' no more helps
us to understand what follows than does the concluding admission
that the man's flow of anecdote was 'despondent but polite'. Or rather,
we cannot move from those qualities to a sober acceptance of the fact
that this chauffeur felt ill after driving a German gentleman to
Baghdad and back, nor can we regard his eager stamping on the
accelerator, in hopes of cutting down a careless child, with understanding sympathy—it would be like trying to understand W. C.
Fields's assertions about children or wives by analyzing Fields's inner
troubles. Nor is there any firmly 'wise' narrative viewpoint of en-
lightenment and civilization from which the barbarian can be
appreciated as quaint and amusing; he is a little too admirably his own
man for that, outdistancing us as he does all the other cars and drivers.

It is possible that encountering a wild body like the Haifa driver

frees the writer from making the sorts of moral and social judgements
he is more inclined to if instead his subject is useless or vicious
English specimens, observed at home and peopling the writer's
fiction. Wyndham Lewis directs no shafts of ridicule or contempt
towards the Berbers or Bretons he meets on holiday, saving them
instead for the Lefties and fakers which inhabit England in, say,
The Revenge for Love. Yet this is not quite the case with Waugh,
for even when the personal type is despicable (John Beaver in *A
Handful of Dust*) or, most far-gone of all, the Bright Young Things
(Agatha Runcible in *Vile Bodies*), we are not allowed to take a knowing
purchase on them, or feel superior to what keeps being too shockingly
and deliberately 'bogus'—to use one of Miss Runcible's own favorite
phrases. The overall effect of this art in these novels is the opposite of
morally reassuring; which is to say that Waugh's books contain
neither villains nor heroes. Edmund Wilson's ranking of him with
Shaw as the two English comic writers of genius in this century reminds us that Shaw likewise gives us no convenient figures of scorn
on whom to release our outrage.

But it is a long way from *Heartbreak House* to *Decline and Fall*
(1928). No doubt the most splendidly outrageous scene from Waugh's
first novel is Sports Day at Llanabba Castle. Already the Welsh band
has appeared ('Ten men of revolting appearance . . . low of brow,
crafty of eye and crooked of limb') and Little Lord Tangent been shot
in the foot by Prendergast, of which wound he is later to expire. Now
appears Margot Beste-Chetwynde in the company of Mr. Sebastian
('Chokey') Cholmondeley who 'though graceful of bearing and
irreproachably dressed, was a Negro'. The following interesting
discussion ensues:

> 'Why, Dr. Fagan,' she was saying, 'it is too disappointing
> that we've missed the sports. We had just the slowest journey,
> stopping all the time to see the churches. You can't move
> Chokey once he's seen an old church. He's just crazy about
> culture, aren't you darling?'
> 'I sure am that,' said Chokey.
> 'Are you interested in music?' said the Doctor tactfully.
> 'Well, just you hear that, Baby,' said Chokey; 'am *I* in-
> terested in music? I should say I am.'

'He plays just too divinely,' said Mrs. Beste-Chetwynde.

'Has he heard my new records, would you say?'

'No, darling, I don't expect he has.'

'Well, just you hear *them*, sir, and then you'll know—am I interested in music.'

'Now, darling, don't get discouraged. I'll take you over and introduce you to Lady Circumference. It's his inferiority-complex, the angel. He's just crazy to meet the aristocracy, aren't you, my sweet?'

'I sure am that,' said Chokey.

'I think it's an insult bringing a nigger here,' said Mrs. Clutterbuck. 'It's an insult to our own women.'

'Niggers are all right,' said Philbrick. 'Where I draw a line is a Chink, nasty inhuman things. I had a pal bumped off by a Chink once. Throat cut horrible, it was, from ear to ear.'

'Good gracious!' said the Clutterbuck governess; 'was that in the Boxer rising?'

'No,' said Philbrick cheerfully. 'Saturday night in the Edgware Road. Might have happened to any of us.'

Read aloud, one marvels at the absolutely perfect speech-rhythms right down to Saturday night in the Edgware Road, or the idiomatic, unforgettable vigour of Chokey's repeated 'I sure am that,' or the emphasized 'just you hear *them*, sir' with regard to his records and love of music. The effect of it all is, in the shop-worn word, hilarious; but in what does the hilarity consist?

It helps little to invoke Ronald Firbank as a way of getting from *Heartbreak House* to Waugh, although Waugh's excellent tribute to Firbank, published a year after *Decline and Fall*, suggests he was very much on his mind.[2] Firbank 'remained objective . . . emphasized that the novel should be directed for entertainment' and mastered certain cinematic techniques of selectivity which concentrated the novel's impact. Yet Waugh is so much less flighty, chic, or giggly than his predecessor, that in a passage like the above, one speech, one line does lead to the next even though no intervening narrator is there to guide us. Such a narrator's absence means that dazzling double-takes are possible, as when, without any pause to assure us that Margot and Chokey have departed the scene, Mrs. Clutterbuck follows hard on Chokey's last 'I sure am that' with her remark about 'bringing a nigger here'. What in a moral satirist might be occasion for bringing out Mrs. Clutterbuck's vicious or vulgar mind, exists here only so it can lead up to Philbrick's rich musings about the Chinks as 'nasty inhuman things'. And the whole scene turns into burlesque when the Clutterbuck governess is allowed to ask dutifully about the Boxer rebellion (no doubt studied in her lessons) in order to set up Philbrick's triumphant revelation about the Edgware Road.

The larger story of *Decline and Fall*, Paul Pennyfeather's anti-heroic ups and downs, is much less interesting than brilliant local successes like this one with Chokey and Philbrick. Everybody is to be admired and applauded, the amount of applause wholly dependent upon the satisfyingness to our ears of the idioms and clichés provided them by Waugh. When Chokey says, soon afterwards, 'When I saw the cathedrals my heart just rose up and sang within me. I sure am crazy about culture. You folk think because we're coloured we don't care about nothing but jazz. Why, I'd give all the jazz in the world for one little stone from one of your cathedrals,' it is immensely, satisfyingly funny, but the joke is not on Chokey, or on the whitefolks listening. Or it is on all of them and both races equally; one might break down the joke, saying: 'Whether or not blacks are highly responsive to jazz, some whites think they are and liberally attempt to draw them out on this their subject. So let's invent a black who loves cathedrals (the white woman's cultural province), then have him declare his beliefs in syrupy eloquence. The result will be highly entertaining— just sit back and enjoy it.' The comedy resists analysis that would push much beyond this point; if the reader has enough style he will recognize Waugh's style and know how much need not be said to 'explain' its workings.

Both *Decline and Fall* and *Vile Bodies* (1930) work this way, representing a pitch of irresponsible satire no artist since Waugh has been able to exceed, although Lenny Bruce, Terry Southern and Thomas Pynchon have made notable efforts. In *Vile Bodies*, Adam Symes goes to look up his putative father-in-law, Colonel Blount, and stumbles onto the set of a movie about John Wesley the Colonel is directing. The following scene may be noted:

> He had not gone very far in his detour before he was again stopped, this time by a man dressed in a surplice, episcopal

lawn sleeves and scarlet hood and gown; he was smoking a cigar.

'Here, what in hell do *you* want?' said the Bishop.

'I came to see Colonel Blount.'

'Well, you can't, son. They're just shooting him now.'

'Good heavens. What for?'

'Oh, nothing important. He's just one of the Wesleyans, you know—we're trying to polish off the whole crowd this afternoon while the weather's good.'

Adam found himself speechless before this cold-blooded bigotry.

Funny enough without the last line, but that line signals a truly irresponsible comic imagination, willing at the drop of a hat to set character or story at naught when compared to the joke that comes from pretending the phrase 'cold-blooded bigotry' can find a solemn home in a book like *Vile Bodies*.

On the other hand there are moments when this novel looks like a conventional one indeed, when Waugh begins to do a landscape, or expatiates on the poetry of fast cars, or makes wise comments on the foibles of his two lovers: 'The truth is that like so many people of their age and class, Adam and Nina were suffering from being sophisticated about sex before they were at all widely experienced.' Here is heard the personality who will be often in charge of Waugh's later novels, most certainly from *Put Out More Flags* on. There is really no way for this knowing, disillusioned, reflectively gloomy figure to exist in unity with the brilliant creator of 'Chokey' or the shooting of the Wesleyans. And in what is in some ways his most interesting book from the 1930s, *A Handful of Dust* (1934), the strain is clearly felt, though not I think to the novel's disadvantage.

Alluding to *The Waste Land*, this book's epigraph cites the portentous lines about showing fear in a handful of dust and serves notice of a deepening in novelistic intention: we are to be moved, not just entertained, by the antics of some vile bodies. And in fact this novel of infidelity, divorce, and grotesque annihilation, published four years after Waugh's own separation and divorce from his first wife, often sounds a resonantly bitter note. It is the first of his books where one can speak of a hero without immediately wanting to put the word in quotation marks, and not only because of the book's extraordinary and memorable ending—Tony Last 'Du Côté de Chez Todd' reading and rereading Dickens aloud to his proud captor. As is known, that ending was originally a short story written previous to the book's main body. Waugh decided that juxtaposing barbarian savagery with the civilized kind treated of earlier would give the book an added dimension of richness; but though one wouldn't willingly give up Mr. Todd and Dickens, there is a case to be made for the ending Waugh wrote for the serialized version of *A Handful of Dust* and published two years later in his collection *Mr. Loveday's Little Outing*. There the Brazilian adventure is entirely omitted, and Tony after his travels round the world comes back more or less to the same world he's left, his wife returned to him out of ennui, but no indication that things will improve or the apocalypse present itself.

At any rate the heroic note, if a defeated one, has been sounded earlier for Tony through a prose that rather feelingly supports him, as in these sentences in which he learns that his wife's treachery extends even to doing him out of his beloved house, Hetton:

> His mind had suddenly become clearer on many points that had puzzled him. A whole Gothic world had come to grief . . . there was now no armour, glittering in the forest glades, no embroidered feet on the greensward; the cream and dappled unicorns had fled. . . .

One could argue that this is sentimental Gothic cliché, appropriate to the simple mind of Tony Last; except that it looks ahead to Guy Crouchback (in the *Sword of Honour* trilogy) with whom his creator has the closest affinities, and that no extenuating circumstances are invoked to explain Brenda's meaningless affair with John Beaver, her lack of response to the death of her son John or the mean-minded hypocrisy of her relatives in trying to do a deal on Tony. Waugh has remarked that the novel contained all he had to say about humanism. What he had to say was that humanism couldn't say very much: to a son's sudden death it agrees that nobody is at fault; to a wife's adultery it says that these things happen; to one's own inner vacancies, which exist beyond the planned renovation of this ceiling or that bedroom, it brings no words. In granting Tony Last the dignity of the language of Gothic, no matter how fanciful or vulnerable it sounds, Waugh opens himself up to possibilities for the expression of deep feelings even if they are sentimental or self-pitying—and surely there is a self-pitying streak in him, the other side of his cruelty and cleverness. *A Handful of Dust* still plays it safe in staying pretty much within the mind of Tony, or at least providing him kinds of sympathy withheld from his wife; it will remain for the later novels, *Put Out More Flags*, *Brideshead Revisited*, and *Sword of Honour* to spread three-dimensional creation rather more widely.

In Part V of *The Waste Land*, fear in a handful of dust surges up, infuses the vision of annihilation and last-ditch tremblings, and celebrates the end of humanism. Eliot could not stay in the position in which he left his protagonist at the close of that poem, fishing with the arid plain behind him; no more could Waugh go back to his first novels' detached strikings-off of contemporary idiocy, though these idiocies will never be absent from the novels he goes on to write. Part V of *The Waste Land*, and *A Handful of Dust*, are marked by not wholly resolved tensions between ways of seeing, of narrating, of valuing—in this sense they are watershed moments. And after writing them, the term 'satire' as essentially descriptive of Waugh's art needs as much adjustment and qualification as when used about Eliot's. Something called the real world will no longer be neatly shaped to the witty demands of a ruthlessly clever narrator. Towards the end of *Vile Bodies*, Nina and Ginger view England from an aeroplane and Ginger begins to recite Richard II's lines about 'This scepter'd isle . . . this England' while Nina looks down and sees, interestingly enough, the terrain of Auden and Day Lewis: 'a horizon of straggling red suburb; arterial roads dotted with little cars; factories, some of them working, others empty and decaying; a disused canal', at which point the plane lurches and she announces she is going to be sick. 'That's what the paper bags are for' replies Ginger, sensibly. But it is too good a line, too marvelous a cinematic fadeout for the novelist within Waugh ultimately to be content with.

Anthony Powell's Comedy

The moralist within Anthony Powell was, on the contrary, firmly held in check; in fact temperamentally he lived miles away from the

Waugh he had known at Oxford and with whom he kept on polite and friendly terms, eventually writing a reminiscence when Waugh died in 1966. *Vile Bodies* appeared in 1930; *Afternoon Men*, Powell's first novel, the next year; both books were about the same size and depicted men and women in motion, to what purpose it was not at all clear. Yet upon reading the opening of *Afternoon Men* one would quickly understand that a very un-Waugh-like creator lay behind this introduction of character and place:

> 'When do you take it?' said Atwater.
> Pringle said: 'You're supposed to take it after every meal, but I only take it after breakfast and dinner. I find that enough.'
> They stayed downstairs where the bar was. Upstairs there was a band, but dancing had not begun to any extent yet because it was still early in the evening. The room downstairs was low with a bar running all along one side of it and some tables and a few divans. The windows in the wall opposite the bar were all open, but they looked out on to a well, so that the room was really quite stuffy and there was a smell of ammonia. Several people they knew were sitting at tables or up at the bar, but they found a place to themselves in the corner of the room and sat down.

By comparison, *Vile Bodies* immediately signals the reader to prepare for troubles, probably comic ones, with its single-paragraph sentence 'It was clearly going to be a bad crossing', after which a thoroughly capable narrator begins the tale in a way tales have often begun before: 'With Asiatic resignation Father Rothschild S. J. put down his suitcase in the corner of the bar and went on deck.' We are not surprised to learn, soon afterwards, that among other things the suitcase contains a false beard. Waugh gets the show off to a bang, already on the first page producing trick after trick from his own well-stocked suitcase. But in *Afternoon Men* there is nothing particularly amusing about anything Atwater or Pringle says or does, and Powell makes sure the atmosphere will be sufficiently leaden or somnambulistic by heavy use of 'was 'as his main verb in the long paragraph—'so that the room was really quite stuffy and there was a smell of ammonia'. Let anyone make what he will of these less-than-exciting details.

Hemingway's name springs to mind as a major stylistic influence:

'In the morning I walked down the boulevard to the rue Soufflot for coffee and brioche. It was a fine morning. The horse-chestnut trees in the Luxembourg gardens were in bloom. There was the pleasant early-morning feeling of a hot day.' This influence was re-marked on by an early critic of Powell's work, G. R. Ellis, who in *Twilight on Parnassus* (1939) gave a perceptive if loosely written account of Powell's indebtedness both to Hemingway and to Wyndham Lewis. Ellis argues that Powell learned his manner from Hemingway and his purpose from Lewis; but although in *Afternoon Men* the Hemingway laconicism and deemphasized presentation exist in man-nered ways, by the time Powell published *From a View to a Death* two years later he had completely made it his own, that is, made it into something else. As for Lewis, G. R. Ellis points to 'Complete objectivity of approach to his characters', and to the presentation of experience 'non-morally' as constituting Powell's debt. But though Lewis did think this was his aim, and at times achieved it in his work, that work had also a very pronounced 'moral' side to it, a most notable animus towards various detestable human types, which had just received its most elaborate expression in his mammoth satire *The Apes of God* (1930). Even if he believed that he had moved beyond creating 'good' and 'bad' characters into a realm where those creations 'are congealed and frozen into logic, and an exuberant hysterical truth' (*The Wild Body*, 1927), he couldn't resist an even stronger impulse to mock and bait the ape-specimens of Bloomsbury-Bohemia which populate the pages of his longest book.

Powell is a master at resisting such impulses. His poker-faced, toneless narration can make what in another writer would be a strongly delivered punch-line calculated to break us up in laughter, hardly noticeable—as in this brief filling-in of Pringle's 'go-ahead' father: 'His father, a business man from Ulster, had bought a Cézanne in 1911. That had been the beginning. Then he had divorced his wife. Later he developed religious mania and jumped off a suspension bridge.' 'He had bought', 'it had been', 'then he had. . . .' the style makes it all sound inevitable, as if the narrator is simply handing along these bits of truth, juxtaposing them but hazarding no more of a causal connection among them than to say, discreetly: 'That had been the beginning.' Or consider a moment when Atwater, returned home from an all-night party, eventually ushers out his female companion and climbs back the stairs to prepare for bed:

> He put the gin in the cupboard in the sitting-room and went into his bedroom and pulled the curtains. The sun came through the curtains, but not enough to see properly, so he switched on the electric light. He cleaned his teeth, undressed and got into bed. Birds in the garden at the back of the house were singing, which prevented him from going to sleep for some time.

End of chapter 4. Perhaps it is the strategic position of 'which' in the final sentence which does the trick. For trick it is to convince us that the birds singing in the garden and preventing him from sleeping is no more, no less than a fact of life, to be recited for no other reason than that it happened that way.

Powell's comedy provides subtle satisfactions that are hard to be clear about. There is a moment in *Vile Bodies* where the infamous Agatha Runcible and her companions find their way into one of the pits at the motor races she is eventually to take part in and come to grief. Earlier, smoking a cigarette, she is asked by an official to put it out:

> There were six open churns behind Miss Runcible, four containing petrol and two water. She threw her cigarette over her shoulder, and by a beneficent attention of Providence, which was quite rare in her career, it fell into the water. Had it fallen into the petrol it would probably have been all up with Miss Runcible.

The second time she tosses one it lands on a leftover chicken leg, there to extinguish itself. In these moments the performance is loud and genial, the invocation of Providence and the coy 'it would probably have been all up with Miss Runcible', beckon the reader to respond in grandly participatory ways. Waugh is not averse to telegraphing his punches, to breezily nudging his audience. By contrast, one of the very best moments in *Afternoon Men* occurs near its end, when the distasteful Pringle, having decided to commit suicide, changes his mind and is fished out of the water and provided with clothes by his rescuers, who then show up later at Pringle's house to collect them. The question, debated for pages by Pringle's guests, is whether to pay the fishermen a pound or ten shillings for their trouble, it being generally agreed that a pound is too much, ten shillings too little. A solution is found when two half-crowns are added to the ten shillings and Sophy, one of the guests, is directed to bear the sum to the fisherman who has been provided with a cup of coffee:

> Sophy took the money and went out again. When she came back, carrying the coffee-cup, Mrs. Race said:
> 'What did he say?'
> Sophy said; 'He just said, "Tar".'
> 'Nothing more?'
> 'No.'
> 'That was obviously the right sum,' said Pringle and, retying his dressing-gown cord, he went upstairs.

The vivid humorous economy of this outcome is of course hardly a matter of imitating Hemingway or moving words around into just the right combinations. Pringle is a moral monster, but we would not have him otherwise; Powell needs the world to be complacent and selfrighteous enough to live up to his witty imagining of it, and by yoking together 'Tar' and the retying of a dressing-gown cord he makes it all coolly unforgettable. But in how astonishingly low a key.

Afternoon Men is a beautiful performance, but Powell's best prewar book and one that is as fine as anything in the postwar *Music of Time* sequence, is *From a View to a Death* (1933). If *Afternoon Men* superficially goes together with *Vile Bodies*, *From a View* in its country-house horse-riding setting and in the violence of its resolutions might bring to mind *A Handful of Dust*, published in the following year to it. *From a View* is a book ostensibly about the fortunes of a 'superman' —Arthur Zouch—his seduction and betrayal of a village girl, his ascension to socially smarter ways, his abrupt death on being thrown from his horse. The main subplot deals with Major Fosdick, a marvelous transvestite whose indulgence in dressing-up in the privacy of his dressing-room is spoken of this way: 'For a good many years now he had found it restful to do this for an hour or two every day when he had the opportunity. . . . Publicly he himself would refer to these temporary retirements from the arena of everyday life as his Forty Winks.' Needless to say this prose opens us up to spacious mock-heroic admiration; no sharp or breathlessly manic laughter is in order. In fact Powell has never bettered the suspended, almost embarrassed reticence with which he freezes his puppets into hysterical truths. Even the most minor of minor characters is accorded his exquisitely suited tribute, as when one of the guests at Torquil Fosdick's notorious cocktail party (the book's funniest scene) is introduced:

> Young Kittermaster, another of Jasper's friends, was at Cambridge. He was tall, with very long legs, and was always dressed in riding-breeches and suède leggings. He had fair, rather sparse hair and thought himself a little like the Prince of Wales. He was called Young Kittermaster because his father, who farmed on a fairly large scale in the neighbourhood, was called Old Kittermaster.

It would be satisfactorily deadpan enough simply to write the sentence about how he fancies himself like the Prince of Wales, then follow it by the splendid explanation of how he came to be known as Young Kittermaster. But Powell lengthens it out, freezing it by interpassing a clause informing us that Old Kittermaster was indeed a pretty successful farmer.

The book's comedy is continuous with glimpses of unease and visionary dreariness deeper than provincial boredom and the supreme directionlessness of lives. At certain moments Powell manages a melancholy poetry which seems to issue from some essentially disillusioned source of energy, as in a rather long paragraph, especially long for early Powell, displaying the sensations of Zouch on waking in the morning from having seduced Joanna in the home of his eventual bride-to-be, Mary Passenger. It is instructive to imagine oneself as the novelist at this point, having created a cynically self-serving hero in whose quest the reader has to participate, since Zouch is at least saner and more intelligent than most of the book's other inhabitants. The question is, how best to have Zouch wake up and steal back to his own room? Here is Powell's solution to the problem:

> The curtain had been drawn only half across the window and now it was light outside. Zouch had slept badly. He had cramp in one of his legs and, as he moved to stretch it out, he felt Joanna's arm resting on his shoulder.... He disengaged himself from her and, getting out of bed softly, he went across the room to the open window. He looked out of it towards the

fields, at this hour unnaturally close up to the house. The morning light brought them just up beyond the lawn. The grey, mysterious English fields. Small pockets of mist hung a short way above the ground and round the roots of the oaks in the park. Farther away the steamy mist grew thicker so that it filled the gap between the trees and hid the artificial water. But beyond, the atmosphere became clear again and the land rolled away upwards to the woods and cardboard hills. A sudden breath of cold air, intoxicatingly fresh, came into the room and he shivered and began to button up his pyjama coat which was open and which flapped around him. He looked at the time by Joanna's watch beside the bed and he knew that he must be getting back into his own room. His dressing-gown was on the floor. He picked it up and put it on, at the same time slipping his feet into his bedroom slippers. Then he leaned over and kissed Joanna lightly upon the forehead. She stirred but did not wake. Zouch opened the door, trying to make as little noise as possible, but the hinge creaked menacingly. He set off along the passage in the direction of his own room. He was not feeling at all well.

It is a strangely affecting, even moving passage, made so particularly through the extended description of morning mists and 'The grey, mysterious English fields.' Just what this does, if anything, to alter or shape the way we take Zouch, his conquest, his 'not feeling at all well' is hard to say. In a sense we see nature through him, sensitively, even as we know it is the narrator, Anthony Powell, who feels and sees here. But it imparts a note of third-dimensionality that is also felt elsewhere in the book, in relation mainly to Joanna's confusions and sadness. It is a bit like the song 'John Peel' itself, not at all the rollicking lilt it seemed like at first, but eventually touching and disturbing—from a view to a death in the morning. Powell's later style in *The Music of Time* sequence is but a step away.

Orwell's Prose Art

On the basis of *Afternoon Men*, *From a View to a Death* and his three other novels written in the 1930s, Powell lays claim to as much 'detachment' from the age's political and public realities—what Wyndham Lewis labeled 'the disasters of the peace'—as any contemporary

English novelist, excepting Ivy Compton-Burnett, could show. At the opposite pole, it would seem, there is George Orwell acting as a seismograph for the decade, indeed for the years from 1933 when his first book was published to his death in 1950. So it is interesting to learn that Powell wrote to Orwell on publication of the latter's second novel, *Keep the Aspidistra Flying* (1936), to express his enthusiasm for the book, thus beginning a friendship which lasted until Orwell's death. They were both Etonians but it is at first glance hard to see what could have appealed to the creator of such artful novels as Powell had already written, in Orwell's rough-and-ready tale of Gordon Comstock's struggle with and eventual capitulation to the Money God. At moments in that novel we hear the voice of what may surely be called 'Orwell', as in this sentence bringing Spring to Lambeth: 'But how absurd that even now, in the era of central heating and tinned peaches, a thousand so-called poets are writing in the same strain. . . . In a town like London the most striking seasonal change, apart from the mere change of temperature, is in the things you see lying about on the pavement.' Yet there is always the story to get on with, and the necessity of subordinating knowing perceptions of things to the simplicities of his angry, bloody-but-unbowed hero.

Orwell came to understand his own writing career as centrally marked by the issue of 'detachment', by the writer's relation to politics in the bad times of the 1930s. The short statement 'Why I Write' (1946) is a retrospective attempt to be clear about what happened to him. He claims that in a peaceful age his motives for writing would have been composed preponderately by what he terms 'Sheer egoism', 'Esthetic enthusiasm' and 'Historical impulse', but that the spirit of the age has instead made 'political purpose' of prime importance; thus he has become 'a sort of pamphleteer', more positively has tried to make, over the years from 1935 on, 'political writing into an art'. He tells us that he wants to hold on, at least in part, to 'the world view that I acquired in childhood'; he still cares about prose style, loves the surface of the earth, takes pleasure in scraps of useless information. Somehow these aesthetic-private responses must be incorporated in books which are also publicly and politically responsible. As an example of the difficulty in such combining he instances *Homage to Catalonia* (1938), written mainly with 'a certain detachment and regard for form', but also containing a long chapter defending the Trotskyists with plenty of names, dates and figures. Orwell remarks that he has been criticized for watering down a good book into journalism whose topicality will be soon out of date and forgotten. Still, he defends it and must leave it in—innocent men were being falsely accused.

Thirty years after 'Why I Write' Orwell is saluted for having made political writing into an art. Yet the feeling persists that there must be a trick in it somewhere; surely it can't be made into an art simply by combining, in discreet proportions, bits of sensuous memories with calls to right action, even if all this is expressed in good prose 'like a window pane', as Orwell said it should be. And so, many appreciators of him have tended to fall back on old-fashionedly moral tributes— Lionel Trilling's 'virtuous man' epithet—or to catalogue the course of his relations to socialism, his fairness and accuracy with respect to the Spanish conflict, his shifting attitudes towards England's joining the war against Germany. My feeling is rather that Orwell's art is truly art, but difficult to describe because it looks artless, sincere and virtuously simple. In that same essay, 'Why I Write', he begins his final paragraph—the one ending with the statement that he only wrote lifeless books or purple passages when his writing lacked a political purpose—by stepping back from the essay:

> . . . I see that I have made it appear as though my motives in writing were wholly public-spirited. I don't want to leave that as the final impression. All writers are vain, selfish and lazy, and at the very bottom of their motives there lies a mystery. Writing a book is a horrible, exhausting struggle, like a long bout of some painful illness.

And he decides that a writer really is driven by some demon beyond reason and understanding.

I am suggesting that for Orwell, making political writing an art involved a similar manipulation, if that is not too sinister a word, of our responses and of his own. He looks at things one way, shows us that there are good reasons for looking at it in that way, then steps back, or aside, and says, but now what if one looks at it *this* way— can one continue to function? Orwell's novels don't very often sound like 'Orwell' because, due to the exigencies of getting a story told and characters disposed, we don't hear enough of the sensitive complicated voice working through its way of taking some experience. That voice emerges clearly for the first time in *The Road to Wigan Pier* (1937) and in 'Shooting an Elephant' (1936). The latter, written for the second edition of John Lehmann's *New Writing* is mentioned in a letter Orwell wrote to Lehmann saying he'd like to do a piece for the magazine but 'I doubt whether there is anything anti-Fascist in the shooting of an elephant!' (Lehmann's magazine was committed to anti-Fascism.) As it turned out the essay is among other things a piece of political writing, at the climactic moment of which Orwell the civil servant finds himself about to shoot an elephant he doesn't want to shoot, because he must act like a sahib and satisfy the flocks of Indians who have come out to see him perform his function: 'And it was at this moment, as I stood there with the rifle in my hand, that I first grasped the hollowness, the futility of the white man's dominion in the East.' This is perhaps a dangerously memorable sentence; at least one would expect the political writer who also aspired to being an artist to think twice before so boldly coming out with his big point, as if the elephant business were merely a pretext or metaphor to be discarded when brass tacks were got down to.

In fact Orwell the writer doesn't discard the elephant, but gives us the inefficient shooting and slow dying of it, then writes a final paragraph worth quoting for the way it concludes things without concluding them too much. Remember that the elephant had trampled a peasant who had ventured in its way:

> Afterwards, of course, there were endless discussions about the shooting of the elephant. The owner was furious, but he was only an Indian and could do nothing. Besides, legally, I had done the right thing, for a mad elephant has to be killed, like a mad dog, if its owner fails to control it. Among the Europeans opinion was divided. The older men said I was right, the younger men said it was a damn shame to shoot an elephant for killing a coolie, because an elephant was worth more than any damn Coringhee coolie. And afterwards I was very glad that the coolie had been killed; it put me legally in the right and it gave me a sufficient pretext for shooting the elephant. I often wondered whether any of the others grasped that I had done it solely to avoid looking a fool.

The rights and wrongs of shooting an elephant have turned into a vacant dispute between older and younger men, conducted in terms irrelevant to the real situation. The 'I' himself is also seen as a help-less, mean figure, glad that the coolie had been killed so that he him-self is legally off the hook. The essay's final sentence, with its casual close—'to avoid looking a fool'—reveals the double light in which Orwell sees his earlier self; at one moment grasping sud-denly the nature of imperialism, at another continuing to act as imperialism's humble servant. The actors in this elephant-saga are all stuck in their parts; freedom is heard only in the dis-illusioned, glum ironies of the writer's voice, while even that freedom of understanding, of the 'wider view', is a precarious one, barely achieved and not very much cause for exultation.

Still, the glum ironies are registered in an extremely winning style which becomes even more so in Orwell's best book, *Homage to Catalonia*—by any standards one of the books from the 1930s which matter most. Political writing as an art here seems to involve, as in the Elephant essay, putting the actor into an impossible position, then adding, 'and yet . . .' There is a pervading sense of exhilaration in *Homage to Catalonia* which makes it also curiously enough Orwell's happiest book, exhilaration such as may be intuited in a moment like the following typical one, ostensibly about the use of passwords in the army:

> They were these tiresome double passwords in which one word has to be answered by another. Usually they were of an ele-vating and revolutionary nature, such as *Cultura-progreso*, or *Seremos-invencibles*, and it was often impossible to get illiter-ate sentries to remember these highfalutin words. One night, I remember, the password was *Cataluna-eroica*, and a moon-faced peasant lad named Jaime Domenech approached me, greatly puzzled, and asked me to explain.
> 'Eroica—what does eroica mean?'
> I told him it meant the same as valiente. A little while later he was stumbling up the trench in the darkness, and the sentry challenged him:
> 'Alto! Cataluña!'
> 'Valiente!' yelled Jaime, certain that he was saying the right thing.
> Bang!

> However the sentry missed him. In this war everyone
> always did miss everyone else, when it was humanly
> possible.

It is of course humanly right to have the peasant lad ask what the
heroic means while performing his task; and one wants to believe, for
humane but also human reasons, that in the Spanish conflict everyone
did miss everyone else when possible. Orwell's voice creates that
possibility while staying within the tones of civilized ironic discourse.
This doesn't mean that the passionate note—in anger or in admiration
—is excluded, but does mean that even matters of life and death aren't
beyond reason, at least not beyond words.

Yet not everyone has been charmed or won over to sensible thinking
by Orwell's making an art of political writing. When V. S. Pritchett
reviewed *Homage to Catalonia* he allowed himself to wish that creative
writers would keep out of politics (*New Statesman*, 30 April 1938).
Wyndham Lewis in his exaggerated and lively essay 'Why George
Orwell?' (*The Writer and the Absolute*, 1952) decided Orwell was
really a Right Winger in disguise and that, living in England, 'A
natural Patriot, he has to act seditiously. His left-wingery probably
was a species of sport, as obviously as his plunge into the underworld
of tramps was the act of a sportsman, not that of a missionary.' 'Where
would he be on the war in Vietnam?' asked Mary McCarthy a few
years ago, and feared that Orwell would be with Kingsley Amis rather
than Joan Baez. An illegitimate game to play no doubt, but it's easy
to imagine Orwell's less than enthusiastic adherence to the notion
of making love not war, or to the sloganeering of liberals convinced
of their own righteousness. Certainly Orwell was fond of sweeping the
board of those who, in a time of national crisis, would talk about
making an equivalent of love rather than war. In April 1940 he concluded a statement of his principles (in 'My Country Right or Left')
with the following challenge:

> It is all very well to be 'advanced' or 'enlightened', to snigger
> at Colonel Blimp and proclaim your emancipation from tradi-
> tional loyalties, but a time comes when the sand of the desert
> is sodden red and what have I done for thee, England, my
> England?

And he claims to sympathize with and prefer this patriotic tradition, 'for even at its stupidest and most sentimental it is a comelier thing than the shallow self-righteousness of the left-wing intelligentsia'. Strong words, uttered in wartime and with Orwell's annoyance at the Left—particularly with regard to Spain and Moscow—to the fore. But the word one fixes on is 'comelier'; patriotism even at its stupidest is 'a comelier thing' than iconoclasm and cynical seeing-through of principle. The user of such a word, about such issues, seems to me to label himself as very much the artist, even perhaps the aesthete, in his approach to messy public matters. He knows that 'England, my England' is bad poetry, and in the next breath says he prefers it to various cynical brands.

Perhaps it is that Colonel Blimp and England, my England, along with Boys' Weeklies, repressive public schools and imperialistic stupidities can be put to artistic uses by someone who delights in words, in the surfaces of things, and who in some perversely un-progressive sense would not have things any less awful than they are. In his fine memoir of Orwell, Julian Symons tells the story of how during World War II he used to lunch with Orwell, Anthony Powell and Malcolm Muggeridge. Symons and the others would grimace their way through the food while Orwell, finishing every bit of some wartime special named perhaps 'The Victory Pie' would smack his lips satisfiedly. Did he really want the food to be any better? His wonderful essay on Dickens at one point considers the sort of school Dickens seems to have wanted, and concludes that 'as usual, Dickens's criticism is neither creative nor destructive'—he sees the idiocy of this but has no use for that. 'What, then, *does* he want?' Orwell asks, and concludes that he wants people to be better and more virtuous, wants a change in spirit, operates wholly on the moral plane. Orwell ends up defending this aspect of Dickens rather than attacking it as not revolutionary enough: ' "If men would behave decently the world would be decent" is not such a platitude as it sounds.' It is not so in Dickens because the moral plane is supplemented, made rich and strange, by the plane of art; so in its way is it with Orwell, another nineteenth-century liberal, as he proudly and defiantly saluted Dickens for being. But with a difference; with the need and the capacities to work himself into complicatedly individual positions in his political

writing that were in fact artistic 'solutions' to what he couldn't resolve any other way.

In 1935, as he tells us in 'Why I Write', he wrote one of those
good-bad poems ('Sharply the menacing wind sweeps over' and 'The
Italian Soldier shook my hand' are others) which stay in the mind and
provide recurrent pleasure:

> A happy vicar I might have been
> Two hundred years ago,
> To preach upon eternal doom
> And watch my walnuts grow;

But, he goes on to tell us, he was born, alas, in an evil time and so
has been dragged into unhappy reality—Hitler, the Spanish war and
other disasters. The poem concludes with an address to the reader:
'I wasn't born for an age like this./Was Smith? Was Jones? Were you?'
No, we are invited to reply; yet how thinly though amusingly trivial
the might-have-been is rendered: Orwell the Vicar, watching his
walnuts and getting in lots of fishing. The truth is that nobody more
than Orwell was born exactly for the age in which he lived; Arnold's
'power of the moment' met the 'power of the man' and they locked
arms in significant combat. The result was a body of work through
which a voice speaks in tones which hadn't yet been heard, about
subjects often close to unspeakable. There seems small chance that
we will choose to stop listening.

Lewis and *The Revenge for Love*

In an essay titled 'Detachment and the Fictionist' (*English Review*,
October and November 1934) Lewis addressed himself at length to
the problem of being a novelist in an age of small disasters which
seemed to be leading up to a huge one:

> I have given it as my opinion that it is particularly difficult,
> at the present time, for a fiction writer, especially, to stand
> above the *mêlée*, and to function as an instrument of impartial
> truth, or anything of that sort. It is even undesirable that, as a
> dramatic writer he should pretend to do so. . . . But I have also
> made plain how necessary I consider it to be to preserve intact

the famous 'detachment' of the artist and the man of science—
even in the midst of faction, even for the purposes of the
crudest and most dramatical rough-stuff.

If this sounds almost indistinguishable from Good Advice to Aspiring
Writers (be engaged, but be detached) Lewis goes on to give it one
further twist:

> But there is more to it than that—it is even desirable to main-
> tain the technique of 'detachment' if for no other reason than
> that, as a partisan, you will be exceedingly ineffective without
> it! You will find, to your great discomfort, if you give yourself
> up entirely to subjective judgement and subjective methods,
> that your one-sided vision will lose all its edge; in order to
> special-plead, even, you must do as an artist, otherwise your
> plea will fall pretty flat.

Orwell's aim was to make political writing into an art; by 1940,
writing 'Inside the Whale' while the world went to war, his main
advice to novelists was to do as best they could what Henry Miller
had done in *Tropic of Cancer*. Since progress and reaction had both
turned out to be 'swindles': 'Get inside the whale—or rather admit
you are inside the whale (for you *are* of course). Give yourself over
to the world-process, stop fighting against it or pretending that you
control it; simply accept it, endure it, record it.' That he did not
follow his own advice but went on to write *Animal Farm* and *Nineteen
Eighty-Four* shows he could not be a happy recorder of 'the world-
process' any more than he could have been the putative happy vicar
of his poem. But he was sure that the world was no longer a writer's
world and that men without art was to be the rule, not the exception.
Whether it had ever been a writer's world Orwell doesn't say.

Lewis, who had grimly predicted this artless world, greatly admired *Animal Farm*, calling it a work of true 'detachment', while he is
harder on Orwell's 1930s work, arguing that the books lacked detachment and slighted the claims of art. In this case the critic did not
neglect to practise what he preached; at least between the 'Detachment' essay in 1934 and the critique of Orwell written after the war,
Lewis produced one novel (*The Revenge for Love*, 1937) that takes
on the challenge of being both very engaged and very detached, that
tries to put reins to 'subjective' judgement and one-sided visions by

presenting and inspecting them through the form of art. It is not merely the outstanding political novel of the 1930s in England, it is very nearly the only one—if by 'novel' we insist that a book take note of the universe of objects and events, that it know also that besides war and poverty the world contains cinemas which people attend and 'thrillers' which they read. *The Revenge for Love* takes on everybody and everything, using them in the interests of an aggressive inclusiveness.

Writing about these years in his invaluable little book *The Thirties*, Julian Symons contrasts the easy tolerance intellectuals gave to Eliot's opinions, with their response to Lewis's and Orwell's:

> Eliot's technical mastery as poet and dramatist was acknowledged, but in the realm of ideals he was regarded as an eccentric reactionary unlikely to do much harm. The writings of Wyndham Lewis and Orwell, however, aroused the fiercest social opposition. They became, as the decade went on, more and more like some terrible *memento mori*. 'If we were not as we are, if we had not been saved, this,' orthodox Artists and Pragmatists thought with a shiver as they contemplated the Fascist monster Lewis and the Trotskyist demon Orwell, 'is what we might have become.'

Although Symons admits that both Lewis and Orwell suffered delusions of persecution, they were also (to the extent that England persecutes its writers) persecuted: a seriously canvassed suggestion that Lewis's works be boycotted by Left Book Club groups; Orwell's insistence that after *Homage to Catalonia* his work was sometimes rejected from places which before had welcomed it. And Lewis recounts with bitterness, in his autobiographical memoir *Rude Assignment* (1950), how *Partisan Review* refused a laudatory review of *The Revenge for Love*, the time being inauspicious (he later felt) for a political novel which told the truth about systems, particularly the Communist one. Yet Lewis himself when he wrote the book must have known it would irritate the likes of James Burnham at *Partisan*; he might also, after reading the book over and deciding it was the 'best complete work of fiction that I have written', have added—'so how could it possibly win the heads and hearts of many readers?'

Lewis advised 'detachment' from the 'dramatical rough-stuff' of which novels, especially in the turbulences of modern politics and public events, had to be made. *The Revenge for Love* has much rough-stuff and studies in some detail the fortunes of a number of figures: the professional communist Hardcaster, shot in Spain and returned to England for publicity value; the unsuccessful artist and wild-man-of-action Victor Stamp; his lover and devoted companion Margot, whose developing consciousness represents Lewis's first achievement in rendering a woman sympathetically; Jack Cruze, professional woman-izer and political *naïf*; plus assorted fellow-travelers, art-forgers, and thugs. Rather than praising or faulting the novel's construction, or even the fairness and subtlety of its satire and criticism of Leftists, I want only to suggest that it is a uniquely disconcerting book which makes other, smoother novels contemporary with it, classifiable as good but undisconcerting stories.

Perhaps the best of such 'action' novels written in the 'thirties is Graham Greene's *A Gun For Sale* (1936). Whether or not one admires the later, more psychologically and religiously problematic books like *The Heart of the Matter* or *The End of the Affair*, this earlier 'enter-tainment' is as assured and efficiently organized a piece of work as Greene ever produced; 'readable' and in truth entertaining in a manner Lewis couldn't have achieved if he'd tried, as in a way he did. Greene's narrative style is carefully oiled, sympathetically showing forth the insides of his characters; it depends on the inter-weaving of their destinies, on juxtapositions and quick cuttings in order to bring out fatal and absurd ironies. In the following sentences Raven, the hare-lipped hero, is about to shoot the policeman whose fiancée has helped Raven escape, but who he assumes has now be-trayed him:

> Raven watched him with bemused eyes, trying to take aim. It wasn't a difficult shot, but it was almost as if he had lost interest in killing. He was only aware of a pain and despair which was more like a complete weariness than anything else. He couldn't work up any sourness, any bitterness, at his betrayal . . . he had been marked from his birth for this end, to be betrayed in turn by everyone until every avenue into life was safely closed: by his mother bleeding in the basement. by the chaplain at the home. . . . How could he have expected to have escaped the commonest betrayal of all: to go soft on a skirt?

And hesitating, he is himself shot: 'Death came to him in the form of unbearable pain. It was as if he had to deliver this pain as a woman delivers a child, and he sobbed and moaned in the effort. At last it came out of him and he followed his only child into a vast desolation.' There the chapter ends, to be followed by a new one which begins smartly in a hotel lounge with the smell of food, local Rotarians and other non-heroic characters.

With its metaphorical continuities clearly laid out, the passage is simple enough; we have no difficulty understanding, in a quite unproblematic way, Raven's pain and despair. The thriller is about to conclude itself in a happy-sad blend of death and qualified reaffirmation of life; we close the book, content to have been so artfully given our money's worth, entertained from London to 'Nottwich' by a writer whose 'detachment' from any special pleading, any public or political ideology, seems clearly enough maintained. Yet in another but no less important way, Greene is not detached enough from his characters—for all his shifting, non-committal camera-eye technique —or from the story he is telling. There is no way, that is, to understand Raven's sobbing and moaning here, his following 'his only child into a vast desolation', except as a thrilling sensational bit of poetic heightening. No other voice plays off against it, devalues or qualifies it; there is only the quick change to a new locale and the easy irony of violent death juxtaposed to mundane life.

A Gun for Sale opens with laconic, tough-baby prose: 'Murder didn't mean much to Raven. It was just a new job. You had to be careful. You had to use your brains . . .' But Lewis, a number of years previously in his comic novel *Snooty Baronet* (1932), had begun that way:

> Not a bad face, flat and white, broad and weighty: in the daylight, the worse for much wear—stained, a grim surface, rained upon and stared at by the sun at its haughtiest, yet pallid still: with a cropped blondish moustache of dirty lemon, of toothbrush texture: the left eye somewhat closed up—this was a sullen eye.

continuing along in that vein until suddenly announcing that 'The face was mine . . . I can't help it if this has opened as if it were a gunman best-seller.' A way to put this is to say that Lewis couldn't write a best-seller, 'gunman' or otherwise, because he couldn't commit himself whole-heartedly and solemnly enough to suspend his own disbelief in story. So *The Revenge for Love* contains numbers of styles, rises to lyric apostrophe or descends to coarsely satiric jeering at its own characters. But Lewis's 'detachment' from his own story does not mean he is indifferent to it or to the figures who for good or evil walk through it and act out their destinies.

It is difficult to suggest the novel's quality from a single passage, but I will attempt it through a modified version of what Lewis himself termed 'The Taxi-Cab Driver's Test for "Fiction" '. This test consisted of putting the opening paragraphs of two novels side by side, then asking whether, after reading each, one would need or want to go on with the book. Lewis placed the opening of Huxley's *Point Counter Point* next to that of James's *The Ivory Tower*, analyzed with some contempt the tone and values he found displayed in Huxley's novelese, then only remarked about the James: 'That is a very different kettle of fish the most unobservant will detect.' Next to the previously quoted paragraph about Raven meeting his death, consider these sentences descriptive of Margot's thoughts after Victor has run over and killed a Spanish Civil Guard:

> They had killed a Civil Guard! She and Victor. This fact at first stunned her completely. She crouched grinning in her corner, her mind flatly refusing to go on with this. . . .
>
> But while she was brooding over these things which belonged to a remote and peaceful zone of her mind, she was gazing all the time, she found, at an enormous Prussian-blue chin. She could hear the terroristic bellow of their horn, accompanied by the whip-cracking and door-banging of rifle-fire. Out of the tail of her eye, meanwhile, she observed a horse arching up on its hind legs with foam decorating its mouth, and the hoarse shouting came to her again of a much-moustachioed dark mouth, strapped down so that it could not open very wide. . . .
>
> Slowly, almost slothfully, within her mind this novel background for Victor and herself took logical shape. She admitted, a fragment at a time, the components of the scenery for this new Act. The reality which had been shut out would have compelled her, by its maddening pressure, to give it admittance, if she had not met it half-way. . . . She saw that the very

worst had happened. And after that, and last of all, she perceived, with a darkening of all the horizon of her conscious
being, that it was herself that had been to blame!

There is much experience behind this moment of hurtling towards
death—three hundred pages of the novel—but even in context it is
difficult to read and take in. The heroine's consciousness is taken
seriously, yet as we observe her beginning to attend to herself and
ultimately deciding it would be better if she'd never loved, never even
existed, there is a strangely exclamatory remoteness about the rendering, as if Margot is surprised at what she's feeling and seeing—and
as if her creator is surprised too.

The Revenge for Love is a novel of action that is about action as
well. Orwell in *Homage to Catalonia* writes about how he, the sometime warrior George, gets shot through the neck, and is disarming
about how his heroism is really 'heroism', about how he shouldn't
have stuck his head up at that moment, about how, as a possibly dying
man he felt this and that sensation, but (he confides to us) that a
man who was truly dying might have felt something quite different.
Lewis's corresponding way of being individual, admittedly a dangerous
way for a novelist, is never wholly to commit himself to a character or
to a literary mode of expressing that character; this accounts perhaps
for the annoyance and uneasiness different sorts of readers have
expressed towards the book. Some are searchers for a 'good read', for
an entertaining vehicle to take them out of daily cares into a well-
managed 'human' tale which is both properly sad about life but
ultimately affirming of it, as Graham Greene and some less talented
writers went about writing and doing. Others prefer an art less committed to what Lewis called 'dramatical rough-stuff', but located more
inside or nearly inside the whale—either linguistically, morally, or
both—than this novel which turns the full force of its exacerbated
awareness (and is surely 'unfair' in so doing) on the universe of
objects and events, Spain and Russia, England on the lip of the mael-
strom.

When Lewis said a few years earlier that the satirist's task was, like
that of men of science, 'to bring human life more into contempt each
day', to demonstrate 'the futility and absurdity' of human life, it
would seem he signed his own death-warrant; certainly it was bad

advertising for someone who had recently published an ill-conceived book on Hitler, while making enemies on the home front with undiminished energy. Perhaps *The Revenge for Love* now bids to be distrusted as a novel which a few people—mainly admirers of Lewis—praise in what must seem like excessive ways. Partly for that reason I have resisted treating it as if it were the finest flower of 1930s fiction, indeed have done little more than try to tease readers into giving it serious attention, especially since its manners towards the ordinary reader of 'fiction' are designed to discomfit and alienate him. Lewis invoked, perhaps unwisely or extravagantly, the name of Swift as a 'pioneer' who did good work 'in the interests of other-worldliness', by bringing human life more into contempt daily. Hard talk, yet made with what at least since *Tarr* he had felt was the artist's necessary contempt towards life as flux, the revenge for or betrayal of love by change and death. Lewis was only able to imagine truly striking human possibilities when he could place them against and make them aware of their imminent destruction, as with the presentation of Margot in this novel.

There is a very elaborate and rhetorically high-pitched final paragraph to this novel in which the Communist agent, Percy Hardcaster, once more in a Spanish prison (in connection with the gun-running episode where Victor and Margot lose their lives) is momentarily struck by the reproach of Margot's remembered voice—'a strained and hollow voice, part of a sham-culture outfit, but tender and halting, as if dismayed at the sound of its own bitter words'. Hardcaster, though not consciously a betrayer, was technically in charge of the operation when the disaster occurred, and he is suddenly stricken with remorse:

> [The voice] was denouncing him out of the past, where alone now it was able to articulate: it was singling him out as a man who led people into mortal danger, people who were dear beyond expression to the possessor of the passionate, the artificial, the unreal, yet penetrating voice . . .

Lewis's novelistic voice here and as it goes on is both artificial and penetrating, ostensibly demonstrating the futility and absurdity of human life while it really does something quite other, shows in its every tone and cadence how much difference speech, in fact lyric speech, makes. Nothing that has happened since *The Revenge for Love*, in the world or in the world of the novel, has made it dispensable or classifiable as an example of anything—even as a 1930s piece of satire and fiction.

IX

Last Things: 'Four Quartets'

'What was happening to the English literary world? Was it dying or merely in hibernation?' Graves and Hodge put the question in their social history of England between the two wars (*The Long Weekend*, 1940) but didn't exactly answer it. Their look at the roster of poets disclosed many distinguished dead ones, including Bridges, Hardy, Housman and Yeats. Eliot is somewhat inaccurately said to have 'either almost or wholly stopped writing poems'. Graves himself was living in Majorca; Auden and Isherwood had migrated to the United States; MacNeice was also there temporarily, teaching and lecturing, though he returned to England at the end of 1940. The *Criterion* had ceased publication in January 1939 with the following statement from its editor: 'In the present state of public affairs—which has induced in myself a depression of spirits so different from any other experience of fifty years as to be a new emotion—I no longer feel the enthusiasm necessary to make a literary review what it should be.' *New Verse* and *Twentieth Century Verse* had likewise closed up shop; *Scrutiny* soldiered on.

Whether by 1940 the English literary world was dying or merely in hibernation is not really the question; but it is instructive to glance further at the list of writers previously considered in this book, asking what happened to them. A number of them were dead: Bennett, Lawrence and Strachey for some years; Ford only recently, in 1939; Virginia Woolf would live on until 1941. In addition to the Auden-Isherwood stateside migration, there was Huxley ensconced in California, dispensing wisdom to those who wanted to listen; while Lewis, who had sailed to America with his wife in hope of making the decent

living he thought would be denied him in wartime England, moved
from Buffalo to New York to Toronto to Windsor, Canada—finding as
usual that life didn't meet the requirements of his imagination: 'When
you read me that letter the other night I found myself envying James
Joyce at Vichy—so much nearer the centre of his world and mine;
with so many more friends than I have too, within some sort of reach.
I feel as if I were in some stony desert, full of shadows, in human form.
I have never imagined the likes of it, in my worst nightmares'—thus
he expressed himself to a correspondent in 1940. And to prove that
writers could still serve God and country, there are the examples of
Evelyn Waugh and Anthony Powell, whose war service can best be
appreciated by reading about it in the novels they wrote later on. A
few spirits kept the home fires burning, in some cases seeing that home
fires caused by German planes didn't burn too brightly: Orwell and
MacNeice worked for the BBC; Spender and Eliot were volunteer
fire wardens; Shaw and Forster uttered occasional wisdom, as elder
statesmen should.

In this altered and diminished literary world, *Four Quartets* took
shape. 'Burnt Norton' had been published in 1935 and figured for a
time as the concluding poem to Eliot's 1909–35 collection; the
succeeding three poems appeared one each year in 1940–42, and were
published together with 'Burnt Norton' in 1943. They have been ex-
plicated and analyzed in detail, most notably by Helen Gardner, but
such analysis has in the case of these poems led to nothing like a shared
response or agreement about their virtues and limitations. With
reference to Eliot's poetic career, it is not simply that an argument
still takes place between those readers who prefer *The Waste Land* to
Four Quartets, or vice versa; but often that lovers of the earlier poems
allow little merit to the latter—conversely one hears the opinion that
Eliot never became fully human until he wrote the *Quartets*. At any
rate the superiority or inferiority of either poem to the other, or to
contemporary work by Yeats, Auden and Frost—other poets who in
the late 1930s and beyond presumed to address, in cosmic or religious
or broadly human terms, the state of man's condition—has not and
probably cannot be demonstrated through comparison and analysis,
Eliot's names for the tools of criticism. *The Waste Land* and *Four
Quartets* are very different kettles of fish, but each of them makes

things peculiarly difficult for the discriminator and evaluator who moves beyond explication and attempts to criticize poetry for what it is and not another thing. These poems put criticism up against it.

1

Four Quartets is a poem of public and historical moment in a sense that other Eliot poems, even 'Gerontion' and *The Waste Land* are not; a poem whose concluding section announced that 'History is now and England', when the 'now' happened to be 1942, can and did speak to readers who may have found themselves in 'other places/Which also are the world's end, some at the sea jaws,/Or over a dark lake, in a desert or a city—' even though the nearest was still 'Now and England'. What it might have meant to open a copy of *Partisan Review* in 1940 or 1941 and read 'East Coker' or 'The Dry Salvages' I can only imagine, but assume that for some it was a more than ordinary day for the post. The poem seized the occasion and spoke to the moment, as well as to the timeless. And though it will not do to take the *Quartets* as solely a war poem, nor to exalt them for referring to England's and the world's clear and present danger, it would be equally wrong to play down the extent to which such reference made them a good deal more reverberant than 'Ash-Wednesday' or the 'Ariel Poems'—not to mention examples of purer or lesser poetry *circa* 1940.

Yet we have been made aware, mainly by the poet himself, of the symbolist character of at least certain passages in *Four Quartets*, like those which begin with 'Garlic and sapphires in the mud' or 'What is the late November doing'. The usual way of dealing with such passages is to admit that there is at one end this extreme limit of language, while at the other there is prosaic talk about the way up and the way down, or Krishna, or the degree of happiness that 'even a very good dinner' can and cannot provide. We appreciate the alternation between 'poetic' bits of undoubted dazzle—though one hesitates to paraphrase them or spell them out into a meaning—and 'prosaic' attempts at further clarification, humble or avuncular or wearily insistent. We instruct ourselves in how 'the poetry does not matter', even as we discount the statement of discounting, readying ourselves to welcome back the poetry mattering in a fresh way. The wonderful thing about the poem is that it does indeed happen; poetry matters by the very ardency of its negations, the tightrope-walking of its teetering affirmations, the momentary grandeurs of its magical gesturing.

Not everyone has been convinced that Eliot succeeds in making the poetry matter enough. Henry Reed's parody, 'Chard Whitlow', is universally admired but is not obviously meant as a tribute to a better poem. At the present stage of critical sophistication about the *Quartets*— sensitive delineation of themes, symbols, musical structure—we can afford to grant this organization and perhaps even be moved by it as an intricate piece of sustained poetic engineering. But the real issue is Eliot's presence, which has seemed inescapably moving to some readers and quite the reverse to others. An early reader of the *Quartets* whose elemental response to Eliot was mainly negative was George Orwell. When his review appeared (*Poetry London*, October–November 1942)[1] 'Little Gidding' had not yet been published, and Orwell would doubtless have moderated some of his contempt for the depressed resignation with which 'The Dry Salvages' ends, given the powerful and determined hope which concludes the final quartet. Still, Orwell wouldn't have liked the Christian way as an answer any better than he did in his review, when he looked back admiringly at early Eliot, comparing to their advantage some lines from 'Whispers of Immortality' with the close of 'The Dry Salvages'. The lines from early Eliot weren't hopeful, but weren't depressing or resigned either— were instead intensely felt moments of horror and repulsion, and were better literature, said Orwell, than the later struggles towards sincerity, towards a transparent rather than a brilliantly superficial poetry:

> If one wants to deal in antitheses, one might say that the later poems express a melancholy faith and the earlier ones a glowing despair. . . .
> But the trouble is that conscious futility is something only for the young. One cannot go on 'despairing of life' into a ripe old age. One cannot go on and on being 'decadent' since decadence means falling and one can only be said to be falling if one is going to reach the bottom reasonably soon. Sooner or

later one is obliged to adopt a positive attitude towards life and
society . . . after a certain age one must either stop writing or
dedicate oneself to some purpose not wholly aesthetic.

Since Orwell found himself actively put off by the religious purpose
Eliot was expressing, it is doubtful that his mind would have been
changed by reading an explication or two of how the poem is organized, of how (if I were to write such a one) the key word in 'Burnt
Norton' is 'Only', used twelve times and always in crucial ways, to
establish the desperate but absolutely necessary sense in which the
poetry matters: from the early 'Only by the form, the pattern/Can
words or music reach/The stillness . . .' to 'The only hope, or else
despair/Lies in the choice of pyre or pyre—To be redeemed from fire
by fire' of 'Little Gidding'. 'Only' is the perfect swing-word, opening
on one side to an inspiriting sense of possibilities glimpsed, eagerly
imagined; on the other side to gloom and depression—after all it's only
words one is employing.

Yet there are passages from the *Quartets* as 'decadent' as anything
Orwell could find in 'Whispers of Immortality' or other early poems
he admired. Compare the stanza Orwell quotes:

> Daffodil bulbs instead of balls
> Stared from the sockets of the eyes!
> He knew that thought clings round dead limbs
> Tightening its lusts and luxuries.

with this one from section IV of 'East Coker':

> The wounded surgeon plies the steel
> That questions the distempered part:
> Beneath the bleeding hands we feel
> The sharp compassion of the healer's art
> Resolving the enigma of the fever chart.

This stanza, one of the first parts from the *Quartets* which originally
drew me into the poem, is as much a grotesque *tour de force* as the
lines about daffodil bulbs and lust. And even if we have been earlier
alerted in 'East Coker' that the poem will include not very satisfactory ways of putting it—'A periphrastic study in a worn-out poetical
fashion'—it is not clear how much serious contemplation we should

give to the wounded surgeon, or to the earth as a hospital endowed by the ruined millionaire.

The lyric's conclusion has especially disturbed readers who feel that in it Eliot goes too far:

> If to be warmed, then I must freeze
> And quake in frigid purgatorial fires
> Of which the flame is roses, and the smoke is briars.
>
> The dripping blood our only drink,
> The bloody flesh our only food:
> In spite of which we like to think
> That we are sound, substantial flesh and blood—
> Again, in spite of that, we call this Friday good.

One could maintain with justice that this is tasteless, embarrassingly heavyhanded (the business about 'good' Friday) and generally over-wrought. One could also show how this lyric is 'only' the place where the poem's images come together and anticipate the conclusion to 'Little Gidding' where the fire and the rose are seen to be one. The trouble is—and this is perhaps the main trouble in criticizing *Four Quartets*—that no standards for 'good' or 'bad', for tasteless or urbane, for successful or unsuccessful poetry exist which somehow T. S. Eliot had not been aware of for some time. Why should one want to point out that a passage or section from the poem doesn't come off very well, when already the poet had anticipated us and shrugged off the offending bit, even agreed with us that, no, it was not a very satisfactory way of putting it, and, yes, the 'wounded surgeon' passage was doubtless too poetical.

And if parts of the *Quartets* go too far in one direction—that of artificial poetry of fancy, with metaphysical conceits or symbolist murmurings put forth we know not how seriously—then the notorious prosiness of other passages has also from the beginning provoked annoyance. All the paradox-mongering, the tiresome wisdom about how down and up are the same way, the complacent satire (compare Pound's at least enlivening obscenity in the Hell *Cantos*) of how civil servants and industrial lords and statesmen all go into the dark, or the too-easy understanding of how people's emptiness is apparent in their behaviour in the tube, or the gibes at 'superficial notions of evolution'

or at anodynes for the 'popular mind' (much more amusing this sort
of thing when done in the Editor's notes in the *Criterion*), or the awful
business about

> The moments of happiness—not the sense of well-being
> Fruition, fulfilment, security or affection,
> Or even a very good dinner, but the sudden illumination—

when one realizes that one doesn't want one's very good dinners
dragged in here, 'understood' and transcended by the high-minded
poet.

Some years after 'Little Gidding' Eliot wrote 'The Three Voices of
Poetry', the most useful of his later essays for illuminating his own
work. The 'third voice' is that of a character in a play; the 'second
voice' is that of 'the poet talking to other people', and this latter voice

> . . . is, in fact, the voice most often and most clearly heard in
> poetry that is not of the theatre: in all poetry, certainly, that
> has a conscious social purpose—poetry intended to amuse or
> to instruct, poetry that tells a story, poetry that preaches or
> points a moral, or satire which is a form of preaching.

But Eliot spends most of his time in trying to describe what the 'first
voice' consists of: that of the poet talking to himself, the lyric as medi-
tative verse, starting from 'nothing so definite as an emotion, in any
ordinary sense . . . more certainly not an idea'. Eliot goes to Gottfried
Benn for assistance and comes up with the notion of poetry's first
voice as originating in an 'obscure impulse':

> He [the poet] has some thing germinating in him for which
> he must find words; but he cannot know what words he wants
> until he has found the words; he cannot identify this embryo
> until it has been transformed into an arrangement of the
> right words in the right order. When you have the words for
> it, the 'thing' for which the words had to be found has dis-
> appeared, replaced by a poem.

There is nothing in this formulation that Eliot had not been saying all
along in somewhat different terms; it was all there in his insistence at
the time of writing *The Waste Land* that Jonson's art was 'creative'
rather than 'critical' and originated from no precise intellectual or
emotional criticism of life. As suggested earlier that point had reference
to Eliot's own poetry at the time, as it still does with regard to the

Quartets. Whatever satiric or instructive or social aim he took or in these later poems there was, as always, his duty to serve at the deepest levels the first voice of poetry.

When this first voice is speaking at its truest, the resulting poetry should be 'glowing'—in Orwell's word used to describe early Eliot—no matter how muted or sober its subject and general tone. The *Quartets* even more than most poems are a mixture of the first and second voices, with the former set off powerfully at certain moments because of the theatrical role-playing of the latter—as 'brilliant' inventor of highly artificial poems ('The wounded surgeon plies the steel') or wearily-pontificating prose directives ('You say I am repeating/ Something I have said before. I shall say it again./Shall I say it again?') All the more rich and undesigning on us come what seem authentic first-voice moments, as this one near the beginning of 'East Coker':

> In my beginning is my end. Now the light falls
> Across the open field, leaving the deep lane
> Shuttered with branches, dark in the afternoon,
> Where you lean against a bank while a van passes,
> And the deep lane insists on the direction
> Into the village, in the electric heat
> Hypnotised. In the warm haze the sultry light
> Is absorbed, not refracted, by grey stone.
> The dahlias sleep in the empty silence.
> Wait for the early owl.

A 'you' is nominally being addressed here, but in fact the voice is talking to itself, creating with great precision and subtle care a scene that seems purely itself, the way it was and had to be—'Shuttered with branches, dark in the afternoon'. In the exquisitely dead line 'Where you lean against a bank while a van passes' is expressed the strange sense of casual yet inevitable activity as the traveler moves toward his beginning (Eliot's ancestors came from East Coker) and the lane 'insists'—a particularly fine example of a word's literal meaning brought alive—on the direction. Here is a poetry all of whose details fit in with each other and in whose overall mood we are invited to participate 'in the electric heat/Hypnotised', but whose particular assertions and observations are so emptied of intentions, of waste-landish outrageousness ('Like a silk hat on a Bradford millionaire') as to come out some place the other side of ordinariness. 'The dahlias sleep in the empty silence': a meaningless and haunting line in which the first voice of poetry has found words to express its obscure impulse.

It is surely a matter of judgement and open to argument whether a spot of poetry inclines towards second- or first-voiced delivery; but the *Quartets* are most moving when one senses the second voice, at its appointed task of instruction and clarification, modulate before our eyes and ears into more private and obscure reverie. In section V of 'East Coker' Eliot tells us about his largely-wasted struggles in the years '*l'entre deux guerres*', engages in humble apologies for having tried to say what had already been better said by earlier writers, and salutes at any rate 'the trying' since 'the rest is not our business'. Then comes this final address:

> Home is where one starts from. As we grow older
> The world becomes stranger, the pattern more complicated
> Of dead and living. Not the intense moment
> Isolated, with no before and after,
> But a lifetime burning in every moment
> And not the lifetime of one man only
> But of old stones that cannot be deciphered.
> There is a time for the evening under starlight,
> A time for the evening under lamplight
> (The evening with the photograph album).
> Love is most nearly itself
> When here and now cease to matter.
> Old men ought to be explorers
> Here or there does not matter
> We must be still and still moving
> Into another intensity
> For a further union, a deeper communion
> Through the dark cold and the empty desolation,
> The wave cry, the wind cry, the vast waters
> Of the petrel and the porpoise. In my end is my beginning.

It begins as the elder's advice to the young, or to the nodding friend, mature in ripe wisdom himself; the distinctions are made in the manner they have been made in the poem thus far. But with 'There is a time', the advice becomes less distinct, the address less focussed and the voice generally more inwards. 'There is a time' is less insistent than Prufrock's 'There will be time' to prepare one's face to meet other

faces; the evening under starlight parallels the evening under lamplight (the two compounds limply echoing each other, though also
contrasted) but instead of linking or disjoining the two 'lights' by
means of a strong word, there is only the unemphatic comma, topped
off with a parenthetical line in explication of what goes on during the
evening under lamplight. Why these three lines should be as affecting
as they are must have much to do with how flat and unmemorable
(the poetry does not matter) they sound, yet how strongly they suggest
and stir up troubled feelings about time passing, youth and age.

Then, as 'here and now cease to matter' when 'Love is most nearly
itself', the poetry appears to give advice about how old men ought to
be explorers and how 'we' must also, at whatever age, be explorers
out into the deep waters. But with the line about old men, punctua-
tion begins to drop off at the end of lines, as if even a comma was too
emphatic, might signal that a design on the reader was being shaped.
Instead the voice floats free, exploring itself in measured cadences.
Nothing particularly interesting or profound is said here; Eliot's
procedure is more like waving a wand, commanding petrel and
porpoise to appear and seem somehow as if they were exactly what
was called for, rather than a trick of alliterative fantasy. Martin
Seymour-Smith who with a few words disposes of the *Quartets* (in his
Guide to World Literature, 1973) as arid evasions of experience,
nevertheless admits that they can be 'sometimes entrancing'. I should
say that such entrancing occurs at a number of places in the poem,
to the extent that it triumphs over its duller, less inspired, more depressed and mundane self.

Such an entrancing moment occurs at the close of section II of
'The Dry Salvages'. In the first, 'lyric' half of that section, Eliot
produces his infamous sestinas about the sea and the fishermen:

> Where is there an end of it, the soundless wailing,
> The silent withering of autumn flowers
> Dropping their petals and remaining motionless;
> Where is there an end to the drifting wreckage,
> The prayer of the bone on the beach, the unprayable
> Prayer at the calamitous annunciation?

It will be remembered, and has been remarked upon with some
severity by critics (particularly by Donald Davie in his interesting

essay on the poem) that in trying to find rhymes for 'motionless'
throughout the next five sestinas, Eliot got himself into grotesque and
embarrassing difficulties—'emotionless,' 'devotionless', 'oceanless',
and 'erosionless' being the sad verbal outcome.[2] This may be, yet
the poet is so caught up in singing the gloomy desolation of nature
at its task of wearing us down, withering all the flowers, and in trying
to think about the fishermen who go out against nature—'Into the
wind's tail, where the fog cowers'—that despite the forced rhymes it
rings through to me as one of the poem's great sequences. But just
as with the wounded surgeon lyric, one may see this as excessive, as
lyric artifice so artificial that a fine poet and critic like Davie judges it
to be a travesty.

That a similar disagreement is unlikely over the end of section II
indicates its deeper poetic resonance; the fact that it doesn't present
itself as a candidate for approval or disapproval is a function of the way
its voice proceeds, builds and climaxes as does music. There is no
pre-established form or determined content in the service of which we
intuit the voice's working. It has been telling us, after the sestinas
about the fishermen, that moments of agony are permanent, that we
appreciate them mainly through others, are less able to understand
our own since 'the torment of others remains an experience/Un-
qualified, unworn by subsequent attrition'; it then concludes:

> People change, and smile: but the agony abides.
> Time the destroyer is time the preserver.
> Like the river with its cargo of dead negroes, cows and
>   chicken coops,
> The bitter apple and the bite in the apple.
> And the ragged rock in the restless waters,
> Waves wash over it, fogs conceal it;
> On a halcyon day it is merely a monument,
> In navigable weather it is always a seamark
> To lay a course by: but in the sombre season
> Or the sudden fury, is what it always was.

This sequence is elegantly paced, poetically entrancing in its development to the final assertion, but its meaning is not clearly stated—
unlike the manner in which the 'second voice' has tried to be clear in
distinguishing our experience of others' agony from our own. Time is
once preserver and destroyer, like the river is, like the original step

(or bite of the apple) into experience. But what about the 'ragged rock'? It is introduced by a nonchalant 'And', as if the connection with what went before—Time, the river, the apple—is obvious, requiring no explanation.

Explicators of 'The Dry Salvages' speak as if there were no problems about what to do with the rock: Genesius Jones calls it 'the terrible love which dominates the poem'; Harry Blamires says it is 'of course the Church', and that ' "ragged" refers no doubt to the unattractive roughness of the Church's exterior and probably also to the Church's superficial poverty'. Even Denis Donoghue's subtler account of the poem founders at this point: 'But the stern voice now says that "the meaning" redeems time and because it is the Rock, is itself'.[3] Donoghue also cites this moment as one of the poem's 'sore thumbs' and indeed is much harder on 'The Dry Salvages' generally than the other *Quartets*. In fact Eliot did not write 'the Rock' but 'the ragged rock in the restless waters'. To say as commentators do that it means 'love' or 'the Church' or even 'the meaning' seems to me a desperately needless attempt to fix, even sanctify (and make rather uninteresting) what in the poem's flux is something else again:

> And the ragged rock in the restless waters,
> Waves wash over it, fogs conceal it;
> On a halcyon day it is merely a monument,
> In navigable weather it is always a seamark
> To lay a course by: but in the sombre season
> Or the sudden fury, is what it always was.

What it always was: what we name 'rock', what a line of poetry alliteratively expatiates on (I remember some boyhood twister in the nature of 'Around the rough and rugged rock the ragged rascal ran') and eventually salutes in the language of pure existence—'is' and 'was' coming together without further nominal definition. There is a rhetoric here as powerful and affecting in its way as the louder brilliances of 'Gerontion' and *The Waste Land*. And when the first voice speaks, as I think it does in this final passage, it is nobody talking to nobody in particular; it is the language pretending to confront and finally be put to silence by something outside itself.

2

Although I have singled out for praise moments from the earlier *Quartets* where extraordinary resonance is felt, moments in which the poetry is neither parsonically didactic nor symbolically opaque, such an exercise is unnecessary with 'Little Gidding' which unless my senses are deceived is of great strength and beauty throughout, offering to the ear and to the mind equal pleasure and edification. If these old-fashioned terms are insufficiently critical, there is also something old-fashioned (or traditional, to hang Eliot's word around his neck) about the core of 'Little Gidding' and of the *Quartets* as a whole. Denis Donoghue rightly invokes eighteenth-century English poems about the vanity of human wishes as ancestral to Eliot's. I think of four lines from Pope's 'Epistle to Miss Blount':

> Let the strict Life of graver Mortals be
> A long, exact, and serious Comedy,
> In ev'ry scene some Moral let it teach,
> And, if it can, at once both Please and Preach.

Admittedly the author of these trim lines had a way to go before producing the anguished turbulence of the final satires and *Dunciad IV;* but he knew already that Life, in blueprint form if no other, was to be long, exact, serious and a Comedy. Eliot's ancestor, in his climactic encounter with the dead Master in 'Little Gidding', is primarily Dante, but we can perhaps be justified in hearing later English moralists behind the great speech about the wisdom of old age, after which the sage departs, fading fast as all is cleared:

> Let me disclose the gifts reserved for age
>   To set a crown upon your lifetime's effort.
>   First the cold friction of expiring sense
> Without enchantment, offering no promise
>   But bitter tastelessness of shadow fruit
>   As body and soul begin to fall asunder.
> Second, the conscious impotence of rage
>   At human folly, and the laceration
>   Of laughter at what ceases to amuse.
> And last, the rending pain of re-enactment
>   Of all that you have done, and been; the shame
>   Of motives late revealed, and the awareness

> Of things ill done and done to others' harm
>   Which once you took for exercise of virtue.
>   Then fools' approval stings, and honour stains.
> From wrong to wrong the exasperated spirit
>   Proceeds, unless restored by that refining fire
>   Where you must move in measure, like a dancer.

And like the language of this passage also, which speaks enchantingly about a time when there will be no enchantment. The greatness of these culminating lines does not reside in their compelling portrayal of salvation; nor do we read Johnson or Pope for their matchless evocation of Heaven or Virtue. What is fine about Eliot's last fire sermon is the relentlessness, the fullness and grace with which the very worst case for old age is put; put in a poetry that does not do dirt on but rather justice to the possible ends—grim as they are seen to be —of human experience.

Speaking about the *Quartets* generally and Eliot's operative presence in them, I would go further and at the risk of special pleading or casuistry suggest the following: that whatever 'unevenness' may be detected—the relative unsatisfactoriness of this lyric, that voice— serves in another sense to make the poem more rather than less interesting, wider in scope and range of feeling, certainly in range of speaking. The *Quartets* catch us up and don't let us escape; one may find, as I have, the wounded surgeon lyric unsatisfactory but one wouldn't prefer it to have been rewritten or tossed out of the poem. It is not the case that a selected *The Prelude* or a compact *In Memoriam* would be the answer to uneasy readers who find themselves not admiring many lines in the finished poems.

In sentences quoted as epigraph to the previous chapter, Lewis provided the Satirist with some unpleasant language in which to see himself, his task being 'to bring human life more into contempt each day. Upon the side of the ascetic, in the interests of other-worldliness, it will carry on the good work of such pioneers as Swift. . . . It will . . . demonstrate the futility and absurdity of human life.' No doubt this function ('a very tolerable one it is' added Lewis) has always been a major function of literature; certainly in English literature between the wars there was among its major figures no shirking of the task. And in Lewis's sense of the word we have at least as much reason to

think Eliot a satirist in the *Quartets* as in *The Waste Land* twenty
years before, those years of *'l'entre deux guerres'*. Yet the definition
leaves out, by necessity, the poetry; and this matters as much to the
reader of Eliot as the poet said it did when, six years after 'Little
Gidding', he asked about the art of Walter de la Mare:

> By whom, and by what means, was this designed?
> The whispered incantation which allows
> Free passage to the phantoms of the mind?

and answered in terms conceived of as particularly appropriate to
de la Mare's subtle and undeclaring cadences, but which with wider
extension also serve for Eliot's:

> By you; by those deceptive cadences
> Wherewith the common measure is refined;
> By conscious art practised with natural ease;
>
> By the delicate, invisible web you wove —
> The inexplicable mystery of sound.

Notes

CHAPTER I

¹ In 'The Progress of the Novel' written in 1929, Bennett announced that 'Among novelists under forty . . . Aldous Huxley rises high above everybody else as a figure in the world of imaginative prose literature.' Huxley found it 'difficult to understand the mentality of a man like Bennett who can sit down and spin out an immense realistic affair about life in Clerkenwell' (*Letters*, 29 April 1924) but was charmed by Bennett and treated him as a distinguished writer.

² W. W. Robson, *Modern English Literature* (Oxford, 1970), p. 6.

³ Wyndham Lewis, *The Lion and the Fox* (Methuen, 1966), p. 65.

⁴ 'When . . . Lytton Strachey, with a Gibbonian period or phrase or word . . . assures us that he feels an amused superiority to these Victorian puppets, he succeeds only in conveying his personal conviction that he feels amused and superior.' 'The Irony of Swift', in *The Common Pursuit* (Chatto, 1952), p. 75.

⁵ 'At about this time the Curate of Littlemore had a singular experience. As he was passing by the Church he noticed an old man, very poorly dressed in an old grey coat with the collar turned up, leaning over the lych gate, in floods of tears. . . . Could it be—? . . . He looked again, and he could doubt no longer. It was Dr. Newman. He sprang forward, with proffers of assistance. Could he be of any use? "Oh no, no!" was the reply. "Oh no, no!" But the Curate felt that he could not turn away, and leave so eminent a character in such distress. "Was it not Dr. Newman he had the honour of addressing?" he asked, with all the respect and sympathy at his command. "Was there nothing that could be done?" But the old man hardly seemed

to understand what was being said to him. "Oh no, no!" he repeated, with the tears streaming down his face. "Oh no, no!" ' (from 'Cardinal Manning', *Eminent Victorians* (Chatto, 1948)).

[6] Quoted in Michael Holroyd's *Lytton Strachey*, Vol. II (Heinemann, 1968), p. 325.

[7] 'D'Artagnan Twenty Years After', The *Criterion*, July 1937, reprinted in *Ezra Pound: Selected Prose, 1909–1965*, ed. W. Cookson (Faber, 1973), p. 425.

CHAPTER II

[1] Gabriel Pearson, 'An American Use of Symbolism', in *Eliot in Perspective*, ed. Graham Martin (Macmillan, 1970), pp. 83–101.

[2] Hugh Kenner, *The Invisible Poet* (MacDowell, Obolensky, 1958), pp. 122–3.

[3] I have taken this approach in my essay 'Reading *The Waste Land* Today' (*Essays in Criticism*, April 1969), pp. 176–92. Kenner's essay 'The Urban Apocalypse', in *Eliot in His Time*, ed. A. Walton Litz (Princeton, 1973) makes good use of the *Waste Land* manuscript to point out that by the time Eliot wrote 'What the Thunder Said' his poem had truly become apocalyptic, the manuscript virtually unrevised. At any rate, coming at earlier parts of the poem through Dryden or Ben Jonson need not be exclusive ways in.

[4] But see Jonathan Culler, *Flaubert: The Uses of Uncertainty* (Cornell University Press, 1974) for a much subtler account of Flaubert's 'fiction'.

CHAPTER III

[1] Roger Sale, *Modern Heroism* (University of California Press, 1973). My own discussion of *Women in Love*, though not as admiring of the book, owes much to him. I should also like to thank my colleagues Benjamin DeMott and G. Armour Craig for insights into *St. Mawr* and *Lady Chatterley's Lover* which I have made use of. Richard Poirier's discussion of *St. Mawr* is to be found in *A World Elsewhere* (Oxford, 1966); Frank Kermode's discussion of *Lady Chatterley's Lover* is in his *Lawrence* ('Modern Masters' Series, Fontana, 1973).

[2] John Carey, 'D. H. Lawrence's Doctrine', in *D. H. Lawrence: Novelist, Poet, Prophet*, ed. Stephen Spender (London, 1973), pp. 122–34.

[3] Keith Sagar, *The Art of D. H. Lawrence* (Cambridge, 1966), p. 155.

CHAPTER IV

[1] For the complicated story of how 'Mr Bennett and Mrs Brown' developed into its present form, and for an account of relations between Virginia Woolf and Arnold Bennett, see 'The Whole Contention Between Mr Bennett and Mrs Woolf', in Samuel Hynes's *Edwardian Occasions* (Oxford, 1972), pp. 24–37.

[2] Unsigned review of *Some Do Not*, *The Nation and Athenaeum* (24 May 1924), p. 258.

[3] R. P. Blackmur, 'The King Over the Water: Notes on the Novels of Ford Madox Hueffer', in *Modern British Fiction*, ed. Mark Schorer (Oxford, 1961), pp. 137–42.

[4] Graham Greene, 'Last Journey' (review of *The March of Literature*), *The Spectator* (17 November 1939), p. 696.

[5] These items by Pete Hamill and Katherine Mansfield, together with ones mentioned later by Middleton Murry and George Steiner can be found in *E. M. Forster: The Critical Heritage*, ed. Philip Gardner (Routledge & Kegan Paul, 1973).

CHAPTER V

[1] 'Stephen Hudson's' (Sydney Schiff's) place in the list can be accounted for at least partly on the grounds that Muir and Schiff were friends. Muir doesn't include Wyndham Lewis in *Transition* (Lewis had published only one novel, *Tarr*, by 1925) but his correspondence contains interesting letters to Schiff expressing Muir's mixed feelings about Lewis. (*Selected Letters of Edwin Muir*, ed. Peter Butter, Chatto, 1974.)

[2] 'Then out of the blue the *Dial* brought out *The Waste Land* and all our hilarity ended. It wiped out our world as if an atom bomb had

been dropped upon it and our brave sallies into the unknown were turned to dust.

'To me especially it struck like a sardonic bullet. I felt at once that it had sent me back twenty years, and I'm sure it did.' (*Autobiography of William Carlos Williams*, Random House, 1951), p. 174.

[3] With Graves, as with Auden later on, I have decided to quote from the *Collected Poems* and *Collected Shorter Poems* rather than from the poems as they originally appeared, except in the case of ones later suppressed.

[4] A. Alvarez, 'Lawrence's Poetry: The Single State of Man' was originally published in *The Shaping Spirit* (Chatto, 1958) and reprinted in *D. H. Lawrence*, ed. Stephen Spender (op. cit.).

[5] Richards's most valuable criticism of Lawrence is found in the chapter on 'Piano' in *Practical Criticism* (Routledge & Kegan Paul, 1929). Quotations from *Science and Poetry* are here taken from the revised version, *Poetries and Sciences* (W. W. Norton, 1970) in which for example, Richard added the reference to *Birds, Beasts and Flowers*.

[6] Kingsmill's remark occurs in his *D. H. Lawrence* (Dodge Publishers, 1938), p. 89. Hardy's essay, 'Women in D. H. Lawrence's Work', is in *D. H. Lawrence*, ed. Stephen Spender (op. cit.).

CHAPTER VI

[1] An illuminating discussion of Empson's criticism is found in Roger Sale's *Modern Heroism* (op. cit.).

[2] 'T. S. Eliot as Critic', in *Anna Karenina and Other Essays* (Chatto, 1967).

[3] The most useful brief account of Eliot's magazine is John Peter's in his essay 'Eliot and the *Criterion*', in *Eliot in Perspective*, ed. Graham Martin (op. cit.).

CHAPTER VII

[1] Fraser says this in his preface to William T. McKinnon's book on MacNeice, *Apollo's Blended Dream* (Oxford, 1971).

[2] *A Reviewer's ABC* (Meridian Books, 1961), pp. 286–7.

[3] Christopher Ricks's brilliant tribute to Empson's poems should be looked up: 'Empson's Poetry', in *William Empson: the Man and his Work*, ed. Roma Gill (Routledge & Kegan Paul, 1974), pp. 145–207.

CHAPTER VIII

[1] My discussion here contains only a cursory reference to Graham Greene, mainly in contrast to Lewis. I find all the novels readable and *A Gun for Sale* and *The Ministry of Fear* more than that. But they don't seem to me in need of much criticism, including *The Power and the Glory*, Greene's most 'serious' early novel. More reluctantly I decided not to deal with Henry Green and Ivy Compton-Burnett. By Henry Green I mean *Living*, certainly his best book. Compton-Burnett is the subject of two very good pieces of criticism by Kingsley Amis in *What Became of Jane Austen?* (Harcourt Brace Jovanovich, 1971), and by Mary McCarthy in *The Writing on the Wall* (Harcourt Brace Jovanovich, 1970). I have nothing to add to what they say.

[2] 'Ronald Firbank' in *Life and Letters*, March 1929.

CHAPTER IX

[1] In *Collected Essays, Journalism and Letters of George Orwell*, ed. S. Orwell and I. Angus, vol. II (Secker & Warburg, 1968), pp. 236–242.

[2] Donald Davie, 'T. S. Eliot: the End of an Era', in *T. S. Eliot: a Collection of Critical Essays*, ed. Hugh Kenner (Prentice-Hall, 1962).

[3] Genesius Jones, *Approach to the Poem* (Barnes & Noble, 1964); Harry Blamires, *Word Unheard* (Methuen, 1969); Denis Donoghue, *The Ordinary Universe* (Macmillan, 1968).

Index

The index is of names and of works discussed in the text, listed under author.

Lane, Homer, 160
Larkin, Philip, 175, 177
Lawrence, D. H., 11–13, 16–18,
19, 20, 32, 61, 70–89, 91, 105–
6, 114–16, 123–33, 135, 137–
140, 143–4, 147–8, 150–3,
161, 179, 180, 209; 'Captain's
Doll, The', 80–2; 'Elephant is
Slow to Mate, The', 126–8;
'Fox, The', 80–2; *Lady Chatterley's Lover*, 73, 79, 86–8,138;
Last Poems, 132–3; *Man Who
Died, The*, 80, 86–7; *Pansies*,
126–7,131–2; *Rhyming Poems*,
125; 'Snake', 128–30; *St. Mawr*,
78, 82–6, 180; 'We are Transmitters',131–2; *Women in Love*,
17, 70, 73–8, 79, 81–2, 86–7,
100; *Unrhyming Poems*, 127–33
Lawrence, Frieda, 72, 78
Lawrence, T. E., 13
Leavis,F.R.,14,15,40,50,58,61,
72–3, 78–80, 82, 117, 134–6,
138, 139, 140, 145, 146, 147,
148–53,162,164; *Education and
the University*, 14, 153; *New
Bearings in English Poetry*,
117, 150, 152; *Revaluation*, 117
Leavis, Q. D., 151
Lehmann, John, 196
Lenin, Vladimir, 165
Lewis, Sinclair, 78
Lewis, Wyndham, 12–13, 16–18,
19–20, 31, 44–50, 51, 54, 59,
61, 68, 70, 72, 79–80, 91, 100,
106, 122, 134, 135, 139–44,
145, 147, 150–1, 153–5, 166,
178–9, 181–2, 189, 193, 198,
200–8, 209, 222; *Apes of God,
The*, 44, 91, 178–9, 189;
'Blast', 44; *Blasting and Bombardiering*, 19, 166; *Childermass*, 44, 179; *Men Without Art*,

18–19, 140, 142–3, 154, 178;
Revenge for Love, The, 153,
182, 201–8; *Snooty Baronet*,
204–5; *Tarr*, 16, 44–50, 52,
54, 68, 91; 'Taxi-Cab Driver
Test for "Fiction"', 205; *Time
and Western Man*, 141–2
Lloyd, Marie, 59
Loos, Anita, 142
Lowell, Robert, 99

Macaulay, T. B., 43–4
MacDiarmid, Hugh, 13
MacNeice, Louis, 20, 156, 166,
169–75, 177, 179, 209–10;
Autumn Journal, 171, 173–5;
'Birmingham', 170–1; 'Epi-
logue', 172–3; 'June Thunder',
174; 'Turf-stacks' 171–2
Mailer, Norman, 27
Mann, Thomas, 79
Manning, Henry Cardinal, 40–2
Mansfield, Katherine, 100
Marlowe, Christopher, 62, 139
Marvell, Andrew, 52, 86, 88,
102–3, 136–8
Maugham, Somerset (*Moon and
Sixpence, The*,) 16, 23, 24
McCarthy, Mary, 198
Melville, Herman, 79
'Men of 1914, The', 12, 19–21
Metaphysical Poets, The, 52, 58,
62, 134
Miller, Henry, 16, 201
Millett, Kate, 81
Milton, John, 87, 89
Mitchison, Naomi, 37
Mizener, Arthur, 93, 95
Moore, Marianne, 118
Morrell, Lady Ottoline, 62
Muggeridge, Malcolm, 199
Muir, Edwin, 32, 114, 117, 123;
Transition, 32, 114